The
Greatest
Search and Rescue Stories
Ever Told

The
Greatest
Search and Rescue Stories
Ever Told

EDITED AND WITH INTRODUCTIONS BY
JOSEPH CUMMINS

THE LYONS PRESS
Guilford, Connecticut
An imprint of The Globe Pequot Press

Printed in the United States of America
Design by Compset, Inc.

Library of Congress Cataloging-in-Publication Data is available on file.

To All the Heroes

Contents

Introduction

What makes a team of Canadian rescue jumpers leap blindly and at frighteningly low altitude into a polar gale? Why did firemen and police officers race into the burning World Trade Center buildings, when everyone else ran for their lives? What impelled Navy SEAL Lieutenant and Medal of Honor winner Tom Norris to steal alone, at night, through an NVA division to rescue a downed and injured American flyer?

What, in other words, makes people risk their lives for others? The happy answer, I think, is that selflessness and heroism are inbred human instincts, ones that just don't get as much publicity as their craven flip sides, selfishness and cowardice.

Helping those in peril began long before the first bucket fire brigade in the Middle Ages, long before St. Bernard of Menthon founded the first mountain rescue group in the Swiss Alps in the 10th century—even long before the Good Samaritan "bound up the wounds" of the injured stranger.

Saving someone's life, basically, just feels good. A fire paramedic in a selection from Steve Delsohn's oral history *The Fire Inside* describes the aftermath of rescuing a child: "You can see the kid walking to school, or you might know their uncle, or you might see the kid's name in the sports section. Maybe he scored ten points in a basketball game. You don't tell anyone, 'Hey, I saved that boy's life.' You just sit back and smile."

The true stories of courage collected in *The Greatest Search and Rescue Stories Ever Told* move from the First World War to the epic catastrophe of September 11, 2001, from windswept mountains and distant seas to the heat of pitched combat and the close quarters of urban mayhem.

While the attack on the World Trade Center and its aftermath (see *Minute-by-Minute at the World Trade Center* and *Under the Rubble*) bought deserved attention to police, firemen, and rescue workers, the truth is that putting their lives in peril is what they do, day after day—see the story from Dennis Smith's gripping classic *Report from Engine Co. 82*.

Civilian Search and Rescue (SAR) units have their counterparts in the military: the pararescue jumpers or "PJ's" of the Air Force and National Guard. The exploits of these almost improbably courageous men are here chronicled in a piece from Sebastian Junger's bestselling *The Perfect Storm*, which describes PJ's jumping into the Atlantic with fatal results during the "storm of the century" in October 1991.

I found the tales of rescue in the high mountains the most harrowing to read about—my palms grew sweaty and I experienced sensations of vertigo as SAR teams tied themselves to sheer rock faces and rappelled down to climbers stranded on ledges only a few feet wide.

Aside from the bravery of the mountain rescuers, there is almost always one constant to these stories: somebody, somewhere, has screwed-up badly. *Outside* magazine reports that "in the year 2000, SAR teams responded to 31percent more incidents in US National Parks than in 1998." The reason? Poorly-prepared people in dangerous areas where they don't belong. Park rangers in the Rockies tell rueful stories of meeting climbers who proudly show off fancy global positioning systems, but haven't even brought along a map or sufficient supplies.

This isn't limited to the United States. A story from Jack Olsen's *The Climb Up to Hell*, which has been described as "one of the best accounts of true high mountain adventure ever written," shows what happened when an inexperienced Italian decided to tackle the extraordinarily dangerous north face of the Eiger Mountain in 1957. (Eiger, by the way, means "Ogre," which should have given the gentleman a clue.)

Possibly the most dramatic stories of search and rescue take place both at sea and during wartime.

Perhaps because we have seen so many movies, rescue at sea has an almost cinematic quality—the thousand-square-mile sweep of the action, the cosmic force of the storm. But there was nothing cinematic for the father and son cowering onboard a small fishing vessel tossed like driftwood in the pitched Gulf of Alaska storm chillingly depicted in a selection from Spike Walker's *Coming Back Alive*. And, if you were a submariner trapped underwater, in the spring of 1939, off the New England coast (*Ready to Surface*) you would find the experience of feeling the air seep out of your lungs as those on the surface battled to lower an experimental "diving bell" to your crippled boat nothing at all like going to the movies.

In terms of wartime SAR, probably the most striking note is the determination of those performing the rescues to save the lives of their comrades at all costs. Case in point, of course, is the famous story of US Rangers and

Delta Force "operators" trapped under intense gunfire in Mogadishu in 1993 (see *Out of the Jaws of Hell* from *Black Hawk Down*) and yet staying to rescue the crew members of the downed helicopter and even the corpse of the dead pilot. Other tales of combat heroism I've included—such as *Precious Cargo*, which tells the story of a raggedy band of 40 Americans in the Philippines saved from the Japanese by the submarine USS *Crevalle*—show how exciting well-coordinated military SAR work can be.

Finally—just because I love dogs—I've included a small section on humankind's best friend. Reading about mountain rescue dogs, or the "mercy dogs," of World War One, who brought aid and succor to battlefield wounded, is enough to bring tears to my eyes, at least.

One final point: the words "that others may live" cropped up a lot during the course of my research. Numerous rescue organizations, including the PJ's, claim that phrase as their motto. I think it captures in one line what lies at the heart of each real-life adventure collected in *The Greatest Search and Rescue Stories Ever Told*. Great heroism (and, sometimes, great heartbreak) is possible when we understand the profound fact that the lives of others are at least as valuable as our own.

Joseph Cummins
October 2002

Part One
Rescue in the High Mountains

The Ogre

From *The Climb Up To Hell*

BY JACK OLSEN

The north wall of the Eiger Mountain in the Bernese Alps, unconquered as late as 1938, has long been known as an extraordinarily dangerous climb. A mile high, covered with ice and rotting stone, the "Ogre" has taken the lives of scores of foolhardy men. A powerful drama unfolded there in August of 1957, as two ill-prepared climbers became stuck halfway up the wall on tiny, wind-swept ledges. While aperitif-sipping tourists watched from Swiss hotel verandas, an international SAR team launched what has been called "the greatest rescue in Alpine history."

★   ★   ★   ★   ★

At dawn the icy Tower of Babel on top of the Eiger summit sprang quickly to life. Gramminger was first up, and began the complex operation of laying out the cable system for new descents. The main problem was to anchor the large, drum-type winch on the shifting icecap. He made it fast with ice-pitons, then tied it to the porous rock of the cornice with several other cables. Another cable was wound around a big block of ice and connected to the winch, and several loose ropes were added on; as a final safety measure, some of the rescuers would grip these ropes tightly, scratch secure stances into the ice with their crampons, and hold on. Gramminger stepped back and surveyed his work. It was an insecure arrangement; he would have given anything for one solid outcropping of firm rock as a cornerstone for the rig. But the top of this mountain offered no concessions to the mechanical needs of the rescue party. They would have to make do.

Friedli watched the Germans set up their equipment and recognized that they were doing a skilled job under the adverse conditions. Still, he was not going to abdicate his own responsibilities in the operation. For all his deep respect for Gramminger and the Mountain Guard, he had serious misgivings about the winch. Under stress, it might tear loose and hurtle down the cliff, impartially taking rescuers and rescued to their deaths below. And even if the winch remained in place, he doubted that it was geared low enough to enable its operators to haul up the men below. At best, it would be an inch-by-inch struggle, taking long hours. And at this stage of the rescue, the life expectancies of the four men down below had to be measured in minutes.

Weighing all these factors, the skilled technician of Thun ordered a backstopping operation of his own. While Gramminger and the Mountain Guard struggled to anchor the winch, Friedli called together a work gang of Swiss and ordered them to extend the length of the level path which had been cut parallel to the ridge on the south side of the peak. Soon Friedli's men had hacked a path almost two hundred feet long, and had even rigged a sort of rope fence on its outer edge. Now men could walk along the trench in comparative safety. If the winch failed to work, the cable could be passed through pulleys over the top and back to crews in the trench, and old-fashioned, dependable manpower could take over the pulling operation. Friedli's move, taken with his usual taciturnity and strictly on the basis of his own forebodings, was a brilliant stroke of planning, even though it seemed to the digging crews in the trench that their leader had simply found a way to keep them busy and uncomfortable.

Overnight, the master plan for this Sunday morning had been worked out. It was known that Longhi was alone on a ledge about one thousand feet down, and it was assumed that the other three were in the tent several hundred feet above Longhi's perch. Reconnaissance pilots, toward the end of Saturday, had noticed Longhi slumping on his ledge. Probably he was in the worst condition of the four. Therefore the tentative plan was to lower a man past the red tent and down to Longhi, give him first aid and a stimulant, and haul him up to the tent. Then other rescuers would go down on the cable and bring the four men, one by one, to safety on the ridge. The only remaining question was whom to send down on the first trip. An Italian-speaking rescuer would have good verbal communication with Longhi and his comrade. But he would not be able to talk to the Germans. A German-speaking rescuer would have the opposite problem. Gramminger and Friedli talked the situation over, and the deciding factor was that the Italian members of the rescue party had no experience with the Gramminger equipment, but the men of the Mountain Guard knew their gear like firemen. Gramminger and Friedli selected Alfred Hellepart, an old hand at mountain rescues, and a man of tremendous strength and courage. At two hundred pounds, he was the heaviest of the Mountain Guard crew, but the quarter-inch cable had a tensile strength of nearly two tons, and Hellepart's bull-like power would be needed below. Gramminger fixed his friend to the end of the cable, strapped on the short-wave radio, covered Hellepart's head with a white plastic helmet, attached a rucksack to his back, and sent him over the side. Friedli took over the radio for the overall direction of the operation, and Gramminger scurried to the anchorage of the winch, there to stand ultimate guard over the life of his friend in case the equipment began to rip loose. Despite the insecurity of the anchorage, Gramminger felt fairly confident that it would stay in place. And if it did not, the other members of the rescue team would hold tightly, and somehow they would work Hellepart back up to the top. They had had to improvise before, and they had never lost a man. Neither, however, had they attempted a rescue one thousand feet down, or from such a treacherous perch. "Well," Gramminger said to himself, "we shall merely do our best." What worried him most was the weather. In good weather, the Mountain Guard could accomplish almost anything. But on this unprotected summit, the slightest break in the weather could mean the end of the whole operation. Even a minor electrical storm could be fatal; the steel cable was also a long lightning rod, and the man dangling at its end would risk electrocution. If clouds came, the important radio liaison with the spotters below at the Kleine Scheidegg would be useless, and the descents would have to be made on a hit-or-miss basis. And if there were high winds, the rescuers would be in danger of losing their delicate stances on the knife-edge of the summit. The weather simply had to remain clear. But a glance at the sky gave Gramminger a chill of apprehension. The sun hung between bilious clouds in a dirty-gray rectangle of visibility. To Gramminger, it seemed a poisonous yellow, a certain harbinger of storm. High black clouds could be seen coming down from the north. He was sure that they would reach the Eiger within hours and begin to discharge their loads of snow and rain and electricity against the face. If they did, the rescuers would have no choice but to beat a hurried retreat down the west flank. There could be no question of risking dozens of lives by trying to remain on the summit during a storm.

It was exactly eight o'clock on Sunday morning when Alfred Hellepart began moving down the mountain into aloneness. As he walked slowly backward on the fifty-degree angle of the summit ice field, watching his friends operate the winch above him, he set about preparing himself psychologically. From long experience, he knew that one had to purge one's mind of all outside thoughts;

the entire concentration had to be on the job at hand, and on the men to be rescued. One could not think at all of oneself; the slightest glimmer of fear could be deadly. Nor could he allow his thoughts to drift back to Munich, to his wife and his eleven-year-old son. From this minute on, they must be forgotten, until he had succeeded or failed in his rescue mission.

Certainly, there was no need to worry about the cable. The experienced Gramminger was up at the anchorage, protecting him as he had so many times before. The men of the Mountain Guard had an almost childlike faith in their leader; they acted on his orders without question or hesitation. In practice exercises, Hellepart had carried two men on his back up the side of a mountain, and the cable had held. He would press a button in his mind and give the matter no further thought.

Now he was halfway down the summit ice field, and he tested the portable radio. The contact was excellent; he could hear Friedli loud and clear, and Friedli could hear him. When he had gone 250 feet, almost to the end of the field, he heard Friedli telling him to make himself secure on his crampons; the cable had to be disconnected from the winch and joined to the next three-hundred-foot length by a frog coupling. Hellepart waited until the go-ahead came from the top, backed over the last few feet of the snow field, and found himself looking down the vast sweep of the north wall. For a moment, despite all his psychological preparations, he felt wild panic. An indescribable feeling of abandonment came over him; he could no longer see the men on the top, and instinctively he looked up at the quarter-inch cable spinning up into the mists, like a thin strand of cotton thread. Below him the north wall fell endlessly away, down and down and down, black and menacing, broken only by a few insignificant snow ledges. Dangling from the cable, he gulped for air, and almost forgot what he had come for. Just then the voice of Gramminger broke in on the radio. "You are doing fine, Alfred," the calm voice said. "Everything is secure for you. Keep control of yourself and remember that there are men on the wall depending on us for their lives." The soothing words brought composure back to Hellepart; he was no longer alone; he felt the strong ties to the men above, all their concentration fixed on him and his task, and he gave the order to continue letting the cable down. Off to his right, he could see a black rift coming up, one of the gaping exit cracks leading to the White Spider. He made a short traverse to the crack, and began wriggling his way obliquely downward. He did not know if this was the right route, but at the moment it was the only one. Two thousand feet below him, he could see the morning mists walking up the wall. For brief seconds, he glimpsed the village of Alpiglen, but then the mists closed together again and blanketed the valley. All around him the wind probed the holes and cracks on the mountain, and the low, hollow "whoo" gave him an uncomfortable feeling.

Now he had to find a secure stance again, to hold himself against the wall while another three-hundred-foot roll of cables was attached above. Friedli's voice crackled down to him from above: "All is well. You will be on your way in a few minutes." The signal came, and he continued his descent. After a hundred more feet, he went on the air to tell Friedli that he was coming in sight of the Spider. Against the low howl of the wind, he talked to the summit, and during that brief conversation he heard another human voice, barely audible at first, then growing louder and coming from the east. He traversed toward the voice and came to a shattered pillar bulging out across the face. He stepped onto the pillar and sent rocks and rubble clattering down the face with his crampons. Still he went on, only partially supported by the cable which now had assumed a sort of J-shape as it followed him on the level course across the pillar. About sixty feet away, he spotted a man in a half-sitting, half-lying position on a narrow ledge pitched with a small red tent. Nervously, he pushed the transmitting button and signaled the summit: "I have found a man."

Across the litter-covered pillar, Hellepart shouted: "Who are you? Are you Mayer, or Nothdurft?" The voice came back *"Italiano."*

Slowly, still sending tons of rubble down the mountain, Hellepart continued the difficult traverse. Now he was within six or seven feet of the Italian, and he could hear the man calling, *"Mangiare!* Something to eat!" Hellepart fumbled in his pocket, found a frozen half-bar of black, hard Cailler chocolate, and tossed it across the edge to the hungry man. The Italian did not even pause to remove the wrapper. He rammed the chocolate into his mouth and began to chew. His mouth full of paper and chocolate, the man called to Hellepart: *"Sigaretta?"* but Hellepart had none. He paused for a moment and considered the situation. He could traverse the remaining few feet of the pillar, but only at increasing risk to himself, since he no longer dangled straight down from the cable. And if he reached the Italian in this manner, he would be unable to make the rescue. The two men, no matter what their condition, could not have effected the traverse back across the rubble without undue danger. Hellepart decided to retreat to the exit crack and ask the summit to pull him up to another position. From there he would try to make a straight perpendicular descent to the Italian. "Take me up," Hellepart called to the summit. "I am going to look for another route." A hard jerk on the cable yanked him off the pillar and out into space. Spinning in mid-air, he fought to turn himself toward the wall so that he could take up the shock of the return impact with his legs. He had barely succeeded in twisting around when he crashed into the wall feet first. "All right," said Hellepart to the summit, "haul me straight up. I will tell you when to stop."

Up he went, inches at a time, for 150 feet, and then set himself into a slow swing until he was able to grab a jutting rock straight above the Italian. "Now let me down," he instructed. As he descended a sheer gully, stones began to shake loose again, and he shouted to the Italian to take cover. Finally he dropped the last few feet and onto the ledge. While the marooned man mumbled *"Grazie! Grazie!"* and put his arms around Hellepart, the German called triumphantly to the summit: "I am with the Italian!" It was nine-fifteen, and he had been on the wall for more than an hour. The Italian gave his name, and Hellepart reported it to the summit. Friedli asked where the others were. Hellepart said to Corti: "Where is Longhi? Where is Mayer? Where is Nothdurft?"

Corti pointed down the mountain. The two men leaned over the edge and called, but there was no response. Hellepart asked Corti in German, "Your condition?" Corti understood—the phrase is similar in both languages—and answered, *"Buona."* But Hellepart, seeing that the man's knees were trembling, ordered him to sit down, and gave him coffee from a thermos, which had been provided by the Poles. Corti was talking in Italian, and Hellepart got the impression from the torrent of words in the peculiar dialect that Nothdurft and Mayer had tried to force through to the top and that Corti had not seen them for several days. He looked at Corti's scarred hand and his bloodied head and decided that the Italian's condition was too poor to permit him to attempt a climb up to the top on a separate cable. Hellepart would have to make the carry on his back. He radioed to the summit for an Italian-speaking man to take the radio and explain the situation to Corti. Cassin's voice came on, and Hellepart handed the speaking mechanism to Corti, who seemed befuddled by it and nervously pushed the wrong buttons. Finally the contact was established, and Cassin could talk to his friend from the Ragni. *"Rispondi,* Claudio," Cassin's voice said. "This is Cassin. Now listen to me: you have not the strength to go up by yourself. Watch how he shows you how to get up on his shoulders! Try everything to make it easy for your rescuer! Drink something when he gives you to drink. Remember, you are safe. Do not lose your spirit!" Hellepart took back the radio as the last words of Cassin crackled through the earphones: *"Coraggio,* Claudio, *coraggio!"*

Hellepart took a final look at Corti's tiny resting place. It was totally cleared of ice and snow, gobbled up by Corti in his terrible hunger and thirst. Some of his teeth were broken and splintered, shattered against the hard, cold ice for a last few useless "meals." Hellepart packed the rucksack, strapped it on the sitting Corti's back, and began lacing him into the webbing of a Gramminger-Sitz. He sat down with his back to Corti's front and pulled the harnesses of the human back-pack around his own chest and up over his shoulders. This left no place for the radio; using snap links to lengthen the girth, he fixed the apparatus so that it dangled across his chest. Bearing the uncomfortable weight, he struggled to his feet and snapped the cable in place. All these preparations had taken nearly an hour. "We are ready," he said to the summit. It was ten o'clock.

Back came Friedli's voice: "We have been rearranging the equipment. It will take us a few minutes more."

Hellepart sat down with his heavy load and waited for the signal. Finally it came. "We bring you up now," Friedli called. "Prepare yourself."

Hellepart wrenched himself into a standing position, but still the cable hung slack above him. "What is the matter?" he called to the summit.

"We are having a little trouble," Friedli answered. Long minutes went by, and then the cable began to tense. Hellepart pressed his feet against the wall and pushed outward with all his strength so that he would keep the cable from running against the wall and prevent it from fouling. Now the wind began to hum across the tightening thread of steel. It sounded to Hellepart like a giant violin string, starting on a low note and gradually whining higher as it tensed, until it had reached a screaming, piercing pitch. And still they did not move up from the ledge. He looked above him at the delicate strand and wondered, for the first time, if it would hold.

On top, Friedli's fears about the winch had only increased as it had become necessary to haul Hellepart back up 150 feet to find a better route down to the Italian. By now there were eight hundred feet of cable reaching down the mountain. Where it made contact with the rock, it had abraded fissures of its own, increasing the friction and multiplying the force required for the upward pull. The men cranking the winch had barely been able to lift Hellepart up to his new stance, and after lowering him back down to the ledge, Friedli discussed the situation with Gramminger. "I do not think we can use the winch to pull the weight of two men," Friedli said. Gramminger agreed. While Hellepart went about his tedious task of readying Corti for the next ascent, the crew on top discarded the winch and prepared to shift over to raw manpower. It was a quick improvisation, made possible only by Friedli's foresight in ordering the pulling path dug into the south ridge. Now the cable would go up to the ridge and through a direction-changing roller placed on top of the rotten cornice. The roller would steer the cable back along the path, where thirty men were scrambling into position. At intervals of twenty feet, pulling ropes were attached to the cable by clamps which could be loosened and moved along to a new position.

Now teams of five were in place at each pulling rope, waiting for the signal from Friedli to begin the haul. A last-minute check was made of the three security brakes on the cable; they were so constructed that the cable could be pulled upward through them, but at the slightest accidental downward movement they would clamp tightly shut. As a final security, Gramminger remained at the big block of ice on the far end of the pulling path to anchor each new length of slack cable to the block as it was hauled in. Now they were ready.

With the voice of a Swiss drill sergeant, Friedli shouted to the men to haul away. They strained backward against the pulling ropes. But nothing moved. More hands were added to the ropes, and the order was repeated. Still the cable did not budge. Fearful that the combined strength of all the rescuers would snap the tensing lifeline to the two men below, Friedli frantically waved the operation to a halt. He did not think it possible that the cable had become wedged into the rock below; the soft limestone on the upper part of the Eiger might increase the friction, but it would not have been solid enough to imprison the cable against all this pressure. He decided that the mechanical equipment must have jammed. If his diagnosis was incorrect, if indeed the cable *was* fouled tightly on the mountain, they would have to abandon Corti and try to find some way to bring Hellepart back up. Nervously, Friedli went from device to device and finally came to one which had fouled. He cleared the jam and ordered the crews to begin pulling again. The cable tensed and whined in the wind, after a few long seconds, the men could feel it begin to move.

Now, at last, the long violin string had hit a pitch and held it, and Hellepart was coming up the mountain, his human cargo heavy on his back, the radio dangling clumsily in front of him. At first, the ascent was not on a true perpendicular line. They swayed from side to side as the cable whipped them about; Hellepart shoved his crampons into the icy patina on the wall, seeking to steady himself, and sent slabs of ice and rock crashing down the wall. Every fifty feet, he had to cling to the wall, leaning as far forward as he could, while the men on the summit secured the cable and moved up to new pulling positions. These were agonizing delays to the strong man of Munich; sometimes he would have to kneel against a tiny ledge, gripping an outcropping of rock with his knees the way a jockey grips a horse, the harsh metal edges of the radio digging into his chest. Sometimes he had to stand upright on scallops of snow, with all the weight of Corti on his shoulders. Once he said aloud, in a lightly annoyed, slightly quizzical voice: "Well, he's quite heavy, this fellow." But Corti seemed not to have heard. He was mumbling, "*Fame! Fame!*" and whenever Hellepart kneeled against the wall, Corti would push his own face into the snow and bite off big mouthfuls.

"Don't gobble so much snow!" Hellepart hollered. "It is bad for the stomach." But the famished Corti took his cold snacks anyway.

After about forty minutes of the torturous rise, the cable rasped over the last foot of the exit cracks and swung the two men onto the summit ice field. Out of the shadow of the overhand, they now could feel the rays of the sun, and Corti reacted peculiarly. "*Que bello e il sole,*" he said in a strangely loud voice. "How beautiful the sun is." Then he slumped forward into a coma. Hellepart recognized this as a shock reaction, and he knew that men in a seriously weakened condition could die from it. He would have to force the final 250 feet of the field. Up he came, staggering like a drunk under his heavy load, while Friedli shouted encouragement from the top. Now Hellepart was taking almost all of Corti's weight, receiving little assistance from the cable which no longer hung straight down to hold them in firm suspension. The men on top knew he was forcing, and increased their own pace, once pulling too far too fast and nearly wrenching Hellepart and Corti face forward into the wet snow of the ice field. Hellepart merely regained his balance, kicked up through the sticky snow, and finally, fifty-nine minutes after the ascent had begun, stumbled with his cargo across the ridge. "Help me out of this!" he shouted to Friedli and pitched forward into the snow. Gasping for breath, while the others wrenched at the harnesses holding Corti and the radio to him, Hellepart felt a slap on the shoulder and heard an unfamiliar voice say, "Good! You have done well!" Relieved of his load, he was lifted to his feet and congratulated all around. "A cigarette!" he said. "I would like a cigarette!" Weak, and afraid he would slip off the summit, he wobbled to the safety of a bivouac hole for a smoke and a rest.

The Terrible Spring

From *In The Shadow of Denali*

BY JONATHAN WATERMAN

Rising more than twenty thousand feet into the sky is Denali, the tallest mountain in North America. As a guide and rescue ranger on Denali, the internationally respected writer and photographer Jonathan Waterman has seen extremes of human heroism. But this selection captures the terrible spring of 1992, when 11 people including legendary Alaskan climber Mugs Stump died on Denali slopes.

★   ★   ★   ★   ★

On May 21, 1992, Mugs came to me in a dream. I woke up wondering why he never got the recognition deserved for his fabulous mountain career. Maybe it was because Mugs never publicized his climbs; maybe it was because climbing was his deeply felt and private ballet.

The real news did not come until several days later in a phone call, but Mugs wasn't the only one. Ten other died. The storm and sorrow of 1992, in fact, surpassed even the eight-man death toll of 1967 on Denali. The summer of 1992 might remain in the history books as the most infamous summer ever on Denali: In addition to all the deaths, there were a record 1,070 climbers on the mountain. And rescues cost the taxpayers $431,345, nearly four times the expense of any previous year. Although more climbers will die on Denali, 1992's events will make most climbers think twice about hanging it out.

At first, the subzero cold prevented most climbers from summiting, an event merely typical of early spring weather on Denali. Then, on May 11, a Fairbanks meteorologist forecasted "the worst storm that'll hit the mountain in 10 years." Within 30 hours more than 5 feet of snow fell at the 7,000-foot base camp; winds of 110 miles per hour hit the 14,300-foot camp. Over a month's time, 22 climbers would be rescued; 18 of them were foreigners.

There were also dozens of minor accidents and rescues, including the evacuation of a Korean who fell while rappelling from the south face. Two Germans fell below the summit, and although capable of walking down with their minor injuries, they sat apathetically at 18,200 feet until Dr. Colin Grissom came to their rescue.

Meanwhile, a 48-year-old Italian climber, Giovanni Calcagno, had pooh-poohed the rangers' advice and arrogantly stalked out of the ranger station, thinking that no one knew how good a climber he really was. Calcagno then succeeded in climbing most of Cassin Ridge with his thirty-year-old companion Roberto Piombo, but at about the time they would summit, the wind began trumpeting like freight trains on top. On May 15, after receiving reports of a body, the rangers flew in by helicopter and found Calcagno's body hanging at 15,400 feet and Piombo's on the 11,800-foot glacier below Cassin Ridge. Piombo's body was slingloaded out, but Calcagno's body could not be retrieved.

At the same time, the rangers tried to evacuate three Koreans from Cassin Ridge; they had been stranded in a 17,700-foot snowcave for a week, radioing for help after the storm blew their tent and food away. Two days later, after the altitude-sick Koreans were nearly decapitated in the rotor, they were choppered down to 14,300 feet. The last Korean climber hooked three backpacks onto the skid below, but the ranger kicked them loose, explaining to the Korean that the extra weight could make the helicopter crash.

When the ship landed, instead of being thankful, one of the Koreans exploded about their packs—containing money and passports—being abandoned to the mountain. There at 14,300 feet, standing in the prop wash of a second helicopter that would take the Koreans to the hospital, Matt Culberson explained to the Koreans that being safe counts more than anything else. But the most irate Korean refused to board the helicopter until the packs were rescued; Jim Wickwire and John Roskelly wrestled the man aboard.

By May 17, the well-acclimated Swiss climber Alex Von Burgen, 42, had carried two loads above his 14,300-foot camp on the West Buttress. Immediately after sitting up to sip the tea that his wife had prepared for him that morning, he died from cardiac arrhythmia. Will Sayre was there, reliving the events of our winter climb, and even thought Sayre knew it was a hopeless gesture, he went into the tent and alternated breathing into the dead man's mouth with hand compressions on the sternum.

Later that afternoon, three Koreans from Je-Ju University Expedition unknowingly began setting up their tent on top of a crevasse bridge at 15,000 feet on the west buttress. Suddenly the 200-by-40-foot-wide bridge broke. Duk San Jan ran down for help.

Roskelly, Wickwire, Matt and Julie Culberson, Ron Johnson, Bruce Blatchley, and Brian Okonek rushed to the rescue. The second Korean, Seong Yu Kang, was buried up to his chest at the bottom of the crevasse; Roskelly and Matt Culberson rappelled 60 feet down and dug him out.

But Dong Choon Seo was hidden somewhere else beneath the collapsed snow bridge blocks. Seo assumed he was going to die slowly, so seeking a quicker end, he began chewing his tongue so he would bleed to death. The blood had clotted until he could barely breathe around the swollen, pulpy flesh that remained in his mouth. The snow around him began reddening, Culberson spied the bloody snow and a foot sticking out; he began sawing apart ice blocks; his shouts elicited a long moan, and finally the Korean's hand reached out and grabbed Culberson's ankle, as Culberson wrote in his journal, "with tremendous force."

After half an hour of working in subzero temperatures, risking another crevasse collapse, Roskelly and Culberson finished digging out Seo, whose arms and legs were pinned by huge blocks of ice. He was quickly evacuated, and in addition to the mess in his mouth, he had a broken back and a myriad of internal injuries.

Of all the rescuers who had seen accidents on the mountain before, Wickwire was doubly relieved about Seo and Kang. Over the past two decades, Wickwire had four partners die at his side. Eleven years earlier, beneath Denali's Wickersham Wall, it was impossible to free Chris Kerebrock from a similar crevasse, so Wickwire was forced to sit and watch him die from hypothermia.

On the morning of May 20, three other students form the Je-Ju University Expedition radioed from 18,000 feet on the west rim that they would soon descend. At 5:00 P.M., the Culbersons—who were descending on the same route—found a long streak of blood on the snow at about 15,500 feet; below they saw three dark objects. Matt belayed his wife down, and when Julie saw the now discernible Korean bodies, Matt heard her shouting, "Oh no! Not again! Why do you guys keep doing this?"

Since 1972 there have been eleven other deaths and several serious injuries here, partly because some climbers continue to proceed up in storms, but mostly because of the perennially tricky snow conditions at 18,000 feet. Guides and rangers now morbidly refer to this chute as the "Orient Express" because of its inordinate number of Korean and Japanese victims.

There was still more. Later that month, four Canadian climbers bivouacked below the summit and became overdue. While flying in a search plane, Roger Robinson spied them descending near the edge of the Messner Couloir at 19,300 feet. Minutes later, the last person on the rope stumbled and fell, plucking his three partners off; all four plunged 2,500 feet.

Dozens of climbers watched from below. "I saw one black dot going about 50 miles per hour down the slope and then you couldn't see any more from the clouds of snow they were kicking up," said Dr. Colin Grissom. "It gave me a real bad feeling in the pit of my stomach."

"It was horrible," guide Michael Covington was quoted in *Outside* by journalist Jon Krakauer. "They were smashing off rocks, bouncing far into the air, and all we could do was stand there helplessly and watch them die."

Colin finally plowed through dangerous avalanche conditions and reached the four bodies the next morning. "It was very, very obvious that they had died on the way down," he said. "I have to say it was a rough thing to witness."

Then Mugs. After taking his client Nelson Max to the storm-washed summit on hands and knees, he escorted Max and Robert Hoffman back down the seldom-climbed South Buttress Route. At that point in the season, only 9 other climbers out of 420 had reached the summit. It is a testament to Mugs's skill that he had gotten so high while escorting clients up in such sordid weather. He had held everything together perfectly when the going was tough—unlike most victims that summer—but when things became easier, perhaps Mugs let down his guard.

The next day, May 21, at 14,500 feet, the three were route-finding down the "Japanese Ramp," a 4,000-foot shortcut swept by unpredictable avalanches. Hoffman stopped at the edge of a crevasse, and since he was unsure how to proceed, Mugs walked past Max and Hoffman without taking a belay, including 15 feet of slack in his rope. Although it was a common mistake, Mugs regularly practiced "casual" glacier travel techniques. He turned around as if to say something, and at that instant a huge crevasse bridge broke with the resounding crack of a rifle shot beneath his feet: Mugs plunged in and dragged Max twenty feet before he could stop. The rope between him and Mugs became slack. For brief seconds everything was silent until the clients began yelling Mugs's name.

Horrified, they peered into the crevasse, buried by tons of dense snow and ice blocks. After getting no reply to their shouts, they cut the rope, and Max rappelled into the crevasse—more than any guide could ask of a client. He dug for long minutes amid dense blocks of snow and ice. Finally, numb with the realization of what the mountain is capable of, they admitted that Mugs had to be dead.

The two started descending the mountain without stove or radio (buried with Mugs), and when picked up the next day in a helicopter—frostbitten and shaking—they quickly showed the rangers Mugs's grave, more than 25 hours after the accident. Max and Hoffman were dropped off at 7,200 feet and taken by airplane to the hospital; Max had frostbite on both feet.

The helicopter, carrying one of Mugs's former climbing partners, Ranger Renny Jackson, returned to the crevasse. Tons of snow and ice still overhung the area, known to previous South Buttress climbers and avalanche survivors as "a bowling alley." Given the steepness of the slope, the falling ice potential, and the amount of time that had elapsed since the accident, it would have been folly to look. Mugs's parents told Jackson's boss it was okay, and the body was wisely abandoned to the mountain.

Back in Talkeetna, a lot of nonclimbers wanted to know why Renny "didn't do more," not knowing that Mugs was a good friend. Renny hated this. No one really understood how bad the South Buttress Ramp is. So Renny went back up in the helicopter and videoed the dangerous crevasse from the air.

Most people could not believe that Mugs would die so ignobly, guiding such a relatively "easy" climb, particularly after everything he had survived in the Alaska Range.

Ranger Ron Johnson broke down when he heard about Mugs. Johnson knew he needed to get down and get some help. It wasn't any one event. Bundling up bodies below the Orient Express, the dead Swiss climber, dealing with the Koreans in the crevasse, keeping the tents dug out, and just staying warm made Johnson lose sleep and start having stress headaches. "Mugs was the final *coup de grace*," said Johnson. "It just got out of control."

Talking with the other rangers accomplished nothing. They would all nod their heads, lift another beer, and say, "Well, you know how it is." They all needed help.

A psychologist was flown up from Washington State for a "critical stress incident debriefing." Since the psychologist did not know "how it is," he forced the rescuers to explain everything. "It allowed me to hear that the things we were experiencing were normal," said Johnson, "and they would eventually go away."

Anchorage journalist Craig Medred wrote that Mugs's death "rocked the soul of the climbing community." And Jack Tackle (who Mugs had helped in the Ruth Glacier rescue of 1979) scribbled me a card while en route to Denali: "to go take some 'mental health drugs' by myself." I am so sad about Mugs, one less hero to make all this alpine climbing worthwhile.

Three days after the accident, a memorial service was held for Mugs on the banks of the Susitna River at a cabin owned by Kathy Sullivan (widow of former Denali guide Ray Genet). Forty locals and guides and rangers stood around kicking sand washed down over the millennia from Denali. The sky seemed more infinite than the ocean; everyone watched the mountain. As climbers and friends took turns telling stories about Mugs, the group alternated between tears and laughter. A mother spoke lovingly of how Mugs tenderly fed yogurt instead of baby's milk to her infant. Another climber remembered what an absentminded driver Mugs was and how he crashed several of his friends' cars. A ranger recalled Mugs's illegal guiding on Denali and how he would tell passing climbers that his bumbling companions were "just friends." No one bore any grudges against the High One, fifty miles away, ripping clouds as the most stunning and luminescent tombstone on earth.

The New York Times, The Anchorage Daily News, Newsweek, Rock and Ice, Climbing and *Outside* covered the tragic events of that summer, but no one got it quite right. One journalist suggested a new adventure-travel theme for Alaskan vacations: "Climb Mount McKinley—and die." And the journals most referred to the mountain by its Republican name, Mount McKinley, instead of the name that Mugs and Herb Atwater used, the name that most Alaskans continue to use.

"Mountain of death," one journal called it, ignoring the fact that more Americans have died on 6,244-foot Mount Washington in New Hampshire, or in automobile accidents, or in senseless gang wars, or from one of many diseases that can snuff you with none of the quick mercy that climbers have found on Denali.

Newsweek asked if climbing the mountain is sport or a "kind of athletic Russian roulette." The journalist then asserted a timeworn platitude that "the old 'because it's there' romanticism that makes people climb mountains lurches into hyper-drive on McKinley."

But no journalist wrote about the banality of city life or how easy it is to become yet another automaton paying bills and working nine to five and being so removed from the primary necessities of life and so far from real fear and natural beauty and human instinct that when death finally approaches in some antiseptic white room, just as you have been waiting for it, you sense that you have already been dead for years.

Mugs knew that climbing Denali is a means of getting in touch with your life and confronting your own fragility, instead of putting it all off and counting your days as atrophied decay. Despite his crevasse travel techniques, Mugs, unlike most of 1992's victims, had a sense of self-sufficiency and respect for the mountain.

The New York Times, with its impeccably objective reporting, referred to "a Utah guide" without even mentioning his name. The paper brushed the truth with its headline: "In the Shadow of Mount McKinley, a Town Lives with Death." The story touched on "the death wall" in the Fairview Inn, but most readers would not have understood the significance of any of the portraits hanging there, so they were not described. Precious few indeed would understand that Ray Genet loved mountains more than anything else in life when he died in a bivouac on Everest; or that the sad-eyed bush pilot Don Sheldon risked his life innumerable times to rescue others because he liked doing it, and probably because he sensed his own crumbling battle with cancer.

Outside magazine also gave it a shot. "Because of his unimpeachable climbing record," wrote John Krakauer, "no one suggested that Stump's death was anything but a freak accident."

Since Allen Carpé's death in 1932, eleven climbers on Denali have died in "freak accident" crevasse falls. Nine of those climbers were of Mugs's caliber and had let down their guard on low-angled glaciers, traveling without rope, with a short tope, or with slack ropes. And Mugs? He was weirdly cavalier about proper rope technique on crevassed glaciers.

When the phone call came verifying his death, I was stunned. But there is consolation in thinking that Mugs had finally gone home, smiling at the storm and saved from those wretched silver-haired years when his memory would falter and his strength would slip and he would have been forced to find the patience to eke out the autumn of his life. No journalist suggested that the forty-three-year-old foresaw being shackled by house payments and being forced to find a "real" job and pace an earth flat and dull without the extreme climbing on the mountains he loved.

Mugs's body remains up there along with the bodies of thirty-two others. Undoubtedly future South Buttress climbers will encounter Mugs's spirit there on the Japanese Ramp; at the very least they will share his enthusiasm for a mountain that the 1903 climber Robert Dunn called an "unearthly castle of opalescent glass." Most other climbers will relive Denali as the zenith of their lives. And surely more climbers will entertain staying on the mountain like Allen and Johnny and Dave and Chris and Mugs have all done.

It is no coincidence that, beginning with Allen Carpé, the Alaskan climbing veterans who have died on Denali all treasured, and in some instances even memorized, Robert Service's poem *The Spell of the Yukon*. Mugs knew it well:

> There's a land where the mountains are nameless,
> And the rivers all run God knows where;
> There are lives that are erring and aimless,
> And deaths that just hang by a hair;
> There are hardships that nobody reckons,
> There are valleys unpeopled and still;
> There's a land—oh it beckons and beckons,
> And I want to go back—and I will.

In my dream about Mugs just after he died, he disapproves of my life with its lack of action and my brooding with words on paper as I worry about paying bills while sitting all day in an office. Mugs often appears in my dreams. He is disappointed that I am not going up Denali anymore, and he tried to talk me into a climbing trip that will last forever, with granite rasping our palms and frozen clouds coursing through our lungs, and where we will look out the windows of heaven at an alabaster ripsawed skyline and pink-orange clouds of a thousand shapes.

It is not stretching the imagination to see Mugs watching the green tundra four miles below disappearing into a gentle curve of the earth. He sees the Bering Sea on beyond like bluing infinity and hangs his legs out over the abyss of the south face while contemplating the air rising and falling through the granite gorge of Ruth Amphitheater—knowing that our planet is all one being as it breathes over him with the heat waves shimmering on beyond the blinding white of the glaciers toward Talkeetna and the budding life and rivers and greenery as far as he can see. Nothing up there is too terrible to behold. There on top of North America, Mugs smells that seared cobalt sky and watches the sun wink through passing clouds. He has found happiness beyond all time and ambition and breathing.

Crash at the Top of the World

From *Heartbreak and Heroism*

BY JOHN MELADY

While not exactly the mountains, the Arctic is one of the most inaccessible and forbidding regions in the world. From his book *Heartbreak and Heroism*, John Melady's "Crash at the Top of the World" tells one of the most incredible SAR stories we've ever read: how Canadian pararescue jumpers leapt from a Hercules transport plane into the teeth of a blinding polar gale to save the crew of a crashed plane just 500 miles from the North Pole.

★   ★   ★   ★   ★

On the last morning of July, 1950, a Royal Canadian Air Force Lancaster bomber prepared to drop supplies by parachute to the northernmost settlement on earth. The place was called Alert, a military listening post on Ellesmere Island, five hundred miles from the North Pole. The plane involved was from 405 Squadron in Greenwood, Nova Scotia, and was flown by D.T. French. Wing Commander French had eight officers and men with him.

The crew on the Lanc expected to be over the drop zone for only a few minutes before flying back to Thule, an American air base on the northwest coast of Greenland. Thule was used then, and still is, as the jumping-off point for the transport of supplies to the listening station. It was a larger and much less forbidding outpost than Alert itself. The men on the plane would be glad to get back there.

On the ground below the Lanc, the crew who would collect the delivery waited in anticipation, and watched as the four-engine aircraft approached.

They saw the cargo doors part, some thousand feet above them, then noticed a bundle come out. A parachute appeared.

Somehow, inexplicably, the chute failed to open.

As the horrified spectators looked on, it streamed back towards the rear of the plane, became entangled in the tail elevators, and remained caught there.

The effect on the bomber was immediate.

It lost altitude, veered out of control, and in a matter of seconds, plunged headlong onto the rock and permafrost below. All on board died instantly in the explosion and fire that followed.

One of those was a young flying officer named Everett McCutcheon of Cornwall, Ontario. He was stationed in Greenwood then, with his wife Joan, who was pregnant, and their little daughter, Gail. Gail now had one parent, Joan was a widow and a second daughter Ann, born some months afterwards, would never see her father. Yet much later, both girls would see firsthand the place where this man that neither knew was killed.

Exactly thirty years from the date of the crash—on July 31, 1980—another aircraft flew over the northern outpost. This time, it was a Hercules from Ottawa, via Thule, carrying a handful of relatives of the men who had died so long before. Among the passengers were Gail and Ann McCutcheon, now married and accompanied by their husbands.

"The plane landed at Alert," says Carl Brand, who was married to Ann. "We were there for a memorial service for the deceased, so we were able to visit their graves and see the stone cairn which had been erected in their memory. It was very moving to honour the memories of those airmen who had sacrificed their lives at our northernmost frontier. The Hercules we went in on did a flypast, as an Air Force general said a few words. Then we were given a reception in the Officers' Mess and flew out."

But the legacy of Alert did not end with the crash of 1950, nor with its remembrance thirty years later. Unfortunately, this most desolate of locales was the scene of another tragedy, this time in 1991. In this catastrophe, five young people would die and several others would be scarred for life, but a third group would demonstrate that even in times of the most devastating heartbreak, genuine, unselfish heroism often comes to the fore. It certainly did in the twenty-four-hour darkness and biter cold of the High Arctic on October 30, 1991, when a Hercules with eighteen people on board went down.

The plane was carrying a tank of diesel fuel to Alert, along with thirteen passengers, but unlike the situation in 1950, it would be landing at the northern base. There it would be unloaded, the passengers would climb out, and the aircraft would depart.

The supply-delivery procedure was quite different from that of earlier years. Now there were three planes ferrying material. All of it came from Thule, where it had been shipped by boat from southern Canada the previous summer. This Thule-Alert operation was a continuous one, yet always subject to interruption because of the changeable polar weather. In the best of all possible worlds, delivery took about ten days in total. "Boxtop" was the code name for these flights.

Shortly before 4:30 P.M. local time on October 30, Hercules 322, or Boxtop 22, was inbound from Thule. At the controls was 32-year-old John Couch, a Gulf War veteran and a seasoned Herc pilot. There were four crew members with him, along with the passengers. Aside from the personal belongings of the people on board, the load was fuel. It was carried in an internal tank in the cargo compartment of the plane. This "wet lift," as it was called, amounted to 3,300 Imperial gallons, weighing just over 28,000 pounds. In addition, there were about 24,000 pounds of aircraft fuel on board, and this, added to the wet lift, made the total weight of the plane almost 135,000 pounds.

The flight for the most part was routine. The weather was good, with visibility for as much as fifteen miles or more. There was no sun, of course, because at Alert there is total darkness from mid-October until March. On the ground, the temperature was twenty-two degrees Celsius below zero, with light winds.

As the Herc neared its destination, Couch talked to the control tower at Alert and assured himself that all was well for landing. He was given the temperature, the wind and their direction, and the visibility on the ground. And, because he could already see the runway lights in the distance, Couch opted for a visual approach.

This decision was unfortunate.

A dozen or so miles from touchdown, the crew apparently thought they were coming in above the frozen surface of the Lincoln Sea, immediately adjacent to the airstrip at Alert. Instead, they were over land that was dotted with hills. But by this time the plane was low—so low, in fact, that it hit one of the hills. The flight was over.

The port wing touched the ground first. This caused the plane to lurch to the left, break apart, and scatter itself in a crude semicircle across a shallow depression surrounded by outcrops of rock. The earsplitting screech of tearing metal cut the frozen silence, only to be followed by the explosion of aviation gasoline and the roar of a fire, fed by liquid oxygen that ignited in the cockpit. Already, all four of the plane's propellers had been ripped off, as the engines on which they had been mounted ground into the ice and stone.

The wings of the plane came to rest in one place, the tail in another, and the cockpit in a third. Human beings, living and dead, were tossed into the snow, then drenched in a massive gush of reeking diesel oil as the wet tank tore from its mounts and broke apart. Roaring flames lit the daytime darkness and billows of black smoke rose into the Arctic sky. Much of the plane was quickly reduced to charred rubber, melted metal and grotesque chunks of debris that defied description. Boxtop 22 was no more.

But here and there in this unspeakable hell were survivors, men and women who had trouble believing they were actually alive; a couple near the cockpit, others back of the wings, two in the oil-soaked snow some distance to one side. All were stunned at the suddenness of events, the chaos around them, and the terrible realization that the plane had just crashed.

Some got their bearings before others. Some were hurt more than others. Some could move and at least two could not—at least not on their own. Some would never move again.

News of the crash traveled fast. When Boxtop 22 did not touch down at Alert at 4:30 as expected, and could not be seen on approach, the radar operator attempted to locate it. The last contact had been a few miles out, but after that, there was nothing. Because Boxtop 21 was also en route to Alert, it was directed to the last known position of the missing plane.

At 4:50, the crew on the second Herc saw fires on the ground.

Ten minutes later, Search and Rescue was notified.

Twenty-six hundred miles away, in Greenwood, Nova Scotia, Warrant Officer Arnie Macauley had just sat down to dinner. He was bone tired, and happy to be home after a long day. For more than seven hours he had been bouncing around in the back of a Hercules C-130, trying to keep an eye on a twenty-eight-man Japanese fishing vessel called the *Eishin Maru*. The ship was attempting to ride out a vicious Atlantic storm, ninety miles off Sable Island. In time, it did; the gale abated, and the trawler and its company moved on.

Twenty-nine-year-old Ron O'Reilly had been with Macauley. He too had been glad to wind down at the end of the day, playing with his daughter and admiring her Hallowe'en costume. He had just finished eating.

Both of these men were SAR Techs attached to 413 Squadron in Greenwood. Macauley, from Medicine Hat, was the team leader. O'Reilly, originally from North Vancouver, had come to Greenwood after the Canadian Forces Base at Summerside, P.E.I. had closed down.

The two men were personable, athletic, and veterans in their chosen profession. They loved being SAR Techs.

"I was still eating when my brother Marvin phoned," says Arnie Macauley today. "All he said was, 'There's a Herc down up in Alert. Get everybody in. It looks as if it's a MAJAID." Macauley's younger brother Marv was a Search and Rescue Hercules pilot at Greenwood; the "MAJAID" he referred to was a military code term for "Major Air Disaster," meaning the crash of an aircraft with more than ten people on board. Arnie kissed his wife Darlene and raced out the door.

"One of the guys at work called me," Ron O'Reilly remembers. "He said there was a Herc down up north and that they needed us all in. At first I thought he was pulling my leg, but he said, 'No, it's for real.' I got dressed and broke a land speed record getting in. I lived close to the base at the time."

While these two men in Nova Scotia were hearing the bad news from Alert, SAR Techs three time zones away were getting a similar message.

"It was just after 3:30 in Edmonton," says Darby Darbyson, who was at the Search and Rescue unit there. "Jim Brown and I were on standby duty on the Herc. We were in the SAR Tech room at the base and he said to me, 'Well, when are we going to get launched?' I knew he was just joking around, so I said, 'By four.' I had hardly said it when the buzzer went off. We jumped up and went right over to the Ops [Operations] Room in another hangar to find out what was going on. The guy I talked to said, 'Get on your plane right now. There's a Herc down at Alert.' I asked how many people were on board, because I knew there were often passengers going up there. He looked at me and then said, 'It doesn't matter. Just get on the aircraft!'

"I said, 'No, we've got to know. How many passengers are on board?' Finally the guy said, 'Wait here. I'll find out.' Then he came back and told me there were five aircrew and thirteen passengers. I was stunned . . .'"

In no time, every Search and Rescue squadron in Canada knew something was seriously wrong in the far north. The news that the plane had been overdue was one thing, but the alarming message that fires had been seen shocked everyone. Each person who heard the news understood, deep down, that a plane crash followed by a fire often, too often, meant no one had survived.

And the arrival time for a rescue mission at Alert was anything but immediate. There were no helicopters there, and the place was far away from all the major SAR establishments in the south. Nevertheless, men and equipment were launched from Greenwood, Gander, Trenton and Edmonton, and later even Iceland and Alaska. The first to go were helicopters from Trenton and Gander respectively, but shortly afterwards, fully loaded Hercules rescue planes from Edmonton and Greenwood were in the air as well. The Edmonton contingent was about forty minutes ahead of Greenwood.

Every person flying to Alert that night knew the distances involved. The northern facility is about 2,500 miles from Moscow, for example, but close to 3,000 from Toronto. Just getting there by Herc would take a long time: roughly seven and a half hours from Greenwood, a little less from Edmonton. Once airborne, the rescuers would have plenty of time to contemplate what had to be done.

"I called Fred Ritchie, our team leader, at home," recalls Darby Darbyson, "and told him what we'd heard. He knew we were going to need a lot of people up there, so he put the MAJAID plan into effect. Then we called every SAR Tech we could find. In no time, the guys were streaming in, and the plane was loaded. Once everyone was accounted for, we left. There were twelve SAR Techs on board. Flying weather out of Edmonton was good; cool and clear."

The situation was much the same at Greenwood.

"As soon as I got to the base, I started opening up the shop and turning on the lights," said Ron O'Reilly. "As I went to get radios and stuff, it just seemed like a stream of orange [the colour of the SAR Tech uniform] coming in. It was amazing because it was rare for everyone in the Squadron to be around at the same time—there would be guys training somewhere else, and things, but when this call came in, just about everyone was there. We formed ourselves into a line, passing gear along and loading the Herc. At this point, we still did not have much information about the crash, so we were preparing for all possibilities. As we loaded what we thought we might need, the Techs on the floor were doing the fueling, and the pilots their flight planning.

"On the way north, we were still getting little bits of information, but not a lot. We learned that there was another Herc from Edmonton on the way, and we were calculating who would get there first. When we realized they would get there about an hour before us, we pretty much accepted that. Then later, when we heard that the weather was getting bad at Alert and that we likely would be part of the search, we started getting excited again. But we were really beginning to realize that this could be a long, hard job."

"The lack of information was a problem at first," explains Greenwood team leader Arnie Macauley. "For instance, we knew there'd been a crash, and that someone had seen flares near it, but at one point we were told that the plane might be down on the pack ice, and that there could be open water, so that meant we had to bring equipment for a water rescue, along with all the Arctic gear. We also loaded toboggans, water, personal survival kits, flares, drop lights, parachutes—everything we thought we might need.

"In all, we had fourteen SAR Techs on board when we left," Macauley continues. "I left four behind on standby.

"Because we knew the flight would be long, our first priority was to let everyone get some sleep, because most of us were dead tired when we started. And we knew, once we got there, we would be busy. The idea was to let everyone sleep as best they could until we were about three hours out, and then get them up and get our gear ready. We had to get the jump gear ready, the drop gear organized, and everyone had to be fed as well. We knew we were going to get up there in the middle of the night. The loadmaster started preparing meals when we were about three hours out. On the way up I stayed with my brother, who was flying the plane. There was a lot of radio communication back and forth and I wanted to monitor it so I could keep my guys informed as best I could.

"We knew as we went along that Edmonton was on the way as well, and that their ETA [Estimated Time of Arrival] would be an hour before us. We figured then that by the time we got there, Fred Ritchie would have a bunch of guys on the ground, so we began concentrating on camp gear and so on."

Meanwhile, on the Edmonton flight, things were progressing as well. Darby Darbyson takes up the story: "We spent quite a bit of time dividing up people and sorting equipment. There was the medical team, then the guys who would drop the equipment. After it was out, they would jump in as well.

"But about an hour out of Edmonton, we were told that a storm was approaching Alert. Then by the time we got there, the weather was really bad. It was storming, the clouds were low, and you couldn't see a thing. We flew over where we thought the crash was, several times, but nothing was visible on the ground. We threw out flares but they didn't help at all. They just reflected off the clouds. You'd throw a flare, turn away for a second, and when you looked back, you couldn't see the flare. It was very windy, snowing heavily, and when we had the ramp down, at the back, really cold."

When all efforts in the air seemed futile, the plane landed at Alert in order to either wait out the storm, or at least see if there might be a break in it. Then, once on the ground, Fred Ritchie decided to split his team. He and others would try to get to the downed plane by tracked vehicle. An earlier attempt to do this by base personnel had failed when they were stymied by a high gorge bordering the Sheridan River, southeast of Alert and tantalizingly close to the crash site. Ritchie resolved to try another route, closer to the sea. The second half of his crew would go back out in the air if the weather improved.

While all this was happening, the plane from Greenwood neared its objective.

"When the time came, we woke the guys," said Arnie Macauley, "and when we were about an hour out of Alert, we heard what was going on there. We were expecting to hear notice of a crash location, status of survivors and whatever, but the next thing we heard was that the Edmonton plane had landed at Alert.

"When we heard this, we thought to ourselves, what the hell is going on here? We did know that a storm had been moving in, that things might not be good, but we never thought it would be so bad we couldn't get down.

"But when we got there, we did the same thing as Edmonton, I guess. We homed in on the site, dropped flares, tried to go down, and basically just scared the hell out of ourselves. This happened because we dropped a flare above the socked-in layer, then dove down through the clouds, thinking we might be able to see something under them when the flare came down that far. But the damned clouds went right to the ground and we almost had a head-on collision with our own flare, the flare we'd dropped up higher.

"But you couldn't see a thing—anywhere. And the area under us was so featureless anyway. We saw snow on snow and nothing more—even with the ramp open and everybody looking out, in the back and up front. Then by this time, we were getting short on gas but there was no room at Alert, so we flew to Thule. We knew that the guys from Edmonton were going to try again."

"We went back up, but it wasn't much better than before," Darby Darbyson explains, "and we kept flying and flying. But then we got some great news from the ground! We began to pick up a transmission from the crash site. Before their batteries down there gave out, we learned that there were fourteen survivors originally, but after a while knew that somebody had died. To save their power, a system was worked out so that the radio just had to be clicked: one click—ten alive; two clicks—twelve alive; and so on.

"The big boost to us was knowing that there were people alive down there, and we wanted to get in to help them. We tried everything we could. There were guys looking out back at the ramp, out the spotter's windows, up in the cockpit. At one point we dropped drift lights, but they were gone immediately, so we knew the winds were really bad. For a second, we thought we'd seen the site, but then we lost it and never saw it again. And we were never sure if it was the crash or just black rocks. By this time, we were completely burned out, so we went back to Alert.

While all this activity was going on in the skies above them, the crash survivors were in increasingly desperate straits. They did their best to adjust to the terrible circumstances: they coped with their injuries, tried to keep warm, radioed for help, counted heads, clustered together, prayed. At first, they thought they would be rescued quickly because most authorities knew they had to be somewhere close to Alert.

But as time passed, and the hours of blackness and suffering dragged on, spirits fell as surely as the temperature in this godforsaken place. And when the wrath of the winter gale eclipsed their world, survival itself was all-consuming. Two of the group, Bob Thomson and Susan Hillier, lay off by themselves, too badly injured to move or be moved. In time, they would be buried in snow. The others dragged themselves to the exposed, more or less intact hulk of the back of the plane, where they lay down, huddled together in a kind of metal cave. Their main commonality was the bitter cold.

"When we landed at Thule, we figured it was all over for us," Arnie Macauley continued. "We expected the Edmonton crew to get in, either in the air or on the ground. So we went to bed as soon as we got there, at a military hotel.

"After we had slept for about four hours, my brother called back to Alert to hear what was happening, and to ask if they needed us back in. They told us they did because the ground party had been forced back and the blizzard was still raging. But old Fred was going to go out again and they needed us to drop flares to guide them. So away we went again. That was when our ordeal really started.

"We piled into the Herc and did a real white-knuckle takeoff out of Thule. There was a crosswind, almost to the limit of the C-130. My brother had to pull off the line there to keep it on the runway, so we did basically a kind of three-engine takeoff. Finally he got the things airborne, and scared everybody on board."

"The weather at Thule was getting worse, too," says Ron O'Reilly, "and we were maxed out on weight. We all knew that the runway there went towards a hill, and I remember it took an awfully long time before the wheels left the ground. Later, I was talking about our takeoff with one of the guys who had been up front. All he said was, 'Ron, you didn't want to be there.' I also was talking to one of the Americans there and he told me that ordinarily they would have closed the airport down, that they wouldn't have flown in that weather. They only kept it open for us so we could continue our search.

"When we got back over Alert, it was clearing near the ocean, but inland there was still a blizzard. Then we could see the lights of the tracked vehicles and had a fair idea about where they should go, so we started dropping flares to guide them. Every so often we would fly back over the crash site to see if we could see anything. We never could though."

Macauley continues: "We established radio contact with Fred and his guys and we guided them as best we could. But they couldn't see fifteen feet on the ground. Their compasses weren't working and they had ended up on sea ice earlier. We didn't want that to happen again, but guiding them was a hell of a lot of work. We did seven or eight hours of that and it was hard on everyone. We'd fly along, then the guys on the ground would get stuck, and a couple of times they went crashing over cliffs even when they had walkers out in front. When they got bogged down, we would go over to the crash site, home in on a beacon that was operating down there and see if we could see anything. We still couldn't, but we did get the ground party over the Sheridan River and onto flat ground and thought they would be our best bet at getting to the crash. They were perhaps two to four miles away.

"All this time, Fred was navigating by the altimeter on his watch, because nothing else worked. He knew the crash was at twelve hundred feet so he knew when the ground started to rise and he got to twelve hundred feet, he might be there.

"Then, one time, when we went back to where we thought the crash was, we were in the right place at the right time. We'd just dropped a flare, there was a slight clearing in the storm, and my God, we saw the tail, the tail of the bloody C-130! There was such a sense of relief for all of us on board. But then we came around again and never saw anything for another hour, and in all, we had been involved in this thing for about thirty hours at that point. Now, though, everyone knew something was going to happen."

"We didn't have enough headsets to go around," said Ron O'Reilly, "and because you can't hear anything in the back of a Herc, some of us were really pretty much in the dark as to what was going on. We were just sitting there waiting for the order to jump.

"During all this time, we were dropping flares, and the ramp at the back was open. Because the guys there were getting cold, we switched around every so often. I went back for a while along about then and had a chance to plug into an intercom outlet and hear what was going on. I remember Gerry Dominie was in the window, I was on the ramp, and Arnie was looking out as well, and Gerry saw something like a tail. Arnie saw something also and they asked me. I said I sort of saw a black object, but I wasn't sure whether it was a tail or not. Then we had another look and it was definitely a tail. That's when we got ready to go."

"We pretty much ignored the ground party at that point," Arnie Macauley explains. "They were still some distance away, and it didn't look as though they would get there soon, so I started briefing my guys on what we would be doing.

"We would go in in three different sticks [groups of jumpers]. The first stick was going to be six people with strictly medical gear, and they were going to go in and set up a triage—to treat the life-threatening injuries first, and so on. The second team was going to be responsible for the perimeter, to get the camp set up and retrieve the gear. The third team would stay on the airplane, drop all the gear and they would jump afterwards. The plan was okay, but then it went all to hell.

"Just as the first stick was about to go, the storm was moving out of there and we couldn't see a thing. But when we did see the tail again our own bloody contrails [exhaust] caused so much vapour in the air that everything would just fog over and cloud everything up again. At one point, we got off course when we thought we were at about a thousand feet, and we saw one of our own flares bouncing along the ground right under us.

"There was a lot going on in the front end, and the guys were working really hard to get the aircraft back over the spot again. Tensions were very high, lots of comments on the intercom, and everybody really frustrated.

"And of course, we all wanted to get on with it because people were dying down there, and the whole world was watching. This has been going on for well over a day now and nobody's in at the crash yet. Here we are, flying around, the ramp's open, it's forty below out there, and a hundred-knot wind is whipping around in the back of the plane. From the wheel wells aft, everything is frozen solid, we're scraping the ice off the windows, and the guys up front are cooking because we had to have as much heat as we could.

"Finally, we dropped another flare, saw the crash and decided this was it. Ordinarily, we never would have jumped in those conditions under two thousand feet, or in those winds. But we decided that the first six jumpers would go out, then a flare would be dropped right after them in the hope that it would come down somewhere near them and give them a bit of an idea of where the ground was. The flare burns for two minutes at two million candle power. Finally, we went out at a thousand feet.

"It was eerie coming down. The flare was an orange glow, and we could see it, but we could sense nothing else at all—other than an unbelievable blast of ice crystals. It took about forty-five seconds to come down, and at the last instant, I saw the tail of the crashed Herc right beside me and I thought I was going to hit it. We had drifted almost two miles coming down. We were really moving.

"One of our other jumpers, Bruce Best, was number two, and he came out of our place behind me, but he hit the ground first. I saw him bounce, then the wind took his canopy and he was off like a shot, so then he collapsed his canopy right away. I remember hitting hard and the back of my head snapped into the ground with a thud. Then I felt myself getting picked up as the canopy started to take me away. It took a bit of struggle to control it."

At last, somebody had reached the crash site.

Macauley gathered his crew around him, made certain they secured all the equipment they carried, and then radioed up to his brother Marv to report that they were down and injury-free. Then the jumpers began stumbling, in pairs, through the snow, ice and blackness towards what remained of Boxtop 22.

"At this point, I don't think any of the survivors knew we were there," Macauley continues. "We swept through the wreckage, yelling as we went, but there was no response that we heard. Two guys went on the left, two more in the center, and Ben House and I were on the right. The guys on the left found a couple of bodies along the way. As we went, we kept yelling to keep from getting lost. The storm was so wild that you could lose a guy fifteen feet away—and we had lights on our helmets. We had radios, but we didn't dare use them because they were pretty much useless. Three or four transmissions in that cold would kill them.

"I came up to the tail section and yelled in there, and for the first time, got an answer. The tail was wide open except for a life raft that was bent up on one side a little, but the whole place was packed with snow. The snow was swirling around, and even with my headlamp I couldn't see much. I got down on my knees because there were a lot of sharp pieces of metal and junk, and for the first time I realized the floor was covered with people. You couldn't move without stepping on somebody. One guy, who I found out later was Mario Ellefsen, was at the feet of everyone, and I kind of fell into him, and he screamed. Later we found out he had a broken pelvis.

"Ben came in then, and we also got two more guys to come over. I was still not really talking to anyone yet but when one of the guys in there seemed a bit better than the others, I introduced myself. He said his name was Paul West. I told him I was Arnie Macauley and that we were all SAR Techs from Greenwood. He revived a bit, but all the others were stuporous. Nobody else made much sense and there was a lot of moaning.

"The first thing Paul tried to get across to us was that there were two others outside in the snow, and that we should try to find them. He thought the last contact with them was seven or eight hours before, but he wasn't even sure of that. He pointed outside and said they were 'over there somewhere, and they're buried in the snow.'

"Two guys stayed at the tail to do what they could, and Ben and I went out with Bruce Best and Derek Curtis to try to find the ones outside. As we went, we were kicking at stuff in the snow, and I remember pulling up about five parkas, because you couldn't tell if it was a person or not. Unfortunately, the survivors never found any of this stuff when they could have used it. This tells us something about the trauma of the crash. . . .

"Anyway, the four of us did an entire sweep up one side and could not find anyone. But on the way back, Bruce and Derek found Thomson and Hillier covered in about three feet of snow. They were alive but were in bad shape—particularly Mr. Thomson.

"I remember being back at the tail of the plane again when the second stick—five guys—came down. As they got closer, the parachutes were silhouetted in the night from the flare they had just dropped. In a way, it was a beautiful sight, with all the ghostly looking orange crystals in the air. When the guys landed, they all grabbed their chutes pretty quickly, and then came over to us.

"As we came down I remember the yellow glow of the flare, and the ice crystals in the sky had this sparkling look," says Ron O'Reilly. "We could see the ground then, but the snow was still blowing. I could see the tracked vehicles and it looked as though they would arrive at the crash site as soon as us, but it was still a while. As we got closer to the ground, we would see dark objects and white objects, so I decided to stay away from the dark objects because they were likely rocks.

"Once you were on the ground, it was a blizzard, and the only things you could see were the strobe lights of the other guys. I remember cutting one of my risers so I wouldn't be dragged away in the wind, and then grabbing my chute right away. As I was doing so, I thought that if I couldn't find the crash site, at least this would be some shelter. Even though we were all together, you could be in a total whiteout in two minutes. I think we all thought the chutes might be needed if we got lost.

"By the time we had our chutes looked after, we were ready to start walking to where we thought the crash was. I remember coming up to the tail, and it was wide open. It was then that Arnie suggested we put the parachutes over the end as a bit of wind break. That helped some."

"The last three guys didn't get to jump," Arnie Macauley explains. "They did one more pass and threw the equipment out, but because they were on bingo fuel they had to get to Alert and land right away. Unfortunately, the equipment they dropped was all lost—$280,000 worth of it. I know because I had to do the complete inventory later. They dropped it in the right place, but the winds were so strong, they took it all. We did see a couple of big bundles go by, but they went as fast as a horse could gallop. We had no way of stopping it.

"The situation in the tail of the plane was really bad. I knew those people had lain down for the last time. None of them could walk; not even Paul West. They were frozen to the metal floor with a combination of sweat at first and condensation, then urine. If we had not been able to get there when we did, I know that where they were was where they would have been found. . . .

"We had a terrible time trying to break them free from the metal. Some we just took out by cutting their clothes. They were in such a hell of a mess, but we had to worry about the hypothermia as well as the various injuries. By this time we had found another body outside, and pilot John Couch as well, who was lying beside Mario. We removed the body at that point. Meanwhile, some of the other guys were working with Sue Hillier and Bob Thomson outside."

After the Edmonton plane had reached Alert earlier on, the crew was fed and given places to sleep. A bit more room was made on the tarmac for the second Herc, when the shortage of fuel made it essential that they come in also. But the amount of rest anyone got through all the hours of turmoil was almost negligible.

"I was in a bed next to a phone," recalled Darby Darbyson. "I don't think I'd even closed my eyes when it started ringing. I grabbed it of course, and somebody told me the Greenwood guys were on the ground and needed help.

"We were out of there—and three of the Greenwood SAR Techs who didn't jump earlier, Keith McKellar, Gerry Dominie and Marc Lessard, climbed into our Herc and we took off. But the weather was still terrible over the crash.

"We jumped from about eight hundred feet, and we couldn't see a thing. Jim Brown went out first, then myself and Shawn MacDiarmid came out behind me. I saw Jim hit the ground, or what I thought was the ground, and I saw Shawn hit. I hit, and even though I had a good landing, I blew into Jim, chute and all.

"When we got organized, we didn't know where we were, and about that time we started to wonder what we'd gotten ourselves into. We later found out we were about two miles from the crash site. It was in the middle of a blizzard, dark, and you could see nothing at all. So we got on the radio to the aircraft and asked them to have the guys at the crash fire off a flare to give us direction, because not one of us knew where to go, nor had any one of us seen the crash as we came down.

"So we stood in a circle, looking out, like a bunch of muskox, but we saw the flare off in the distance. In order to keep from getting lost, we decided to leapfrog towards it. Two guys would walk a short way, then two more would walk to them and go a bit beyond. Then two more would come up and so on. We kept doing that, lining each pair up, and yelling back and forth all the time to keep from getting lost. Every so often, we'd ask for another flare to keep us in the right direction. We always had to talk to the plane and they talked to Arnie, because there was a hill between us and the crash site.

"Then as we started getting closer, we could see gouges in the snow and pieces of wreckage. After we'd been walking for about two hours, and some of the guys were hurt doing the jump, we were pretty happy to be getting close to where there were people. Walking across the tundra after being lost was not a lot of fun. We were lucky there wasn't another search for us. This was my first operational jump, and I told myself I would never do another one like it. The next time, I would know where I was jumping, and at least what I was getting into. We pushed it and were lucky.

"We came to a ridge line that was between a hundred and as much as two hundred feet high, which the aircraft had hit. Then we walked down a slope, into a bowl and came to the site. There was a mass of metal everywhere, but apart from the tail, it was hard to tell that it had been an airplane. The whole scene was so strange. There was no light other than the headlamps of the SAR Techs who were there, and occasionally the light from a flare up above that our Herc was dropping to guide the ground party.

"The first guy I saw was Ron O'Reilly, and I remember asking him if there was anyone still alive—the place looked so bad. He said, 'Oh, yes there is. Glad you guys made it okay.' So were we."

For the SAR Techs at the scene, the next hours began to run together. Those I interviewed for this book remember some things in vivid detail, but other matters, faces, and even a few of their efforts have been forgotten. For one thing, they were all desperately tired, but without exception kept going long after human beings are supposed to give out. Their actions in that frozen hell were exemplary. Had they not been there, not a single person on Boxtop

22 would have come out alive. Yet every man who risked his life to get to the crash site downplayed what he did, deflected the credit, scoffed at praise, and in various ways said simply: "It was my job."

For so long in the operation, things had gone wrong. The storm never really abated in all the time the rescue teams were trying to get on scene. The ground parties kept getting lost, and almost died in their journey. The last group of SAR Techs who jumped could easily have perished on the trackless tundra. The equipment blew away almost as soon as it left the planes. The litany of problems seemed endless, but then—mercifully—it did end.

"They [the problems] began to end when a couple of my guys, Jean Tremblay and Rob Walker, found a toboggan jammed into some boulders somewhere," recalled Arnie Macauley. "They brought it in, took a tent out of it and were beginning to set it up, just as the last group of jumpers came over the hill. The tent was a six-man SAR tent, about six feet wide and ten long, and there was also a lantern. They set the tent up, got the light in there, and finally we had some place to put Hillier and Thomson, to get them some protection. At about this time, Fred Ritchie and the two tracked vehicles from Alert arrived.

"We had been at the site for two hours and forty-five minutes when the bloody ground party pulled over the horizon. I know when I saw old Fred, I was never so happy to see anyone in my life. They had more tents, cases of pop, chocolate bars, Coleman stoves, all the things Base Alert had given them. We set up more tents, got some people melting snow for water, started to warm up our IVs because they were frozen solid, and began moving people inside."

"The tail section was an unbelievable scene," Darby Darbyson says, with a perceptible shudder. "The parachutes were over the opening when I went there, and then inside, there was another chute over the people. It was hard to distinguish where they were, and you didn't want to step on people. I'll never forget the moaning. It was like walking into a meat-freezer. Then everyone would be absolutely silent.

"I went to one guy, Mario Ellefsen as I later found out, and started to feel around to see what I could do for him. He was in severe pain, and his clothes were frozen to the ramp. He said his back hurt, and this was because his pelvis was broken. We had to try to figure out how to get him loose without hurting him any more than necessary. Finally we shot him up with morphine, cut his clothes off, put him into a sleeping bag, and carried him to one of the tracked vehicles. Ben House started an IV in him and we got him into MAST pants [anti-shock trousers] to stabilize his fractures. At least now, his broken bones weren't grinding on one another. He was conscious all the time."

"Once we got one or two out of the tail, we had a bit more room in there," Arnie Macauley continues. "But before we were able to give them morphine, we had to be able to monitor them because they were in such a sorry state. Morphine is a respiratory depressant, so if you give it to somebody who is too weak, you could stop them from breathing and kill them. That's why we had to be so careful. And of course, everyone in the tail had been drenched in the damned diesel fuel, and that, along with the sweat and condensation and urine, made it so bad for them all. That was before you even considered their broken bones and burns."

"I remember working on one guy who was in bad shape," Ron O'Reilly says. "He told me he had to pee in the worst way. I told him to go ahead, that we were going to cut his clothes off anyway. I guess that okay wasn't the best, because right afterwards, he relaxed and was right out of it. Then he didn't respond anymore. I knew he likely had a fractured skull, but I didn't know whether it or hypothermia was the bigger problem. Anyway, we got his clothes off, I did a rectal temperature check to see what his core temperature was, and we got him into a sleeping bag, and started an IV.

"Working in a tracked vehicle was difficult because we were in such close quarters. I recall bumping into the doc's [Doctor Wilma de Groot, a crash survivor] broken ankle, and she wasn't too happy. But when I gave her some morphine, she was happy.

"And we were really getting burned out by this time. I'm not sure of the number of hours, but it seemed like a couple of days without sleep. When you were outside, you were in the cold, but after working in the warmth of the tracked vehicles for a while, the adrenaline rush began wearing off and you felt so sleepy. I remember trying to get an IV into one person, but I was falling asleep and couldn't see the vein. I got someone else to do the stick for me and I got out for a few minutes in the cold to wake up."

While his men were doing their best to save the lives of those they worked on, Arnie Macauley was on the radio, talking to the base surgeon from Edmonton, who was now at Alert. Macauley knew that soon a Twin Huey helicopter, also from Edmonton but being partly assembled at Alert, would be in for the survivors, and he wanted to do all he could to prepare the personnel at the northern base for what they could expect. He knew too, that a field hospital was ready there for them. Finally, the helicopter arrived.

"We knew the Twin Huey could only take four stretchers at a time, so we picked the most serious for the first flight out," Macauley explains. "I think the next was two stretcher cases and three survivors who were ambulatory, and so on. Anyway, we got all the injured out in three lifts. Six SAR Techs had gone with them, and then the Huey broke down.

"Fortunately, it didn't cause a great problem because we had been told two American Pavehawks [helicopters] from Elmendorf [in Alaska] had been taken to Thule, and they would be in to help us bring everyone else out. Well, the Pavehawks arrived okay, but because of their size, when they landed their rotor wash smashed down all our tents and broke them up. We were damned lucky we didn't need them anymore.

"But at the very end, there was another problem. I wanted to send everyone who was left out on the last flight—including the bodies of the five victims. Well, the American pilots didn't want to take the bodies, so I talked to somebody higher up in Alert. Alert talked to the pilots, and the bodies were taken."

And so the saga in the far north came to a conclusion. The exhausted SAR Techs, navigators, pilots, flight engineers, loadmasters and so many others could relax at last. The men who flew the helicopter from Trent to Eureka on Ellesmere Island could enter the realm of legend—but that is another story.

And now there are two memorials at Alert. Each is a reminder of something terrible that happened there, first in 1950 and again in 1991. The stone cairns stand together, on the windswept wilderness at the top of the world.

Not Enough Time

From *The Falling Season*

BY HAL CLIFFORD

In 1992, writer Hal Clifford decided to tell the story of one of America's premier mountain rescue teams, Mountain Rescue–Aspen. In order to do so, he was told, he would have to join the all-volunteer unit. He did, and the result is his extraordinary book, *The Falling Season: Inside the Life and Death Drama of Aspen's Mountain Rescue Team.* The section below describes the gut-wrenching emotions that overtake the members of the team when they arrive too late to help a hunter fallen deep in the Rocky Mountain backcountry.

★   ★   ★   ★   ★

Just from the whole way the situation was going, the way the day was going, it just seemed like there was some reason for me to be out there. I just felt like there was a possibility I was going to find him. We were in our [search] area, so we had to really look, we had to pay attention to clues, any kind of findings, and so all of a sudden things started getting more and more focused, more and more energized. We went up this really intense, steep, rough terrain with heavy packs on, and I wasn't at all physically exhausted. It didn't bother me a bit.

—Lori Hart

The call comes on a glorious Indian summer day in mid-September: a search for a missing hunter in the Hunter-Frying Pan Wilderness. John Zell, working far up Castle Creek at the Lindley Hut hauling firewood, is scornful. "AFH," he said, "Another Fucking Hunter. I'm not going to bust my ass for a lost hunter."

Hunters are almost always fine, John says, usually sleeping in their tents when rescuers find them. Although many team members hunt themselves, some—especially John—see hunters as generally boorish and incompetent.

Down at the rescue cabin, however, David Swersky and Tom McCabe are thinking very differently. The hunter isn't only missing—he'd last been seen Sunday. This is Wednesday.

Mark Lobsinger, thirty-nine, and Terry Phillips, forty, both Oklahoma residents, hunt together every year near Aspen. Mark, a father of five children, has a terrible sense of direction and often gets lost. But he is in good physical condition. He trained to be in shape for the venture, which coincided with Colorado's archery and muzzle-loading rifle seasons for elk and deer. The two men set up camp among the rocks near Scott Lake, a pool perched at twelve thousand feet, just above the timberline in the Williams Mountains. Two ridges east lies the Continental Divide.

On Sunday they set out to hunt in different directions. When Terry returned to the tent that evening, Mark wasn't there. Terry wasn't worried; they had agreed that if one of them was trailing an animal he wouldn't be back. Terry wanted to hunt on the next ridge east. He left Mark a note saying he was going to set up his own tent a few miles away, and headed out.

That night it snowed, but when Terry looked through binoculars at Mark's camp Monday morning, the tent had no snow on it. He assumed Mark must be there, and went on hunting, eventually killing a deer Tuesday. Only after hiking back to Mark's camp Wednesday morning did he find Mark had not returned. By early afternoon, Mountain Rescue knows it has a problem.

"When you're notified on a Wednesday that somebody was last seen on a Sunday morning, and in between two big storms came through and the temperature plummeted and this guy's from Oklahoma, all of a sudden you think, 'This guy's dead,'" says Tom. "My gut feeling is this is not good, this is serious, we need to move immediately."

Tom heads to the airport, where he joins Rick Deane and takes off in One Five Charlie to search from the air. David calls Richard Dick, a wiry, weathered man of indeterminate age who wears sharp-toed cowboy boots, favors snap-button shirts, and flies a Bell 47 Soloy helicopter as well as anyone in Colorado. It will take the better part of an hour for Richard to fly from his home in Montrose to Aspen.

By the time Scott, John, and I reach the cabin after a morning of stacking firewood at the Braun huts, David Swersky has already sent eight searchers up Highway 82 toward Independence Pass. Mark Lobsinger disappeared in a valley known as Lost Man; on the wall of the comm room, the eastern flank of the Williams Mountains above the valley is carved up with Magic Marker like a butcher's diagram of a pig. Each of the four search teams will try to cover one pork chop before dark, then make camp and start again in the morning.

"I still had hope," recalls Jace Michael. " 'Hey, maybe he's bivouacked somewhere; he might be injured and we can find him.' I think we all kind of felt that way, and I think we all evaded that final decision that he's dead, we won't find him alive."

When Richard Dick is only a few minutes from the airport, David sticks his head out of the comm room and looks at me and Kevin Hagerty, a blond, sunburned carpenter and ski patroller. One of the team's rescue leaders, Kevin is universally known as Hags.

"You're going," David says. We climb into Kevin's battered pickup truck, pushing tools out of the way, and drive the three miles to the airport. The day is calm and warm, the valley filling like a bathtub with limpid, late afternoon light. But we are sweating in our gear. We must wear as much as possible, in the event we somehow are separated from our packs during the helicopter flight. Although we strap the backpacks into the cargo racks on the side of the helicopter, sometimes packs and rescuers fly separately to keep from overloading the tin machine at high altitudes. There is no guarantee they will end up in the same place.

We fly slowly east up the valley, fifteen hundred feet above the winding road. The three of us fill the Plexiglas bubble of the cabin, which affords a view from our toes to the rotor mast behind our heads. Kevin connects the headsets and dials in the Mountain Rescue radio frequency so we can hear the ground teams. Our plan is to be dropped in high, up on one of the thirteen-thousand-foot ridges above Scott Lake. As the other teams search up, we will comb the high ground, then bivouac for the night. In the distance we see a flicker in the sky—One Five Charlie banking in a turn as Rick and Tom crisscross the Williams Range.

We were looking for footprints, and we followed tracks. Unfortunately, because of the number of people who happened to be working that area—guides had taken a variety of people in there—there were horse tracks and people tracks all over the place, and we were trying to fly them down and see where they led us. They led us into some pretty far-flung drainages, and then you're looking for any individuals, you're looking for color, you're looking for movement. It's real basic, but it's surprisingly difficult from an airplane to see things, even when they're trying to get your attention. And if they're not trying to get your attention, if they're unconscious or down in a snow cave or something like that, when there are very few visual clues, it's a whole lot more difficult than you might think.

—Tom McCabe

Sloan Shoemaker is driving back from Boulder when he passes the Lost Man trailhead and sees Rescue 1 parked there. He stops to help and soon is running the staging area. Now, when we are only a few miles from the mouth of Lost Man Creek, his voice comes over our headsets in the helicopter. "Cabin, this is staging," Sloan radios. "Team Two reports contact with the victim at 11,300 feet in Jack Creek."

"What's his condition?" Tom breaks in from One Five Charlie.

"Go to channel eight," interjects Dave Lofland. He is half of Team Two, along with Lori Hart, who is on her first mission. I open a topo map and point to Jack Creek, a Lost Man tributary south of Scott Lake. Richard banks the helicopter into the mouth of Lost Man Valley and the shadow cast by the Williams Mountains. Kevin fumbles with the radio to find the alternate channel. Dave's cryptic comment is not a good sign. Team members learn to guard their conversations on the assigned Mountain Rescue radio channel, assuming that reporters or others are listening in. More obscure channels are used for bad news.

By the time Kevin changes channels the brief discussion between Dave and Tom is over.

"What do you think?" I ask.

"I don't know," Kevin shrugs. "He could be alive."

Down in the Lost Man Valley, we see searchers heading up the trail, bright in their red climbing helmets and yellow Nomex shirts. Richard flies past Jack Creek, circles around, banks left and into it. Our altitude is 11,500 feet, only slightly higher than Dave and Lori's reported position. As we turn west the setting sun fills the cockpit, refracting off the Plexiglas bubble and all but blinding us. Richard flies toward a cliff band that protrudes from the ridge north of the creek; the terrain comes up sharply before us. With only a few hundred feet to spare he gets the bird under the ridge's shadow, and for a few seconds, we can scan the scattered openings in the timber along the creek. Then he banks hard left and heads back out.

He repeats the maneuver, and this time, looking down between my feet, I see a body clad in yellow, sprawled on the ground near a tree. It is face-down, left arm and leg cocked out. Dave Lofland is standing near it, looking up. It is a singular experience to look down at a dead man, but—as I had been the winter before on Peak Twelve Four Thirty—I am wrong about what I am seeing. It is only a rain suit Dave laid out to attract our attention.

"That was full power coming out of there," Richard says softly as the rotors chop at the meager air and pulls us back over Lost Man Creek. Kevin calls Tom—what do you want us to do? Set down and stand by, Tom says. Richard puts the helicopter down in a clearing near the mouth of Lost Man Creek, and we wait, rotor spinning.

> I wasn't sure if I was going to see someone walking through the woods or someone lying down in the woods or someone lying there moaning and groaning. I wasn't really sure what I was looking for, except for a person who could have been miles away. I had so much energy I felt like I was going to create this person if I didn't find him.
>
> —Lori Hart

> Mostly what you're looking for is evidence, for signs. It's going to be a coincidence if you run into the person. You need to look for boot tracks in the snow, look for empty pop cans or cigarette wrappers and that sort of thing, just any sign that someone has been there and that that someone is the person you're searching for. Hunters are the worst, because every guy out there is wearing camo. I've found with hunter searches you interview a lot of hunters, and if there are a lot of hunters in the area, they're all wearing Vibram-soled boots. And they're never glad to see you.
>
> —Dave Lofland

To start their search, Dave and Lori split off from the Lost Man Valley and start hiking up through spruce along Jack Creek. There is no trail and the terrain is steep; sometimes they scramble on all fours. After the better part of an hour they break out onto a small, open rib along the north side of the creek. Ahead of them a cliff band rears up. Below and to the left is the creek, a one-step-wide stream burbling down through smooth granite boulders and a fringe of conifers along its banks.

Dave heads right to traverse the base of the cliff band. Lori walks along the rib, looking down into the creek. They have only one radio between them, and agree to keep in voice contact. Every few moments they call Mark's name. As she trudges up the open rib, Lori alternates between watching where she is walking and looking down toward the creek. Suddenly, framed between two trees, down in the shadows of the watercourse, is an incongruity.

"I see this orange hat," Lori recalls. "I'm yelling, 'Mark, Mark, DAVE! DAVE!'"

Dave runs back to Lori, who points to the hat. For a moment neither is sure of what they see in the evening gloam.

We started to take a couple steps in that direction and I said, "Oh my God, there's a boot, there's a leg, and there's another leg. That's him, Dave." We both just started yelling his name, and there were millions of thoughts, there were light-years of thoughts that went through my mind in the fifty yards that I had to go from that point. You know what it's like to be in a dream when you're trying to run away from somebody, you're trying to run and you can't get anywhere? I wanted to get there, but I really didn't want to get there. I wanted to arrive, but I wasn't sure what I was going to find.

My legs were moving but my mind was resisting, and I started thinking, "What am I going to find?" All we could see were the boots and the legs, because he was in camouflage, and I was beginning to come into view of the chest and the short-sleeved shirt. I still couldn't see his face. What was going through my mind at the time was, "Okay, is this person going to be mauled, is he going to be shot, is he going to be dismembered, is he going to be alive, is he going to be moaning and groaning, and am I going to have to save him?" I was scared. I was scared.

—Lori Hart

Mark Lobsinger is not alive. His blue eyes are stuck half-open, staring at some place neither Lori nor Dave can see. He is lying on his back by the stream, one foot hooked under a log, tucked between a rock and a tree. If Lori hadn't looked through the gap in the trees when she did, searchers might have wandered for days without finding him. He is stripped down to his white T-shirt, laying on another shirt. His jacket is off and lying nearby, as is his pack.

"At a glance I just knew," Dave recalls. "He just looked dead."

Lori kneels down to check for vital signs, but finds none. She cannot close his eyes. This bothers her immensely. The two of them step away from the body, climbing back up into the sun. Dave keys the radio and calls Sloan at staging, reporting only that they have "made contact." He knows everyone in the field is listening, including Terry Phillips, Mark's hunting partner. He is hiking with Jace and Ron Bracken, taking them up to the camp by Scott Lake. The three men are climbing a steep avalanche path below the camp; they're spread out and searching for clues when Jace hears Dave's radio report.

Jace has spent much of the afternoon with Terry, talking to him on the trail, helping relay questions from Tom about how Mark might behave if he is lost, learning about who these two men are. The hunting trip is an annual high point for Mark and Terry, an opportunity to watch the birds, identify the flowers, and just be together. "As I got to know Terry, I got to know Mark, too—wife, five kids, all that stuff," Jace says. "I liked being with Terry."

Jace wasn't worried about finding a body. "As far as handling bodies, dead people, I'll do it," he grins, mentioning his former job in a mortuary. "I'll pick up the pieces, I'll do anything. I'll handle a thousand bodies. It's not going to bother me." What he hadn't counted on was handling Terry.

I had the only radio, and it came across that they'd found him. When Dave said, "Switch to channel eight," I knew right then he'd found Mark dead, that he was a "Frank." So I switched over and listened in and just confirmed it. I was walking over toward Terry. I yelled out that they've found him and we'll get some stats in a minute. So I turned the volume down and I was walking over toward Terry, and Terry was like, "Well, how is he, what's going on?" So I just listened and confirmed what I had thought. That was the hard part, telling Terry, "I'm sorry, your friend is not alive." He sat down and started to cry, and so Ron and I just sat there with him.

It was hard for me to get those words out. The exact words I said—I said, "I'm sorry, your friend did not make it." Those were the hardest words I've ever had to say.

—Jace Michael

The Aspen airport shuts thirty minutes after sunset, and we are burning daylight as the helicopter idles on the ground. After twenty minutes Tom McCabe calls Kevin—fly a team up, get Mark's body onto the helicopter, and get him out. Richard lifts off and flies to the junction of Jack Creek and Lost Man Creek, landing in a small meadow by a stand of old spruce. A half-dozen searchers are congregated there by now, crouched low, backs turned to avoid the rotor wash. As we set down I look at Kevin. Richard, after his earlier passes into the valley, doesn't want to land more than one passenger, and no packs. The air is too thin, the landing zone too small for the little helicopter to carry a full load. "You go up," Kevin says. "I'll take off the packs."

We fly a mile up the valley. After circling twice, Richard settles on a tiny clearing a hundred yards from the creek. A tall spruce marks one side, a dead snag the other. The air is calm, and he carefully settles into the hole between the trees with only a few feet to spare. Three feet off the ground he holds the hover and spins in a slow circle, looking for rocks and uneven spots before touching down. Richard nods to me, and I carefully unclip the seat belt and shoulder harness, open the door, latch it firmly behind me, then crouch and scuttle downhill and away twenty yards. I turn and give him the thumbs-up.

After he lifts off I stand up and find Dave hiking up from the creek. After determining Mark is dead, he set about trying to find some sort of identification, just to make sure this is the man we're seeking. Going through Mark's pack, Dave finds a note, penciled almost illegibly on a topo map of the area.

"Things aren't going so good here," the note begins. Mark explains how he had fallen and broken his hip, trying to get back to his camp. Unable to move, exposed to the snowstorm, Mark knew he was going to die. At the end of the note he listed the names of his five children. "I love you," he concludes. "See you in heaven."

> At that point Dave said, "I can't read this." All of a sudden he [Mark] had this human quality. I knew he had loved ones. Then it was harder, because he was no longer just a body. He had people who loved him out there, he was writing this note as he was dying. You knew he was in pain, you knew he was dying, and that was—that was really hard for both Dave and me. That was when I just wanted to bless his soul. I'm not real religious. I think I just said, "God bless you," and that's about it. I felt like I wanted to say something to him.
>
> —Lori Hart

A whistle lay near Mark's body. He had probably blown it, but there was no one near to hear. His right hand was across his chest, clenched in a fist—but it held nothing. The note answered some questions, but it raised others. Where had he fallen? What had happened to his bow, his black-powder rifle, the poncho and binoculars we knew he carried? How had he come to be here, in this quiet, sheltered spot by a small mountain stream?

There is no time to figure it out. I pull out my radio and call Sloan. The helicopter is flying to the trailhead to pick up gear. Mark weights 190 pounds, and we need to get him up the slope to the tiny helispot.

"We need a three-hundred-foot rope, uphaul bag, extra webbing, bivvy bag, and a Sked," I tell Sloan.

"Bivvy bag?"

"Large, dark, heavy-duty, long-term bivvy bag."

"Copy that."

In a few minutes Richard is back. Crouching under the rotor wash I pull the gear from the side baskets and begin to rig a simple uphaul system, while Richard ferries first Ray, then Jace to the tiny landing zone. Once Jace arrives, Richard steps out of the helicopter, leaving it running, and walks over. "You've got twenty minutes," he says.

Everyone is sweating, running up and down the hill, getting Mark into the body bag, then lashing the body bag in the Sked, a flexible, plastic sled that wraps around a victim like a taco shell. We tie one end of the haul rope to the Sked. The rope runs through a pulley attached to a tree by the landing zone, then around obstacles, while Jace, Ray, and I grab the other end of the rope and, by pulling downhill, haul the Sked uphill.

At the top of the hill we pick up the Sked and heave Mark onto the helicopter's starboard cargo basket. There's a special weight to a body, an unmistakable thickness, that you never forget once you have felt it. We lash the whole package down with bungee cords, avoiding the screaming turbine and hot jet exhaust only a few inches away. As we step back Lori comes running up the hill, out of breath. She has Mark's shirt and pack. Richard puts them on the passenger seat.

We retreat down the hill and listen to the turbine wind up, to the bite of the rotors as Richard changes the pitch and the machine strains against the load. The helicopter lifts off gently and Richard slowly spirals 180 degrees as he climbs to treetop level, his tail rotor passing within five feet of the big spruce. As he flies over us, he waves once. Everyone watches the body on the side of the helicopter, tails of webbing fluttering in the breeze, as the machine, silhouetted against the clear, almost colorless eastern sky, curls with unspeakable beauty down and around the ridge.

Suddenly I am aware of how quiet the wilderness is, how serene this place. People unclip helmet straps, swig from water bottles. There is relief in the air, and laughter. This is a good place.

"It was a beautiful evening," Lori says later. "I was really aware of that. The skies were clear, the stars were starting to come out. I really felt alive."

Of all the people who worked on Mark's body recovery, Jace is the most upset, and he is surprised. "I'd sit there and cry," he says, "and not know why." Like John Zell before him, Jace has learned what it means to get too close to a victim. Jace is unable to attend the debriefing—he has previously scheduled a trip to Chicago and is out of town. Talking to his mother helped, although not enough.

> I wanted to talk to someone on the team. It just didn't work out. I wanted to talk to someone like David Swersky, or Tom, someone who's been through that stuff and could kind of help me out with it. I didn't know why it was bothering me. I'm still not sure if I understand why it was bothering me. It wasn't like I couldn't sleep—I could sleep fine. If I got to thinking about it, emotionally I would get upset. I talked about it a

lot with my girlfriend, Barbara. She's not been through a lot of things like this, but she just tried to help me understand why this was bothering me, because I could not explain it. I could not say, "Well, this is why it's bothering me." I was just more attached to it.

—Jace Michael

Two weeks after Mark's death, Jace takes his dog and hikes back up Lost Man and Jack creeks. Sitting where the helicopter had landed, he raises his binoculars and begins scanning up the valley. Almost immediately he spots a hat on a rock, a hundred yards away. Next to it he finds a coin purse, binoculars, and Mark's rifle, still loaded.

"I knew what happened when I found the rifle," Jace says. The firearm lies at the base of the cliff band. Jace climbs forty feet to the top. "I went to the point where he was when he fell. I know I stood right on the spot where he fell, where he slipped off. And it was straight. He might have bounced against a rock, but it was a pretty straight fall. There was nothing to grab."

In his mind, Jace puts the story together as best he can. Caught in an early season storm, Mark—already beset by a bad sense of direction—tried to make it back to camp, perhaps coming up out of Jack Creek. But as he climbed above the timberline he became disoriented. The snow was heavy, the storm blowing hard. His cotton clothes were probably soaking wet, and he was cold. His poncho, whipping in the wind, wasn't doing him much good. He decided to wrap it around his bow and stash them somewhere for later retrieval—he was carrying too much gear and his situation was getting desperate. Unable to find his camp he stumbled back down, headed for the road a few miles away. Perhaps it was dark, perhaps the snow obscured his vision, perhaps he simply misjudged and slipped off the top of the cliff.

However it happened, when he got to the bottom he thought he had broken his hip. Now his situation truly was desperate. He left his gun and binoculars where he fell. He took a few snacks from his pack and ate them, lucid enough to realize he was going to need the energy, then left the wrappers behind. He started to crawl downhill. He may not even have intended to end up at the creek. He could have slid inadvertently down the last slope to the shelter of the trees and boulders. But there he rested, a little way out of the wind and storm. He found that by hooking the foot of his bad leg under a log and pushing with his other leg he could put some traction on his bad hip and relieve a little of the pain. He drifted in and out of consciousness as the hypothermia got worse. He was able to write his note with a pencil, and perhaps he blew his whistle into the impervious storm.

In the end, just before he died, he felt marvelously warm. Too warm. He pulled off his coat. He tucked his shirt under himself, and he lay back to sleep.

> It made me feel a lot better. And I was doing this for the family, too, you know. They were kind of strapped for money and stuff like that. His rifle was a .300 Mag, it was a six-hundred- or seven-hundred-dollar gun. It helped me. I didn't like the feeling that some of his stuff was still out there, some Joe Blow could just walk by and say, "Oh, here's a rifle," and take something. It just didn't seem right to me that the stuff was still up there.
>
> —Jace Michael

Nine months later, Mark's widow, Denise, and a friend come to Aspen to see the place he died. Linda Koones and David Swersky lead them up Lost Man Creek.

"She mentioned that she had asked him not to go on the hunting trip this year, because at the time they had a seven-month-old daughter," David says. "She just wanted him to stay home with their daughter and maybe go next year. So she had a lot of anger about why he ended up even going on this hunting trip when she had asked him not to. Underneath that anger there was a lot of hurt that she had asked this and he hadn't listened, then he had gone and died. She was pissed. I think it was really good for her. I was perfectly willing to be a sounding board and let her get out whatever she had to and come to a conclusion on this episode."

No Place for People

From *High Drama*

BY HAMISH MACINNES

Contained in Hamish MacInnes' stirring book of mountain rescue stories from four continents is this gem by the well-known American mountaineer Pete Sinclair. "No Place for People," occurs in 1962, in the Grand Tetons, when Sinclair was working as a ranger. It concerns his extremely dangerous but sometimes humorous attempt to rescue a group of stranded East Coast mountaineers ("Appies," in Sinclair's caustic phrase) off a very serious Grand Teton peak during a blinding storm.

★　★　★　★　★

An account by Pete Sinclair:

The back room of the Jenny Lake ranger station served as a country store on stormy days or rest days. The cabin had a stove because in the winter it was used as a patrol cabin; there was also running water. It was a good place to make tea and to talk. Leigh Ortenburger spent quite a bit of his research time there when he was in the valley and since he was our historian, the back room became one of the two storytelling places in the valley. The climbers' campground was the other one. Once Yosemite climbers started coming to the Tetons to rest from the intensity of the Yosemite walls, the campground and ranger station became the communications hub of American climbing through most of the 'sixties.

Late in July, 1962, there was one storytelling session going on with Leigh Ortenburger and Dave Dornan in the group. Dave wanted me to work on No Escape Buttress with him. Mount Moran's south buttresses presented Teton climbers with a chance to do something that resembled Yosemite wall climbing. The easternmost of these buttresses, No Escape Buttress, was the last and most difficult of these problems. I was not in any way prepared for a climb of this difficulty but I had to try. Dornan wanted this climb. He was born in the valley, and had been a climbing ranger with me and was now an Exum Guide. He had accepted the Yosemite challenge. That is, he did not expect to become as good as Chouinard or Robbins but he wanted to be good enough to carry on a conversation with them.

There were encouraging signs in the heavens as we rowed across Leigh Lake in a rotting plywood skiff, one rowing, one bailing. I had never seen clouds so massive or as black as those which were piling up on the Idaho side of the range. Such clouds in the morning indicated that this was not to be an ordinary storm; we were sure to be stormed off the climb. The prospect pleased me, we'd do a couple of pitches and then go home. That would give me time to psyche myself up for a serious attempt later. As it turned out, I was to be busy for a while.

In a different part of the range, another climber was discovering that he had backed himself into a commitment which was to prove very serious. Ellis Blade had led a group of nine Appalachian Mountain Club climbers up Teepe's Snowfield on the Grand Teton. The snowfield is steep though not extreme. But the snowfield had become Blade's personal Rubicon.

Dornan was near the top of the first lead when the storm hit us. He rappelled off and we ran for the lake. Crossing the lake in that storm is one of the sillier things I've done. Fortunately, the energy of the storm was released in impulses rather than as a sustained force. The wind and rain combined to beat the surface of the lake down instead of lifting it into breaking whitecaps or we would have been in trouble. Dave, chortling because he was no longer a rescuer, remarked that if there was anybody in the mountains, my day was over. I wasn't much worried. This storm was severe enough that the most desperate vacationing climber with one day left on his vacation and fifty weeks of being chained to a desk facing him, could not pretend that it was a passing summer shower. It was not only violent, it was cold. There was a smell of the Gulf of Alaska about it. You could tell that an Arctic air mass had penetrated south.

I looked forward to a few quiet days in the ranger station as Dave and I walked and hitch-hiked back to Jenny Lake. The climbers would be out of the mountains and the campers would be heading for motels or the desert. The back of the ranger station would be warm, full of climbers drinking tea. The guides would be in, looking at our photographs of the peaks, planning one more climb, swapping stories.

When we got to the ranger station I was told that the other ranger on duty, George Kelly, had been sent out to check on an overdue party of ten from the Appalachian Mountain Club. This was an annoyance but couldn't be serious. Ten peoeple can't just vanish in a range as small as the Tetons.

The failure of the Appies to return as they had planned was irritating to us. People often get benighted in the Tetons in circumstances like those attending this climb: a large party, composed of people of varying experience, climbing a route that is reputed to be easy but is seldom climbed. In fact, those circumstances are guaranteed to produce a bivouac. At the ranger station we would normally give the party plenty of time to extricate itself from the route and get back before we did anything dramatic. Often there was another party in the same general area who would spot the late party. From where they were last seen, we could make a reasonable guess of how long it would take them to get back. If the missing party exceeded our estimated time of return, as well as their own, then we'd set things in motion. Even then we wouldn't scramble a full-scale search. Our first action would be to send out one ranger, or two if there was to be technical climbing, and combine the search with some other activity such as a patrol, if possible. We might also pass the word around to one or two key rescue types that such and such a party was overdue. What that meant to them was that they'd be where they could be easily reached and maybe pass up the second beer until the word went about that everybody was out of the mountains.

Sometimes the worried family or concerned friends who were waiting in the valley would take exception to this stalling for time. But there really is no other way to do it. If we'd scrambled a full-scale search and rescue operation every time a party was overdue, the expense would have been enormous but, most important, tremendous pressure would be put on the party in the mountains to get back in the time estimated and the result would be many more injuries and deaths.

In the case at hand, we actually did not stall as long as we normally would have. There were a lot of people in the Appalachian Mountain Club encampment who were concerned enough to bring down word to us of the overdue party. They certainly expected a response from us. Second, the storm increased the possibility that the party could be stuck for some time. One detail was worrisome, the party was not well equipped for cold weather. So, very soon after we were notified, Ranger George Kelly was on his way in to the mountains on a patrol. He would start by organizing a search party from the Appalachian Mountain Club encampment. It's not that we didn't worry. We always worried. Worrying was a major component of our work. It is not difficult to imagine the worst, even after a hundred repetitions of one's imagining's turning out to be worse that the reality. We worried, but we had learned an orderly, logical procedure to follow in these cases and kept our imaging at a distance.

The leader of the party was Ellis Blade, not himself an Appie but a recognized leader. Blade was not really what Europeans would regard as a guide. Americans do not hire guides in America, they hire authorities. Glenn Exum, the founder of the Exum Guides, has a kind of genius for spotting young men who carry an aura of personal authority. And that is part of the reason for the success of his guide service, a success which is unparalleled in America. The Exum Guides at that time ranged in age around late twenties to early thirties. Blade was in his fifties. The rest of the party varied greatly in experience. Steven Smith, quite young but a good rock climber, was the assistant leader. The other able rock climber was Lester Germer, who was sixty-five. Charles Joyce was a good recreation rock climber, very respectful of the Western mountains because his experience had been mainly on the cliffbands of the East. Janet Buckingham was an experienced hiker, with Lydia and Griffith June, Charles Kellogg and John Fenniman in various stages of learning rock climbing. Mary Blade, Ellis's wife, was also along and was an experienced mountaineer. The route they were to climb was known as the Otter Body Route, after the shape of a snowfield in the middle of the east face of the Grande Teton.

The party got off as planned at four A.M. Thursday morning, a good sign. There had only been a couple of minor problems in the days prior to setting out. Blade hadn't been able to generate much enthusiasm for conditioning climbs. The time to get the party into condition had been scheduled, but things hadn't quite worked out. This is not surprising in view of the fact that the encampment was the size of a tribe, but one with random membership. Going into the wilderness to set up a new society is an American passion, but it takes a lot of energy just to eat, sleep and talk in a situation like that. There are new people to meet and hierarchies, liaisons and enmities to be established before the group can truly focus on its stated purpose. It requires the genius of a leader like Shackleton to select team members who accomplish the settling-in work quickly and in such a manner that the resulting organization is the one that's needed to do the job.

The problem, other than conditioning, that Blade might have had on his mind at four A.M. that Thursday morning was that Steven Smith, the young assistant leader, was suffering from an attack of no confidence. He didn't like the looks of the weather. He had vomited the evening before, and had confided his doubts to Charles Joyce. Blade was fifty-four and Steven Smith was twenty-one. They never became co-leaders in any meaningful sense. It was Joyce who broached Smith's worries to Blade. If there was to be any rapport established between these two, it would have been up to Blade to establish it. Presumably part of his responsibility was to train the next generation of leaders. It is also true that mountaineering in America was undergoing a tremendous growth in rock-climbing skills; hundreds of good young climbers were, within three years, learning to do moves on rock routes that older climbers had thought only feasible on boulders in campgrounds. Blade would be an unusual man indeed if he did not feel his authority somewhat undermined by this new generation.

As for Smith, it's possible that he had a touch of the 'flu or had picked up a bug from the water. It happened to me at least once a season in the Tetons and to all the guides and climbing rangers I know. Whatever the cause of Smith's loss of confidence, the events of the first day conspired to keep it that way. They did however make an early start.

Four and a half hours later, at 8:30, they started up Teepe's Snowfield. A pace twice that fast would be regarded as slow by most climbers. Blad had plotted the climb with a five-hour margin of daylight. Half of his margin was gone before the party roped up.

Janet Buckingham broke out of her steps in the snow, and although Smith held the fall easily, Janet's feet flailed away at the snow uselessly. Anybody who has taught climbing beginners is familiar with the scene. The student or client literally loses contact with his/her feet and thrashes away hoping that a miracle will occur and one of them will stick. Perhaps Smith didn't know how to deal with the situation, perhaps he hadn't the chance. It was Blade, leaving his own rope, who talked her back into confidence in her steps again. The incident with Janet would have been soon forgotten by all involved except that disturbing incidents began to accumulate.

The lead rope of five made it to the top of the snowfield half an hour before noon. The second rope, Smith's, didn't join the lead rope at the top before lunch. They stopped on an outcropping about three rope lengths below. This area is scarred by debris fallen from the cliffband and two snowfields above. This detail did not go unnoticed by Joyce at least, and he was the one who spotted the falling ice first and gave the warning yell. One block carried away Fenniman's ice axe. Another glanced off Kellogg's foot. Joyce had two blocks to dodge and only managed to dodge one. He was hit hard and knocked into the air. Though briefly stunned he was uninjured.

To this point, Joyce, though he was Smith's confidant, had been maintaining a neutral stance on the question of whether the climb was advisable or not. After being hit, he still wasn't as shaken as Smith, whose hands were trembling, but he was now of Smith's opinion that this was an ill-fated climb and they ought to go down.

Blade had gone down to check that everybody was all right and then quickly climbed back up to his rope, before a discussion could ensue. The lower party, wanting to get out of the track of falling debris even more than they wanted to go down, followed quickly.

While they were getting underway, Joyce said to Smith, "Let's get out of here." Smith replied, "He'll kill us all."

As the entire party reached the top of the snowfield, a storm hit. It was noon. This was not the familiar late afternoon thunderstorm but the arrival of one that had been threatening since the previous evening. The party took refuge in the moat between the top of the snowfield and the rock which at least sheltered them from the wind. Smith finally confronted Blade with his desire to retreat. Blade responded that the snowfield was hardening and had become dangerous. As the heavy rainfall and hail from the first huge cumulus cloud passed and the rain moderated, Blade gave the word for everyone to put on their packs and start moving up. Joyce sought out Smith.

"What's he doing? Is he nuts? We've got to go down. You're a leader. Tell him we've got to go down."

Eventually it would be Joyce who would take command and make the decision to go down, but that was to be two days hence.

The party traversed the top of the snowfield to the base of a rock couloir. Blade sent Germer ahead to scout the route, asking him to report "how it would go". The wording is significant. Phrased that way, it is not the same as asking "Ought we attempt it?"

This couloir, carved in the interstice of the east face and the east side of the Grand joins the Otter Body Snowfield to Teepe's Snowfield. It is rather alarmingly free of the debris which packs the bottom of most Teton couloirs. It is too steep, too water, ice- and rock-washed to hold anything much in it for long. Obviously the rock is not particularly sound which is why a couloir developed. Griffith June saw the couloir first as a bowling alley and then found in his mind the inscription from the *Inferno*, "Abandon hope, all ye who enter here." Wet, cold, late, tired with weather threatening and tension in the group growing, it can not have been a cheerful party that geared themselves up for rock climbing.

Germer returned with his report which he recalls thus: "I told him it looked easy. I know now he was asking for advice, and I gave him a rock-climbing opinion. It was easy rock climbing. I was not considering the safety of the party. The camp had chosen Blade as a leader, but I should have said something." Possibly there was something else at work here. The opening sentence in the description of the route in Ortenburger's, *A Climbers Guide to the Teton Range* (1965 edition) is : "Petzoldt (who did the first ascent) ranks this as one of the easiest routes on the Grand Teton." Twenty-seven years after the first ascent, an Eastern cliff climber of Germer's stature could not in good conscience rate this climb as more difficult than the first ascent party found it to be. Unless Blade had reason to think that he was seriously off route, which was unlikely, he knew what Germer's reply was to be.

Ellis Blade retorted when Smith once again said that they ought to go down, "I've been on that glacier before in weather like this. It's as hard as ice. If we go down someone will get killed."

Smith pressed the point, "We can't climb the mountain now."

Blade's response was, "You keep your mouth shut."

"Well, I'm assistant leader of this group," said Smith, "and I think my opinion should be considered."

"Well, don't you forget that I am the leader and I know it is safer to go up."

In the hours that follow, they all got soaked, Lydia June had a shock from a lightning bolt, Smith avoided a rock avalanche only by leaping across the couloir into the arms of Griffith June, and Kellogg was hit by a rock which drove his crampons through his pack and into his back. Griffith June considered leading a splinter group back, a serious responsibility. He had the authority within the AMC organization, but not as a mountaineer, and they were very much in the mountains now. He urged Blade to lead them back but Blade replied that they were committed.

Blade now climbed quickly and well, getting the party three-fourths of the way up the couloir. Griffith June arrived at a huge boulder two pitches from the top, big enough for them all to sit on. Joyce secured them with pitons and they all bivouacked there except Blade who had reached the wide ledges and easy slabs at the top of the couloir. There was no reconsideration of Blade's decision. There were complaints, perhaps fewer than there might have been had Mary Blade not been part of the group. A decision to go down would have been a decision to abandon Blade on the mountain.

Three inches of wet snow fell during the night. They had no down garments, no dry clothes, and virtually no food. In the morning, Germer asked Smith what he thought, Germer didn't like the rotten rock and had been weakened by the bivouac. Smith replied that he didn't know the route.

It took all of the next day, Friday, to get the party up the remaining two pitches to the top of the couloir. Joyce and Fenniman climbed up to Blade. June slipped on the ice just below the point where the angle of the couloir eased. He tried repeatedly and fell repeatedly. He cut steps, almost made it, fell again, this time further and over an overhang. There was danger of his being strangled by the rope. Smith muscled him over the bivouac pillar where June collapsed exhausted.

Germer then went up and set up an intermediate belay position where he stayed until all six remaining climbers were up the couloir. (This was during the time when Dornan and I were being driven from Mount Mornan a few miles to the north.) Though fit enough, Germer was in his sixties and this was too much; he had lost all reserves. His hands were claws; he clutched a piton in each and made it up the ice.

Blade moved on but was called back. Germer announced he was dying.

Blade assessed the situation and had a new plan, but not a new direction. There can be an infinite number of situations, tactics and explanations but there can only be one conclusion. He, Joyce and Smith would go up. They might find climbers on the top. If not, they'd go down the Owen-Spaulding Route and get help.

There was twice as much snow above them as they climbed Teepe's Snowfield and beyond was another cliffband.

When duty ranger, George Kelly, got to the AMC camp at the Petzoldt's Caves, there was no word of the missing party. By the time he radioed this news down, we were back in the ranger station and instructed him to organize a search. We were getting a little nervous. The search was to a certain extent window-dressing. These people couldn't be sent up on any difficult terrain. In other words, any place they could be allowed to search would be a place where the missing party could get out of by themselves. What they could do was to look and listen. They did and what they saw was three members of the party up on the Otter Body Snowfield.

The need for a plausible explanation for what was happening with that party was increasing by the moment, while the prospects for getting such an explanation were decreasing. At their present rate, it would be two days before they got to the top. We were at first inclined to believe that these three could not be from the party we were seeking, but a review of the facts available to us convinced us that they had to be three of the ten. There was no way to make sense of it. It was hard to believe that if there had been an injury, accident or fatality someone couldn't have gotten out to tell us. If there had been some kind of horrible disaster and these were the only survivors, that would explain why we hadn't heard from them, but not why they were going up. Only one thing was clear, we had to get serious about finding out what was going on.

There had been a short rescue the evening before involving a client of the guide service. The guide service had provided most of the manpower for the rescue. Barry Corbet was one of those who had helped. He was to take a group up the Grand on Saturday but another guide had taken his party to the high camp at the Lower Saddle earlier in the day while he got some rest. He was on his way up to join them when he met George Kelly and was pressed into service. As they followed the track of the party up the snowfield and into the couloir, the storm renewed itself. Barry was equipped and George wasn't. They were, as we later determined, within 400 feet of Blade's group when they turned back, Barry to join his party.

Doug McLaren, a district ranger and member of the rescue team when it was originally organized a decade earlier, was our supervisor, though no longer an active climber. It was he who organized and coordinated rescue activities. Doug ordered a pack team to move as much equipment as we could reasonably muster up to Garnet Canyon. Garnet Canyon is the cirque rimmed anticlockwise from north to south by Disappointment Peak, the Grand Teton, the Middle Teton, the South Teton and Nez Perce. Doug, Sterling Neale, Jim Greig and I left in the advance party at seven P.M. Rick Horn and Mike Ermarth, the remaining strong climbers on the park team were to follow with more equipment. All the available Exum Guides volunteered, Jack Breitenbach, Pete Lev, Fred Wright, and Al Read; and they were joined by four other volunteers, Dr. Roland Fleck, Bill Briggs and Dave Dornan, who were soon to become guides, and Peter Koedt, who later helped me in organizing the Jackson Hole Mountain Guides until the Vietnam disaster forced him into Canadian exile. These guides and volunteers were to come up in the morning. Another guide, Herb Swedlund, was holding at the Petzoldt's Caves, awaiting developments. The majority of the professional mountaineers in America at the time were to carry out this operation.

The four of us got a little sleep at the end of the horse trail about an hour's climb below the encampment at the Caves and started up around four A.M. We arrived at the top of the snowfield at about 10:30. Here I made a serious mistake in route-finding. The party had to be either on the cliffband between Teepe's Snowfield and the Otter Body Snowfield, or possibly at the top of the Otter Body just above the point where the three climbers had been spotted. There were two obvious routes up the cliffband. One was the couloir to the right of the cliffband, dark, wet, rotten, and the other was a nice sunlit rock line straight up from where we were.

I'd never been here before, but I'd been nearby six weeks earlier, looking at it from a col about 400 yards to our left at the southern edge of the snowfield. I had come to take a look because the climbing pressure on the standard routes was becoming such that I was interested in finding another easy way to the summit to recommend to those climbers who mainly wanted to get to the top of the mountain. What I had seen in June was far from being the easiest route on the mountain. The sun reflected off the snow into the couloir to reveal a mass of contorted ice, as if a section of rapids in the Grand Canyon of the Snake had been instantly frozen and set up vertically in this evil-looking crevice in the mountain. Debris, both ice and rock, cascaded out of it. It seemed the picture of unpredictability. There was no pattern other than a headlong, downward plunge. The mountain seemed to be saying, "Here I keep no pacts." At the same time, I did note the comparative warmth and orderliness of a sunlit route up an open chimney just to the south of the icy corner. I had decided this was the route Petzoldt had gone up and though it may have been easy for him, it wasn't easy enough for the type of climber I had in mind. I descended from the col without bothering to traverse the snowfield to take a closer look.

Now the ice was gone and water poured down the couloir. My comrades were of the opinion that the route went up the couloir. I said that was impossible, anybody could see that that was no place to be. It was not a place for people. My memory of my first look at the couloir in June colored my present perception of it considerably. Thus I persuaded them to follow me up the route I had seen, which is in fact not the Otter Body Route but the Smith Route.

The discussion had planted enough doubt in my mind that I wanted to make sure the climbing went as easily as I had claimed it would. I've never worked harder to find the easiest possible line. I scanned the rock almost frantically and climbed with as nonchalant a motion as I could. However, the climbing, while easy, was not trivial and at the point which in the guidebook account of the Smith Route is described as "the difficult overhanging portion", the climbing became seriously non-trivial. As we paused to deal with this shocking appearance of fifth-class climbing on what was supposed to be a third- and fourth-class route, we heard voices unmistakably coming from the top of the couloir.

We rappelled down and decided that only two of us would go up to investigate, partly because of the rockfall danger and partly because the voices we heard seemed to be singing! Sterling Neale and I had traveled together, worked together and climbed a lot together. I wanted him to stay at the bottom with Doug because it looked like that was going to have to be the organization point. I didn't know what the tremendous barrier was between where we were and where they were, but there must be something keeping them from descending. Sterling could practically read my mind and I wanted him where he would be in a position to do something if things got complicated. Also, Jim Greig was bigger and stronger than either of us and there were at least seven of them up there someplace.

Angry because of my mistake, I climbed carelessly and managed to break my hammer soon after we got underway. I remember the climbing as being more difficult than does Jim. The last two pitches, bypassing the overhand and crossing the ice, could be psychologically intimidating to a climber, or a party, not in good form.

The route lay up the right-hand or east side of the ice at the top of the couloir. The party was on the slabs at the 'tail' of the Otter Body, about thirty feet above and half a rope length in distance. There was about seven inches of snow on the ice almost heavy and wet enough to adhere to the ice while bearing our weight. We weren't able to protect the pitch in a manner which could stop a fall short of the overhang. We had neither ice pitons nor crampons. A rope from above would be just the thing.

For the first time, we returned our attention fully to the party we'd come to rescue. They seemed surprisingly calm. Did they have a climbing rope? They did. Would they toss us an end? They would. The young man Fenniman stiffly approached the lip of the ledge with a rope. He seemed a bit perplexed. We instructed him to give the coil a healthy swing and toss it down to us. He swung the coil back and then forward but failed to release it. He did the same thing again. And then again. And again. There was something odd about the motion. He wasn't swinging the coil to get up momentum, but swinging indecisively almost as if he wasn't sure he wanted to cross over to them and disturb the calm which reigned there. The swinging motion became mechanical. He'd forgotten that he was not only to swing the coil but also to release it. We hadn't told him that he had to do both. We told him. The coil, released in the middle of the swing instead of at the end of it, dropped in front of his feet. Jim and I exchanged glances. Perhaps if he climbed down the slab to the next ledge toward us?

"I won't! I won't!" He spoke not directly to us but first to the air at our left and then to the rock at his feet.

"Stay where you are!" we said in one voice we just managed to keep from rising. We were in for it, no doubt about that, we'd really gotten into something which promised to be very strange.

Jim "went for it" and we made it across and joined them on their ledge. They undoubtedly had been badly frightened and were probably making an effort to recover their wits. Possibly they were somewhat embarrassed. The resulting impression on me was of an unnatural calm. It seemed to be an effort for most of them to acknowledge our presence. There was a polite smile, a curious, almost disinterested gaze, the sort of thing I'd experienced in New York subways. Mary Blade seemed positively cheerful. They'd been singing, she told us. She also told us that Lester had been having a difficult time. Lester wanted to know if we'd brought any strawberry jam. We hadn't. We should have. According to Lester that's what we were supposed to do, bring strawberry jam and tea. He was a little put out with us and seemed doubtful that we knew our business.

I was offended. My first thought was, "Jesus Christ, Lester, if I knew what we were going to find up here I would have brought the Tenth Mountain Division!" I had just enough presence of mind to realize that I was feeling defensive and said nothing. The Grand Teton National Rescue Team was and still is the best rescue team in the country. Where did Lester imagine he had gotten the authority to lecture us? From a book, a book on European practice? I had a picture of the members of these large climbing organizations sitting around in their meetings imagining rescues with the old New England obsequiousness toward things British and Continental. The European teams were unquestionably better than ours. Gary Hemming used to urge me to go to Europe and learn from them and I wish I could. But what we'd been able to glean from books we found inadaptable to our circumstances. There was a more immediate reason for my defensive response to Lester's suggestion that we didn't know what we were doing. What were we going to do?

I signaled to Jim. Under the pretext of moving to a better radio transmission site, we climbed up to the next ledge and walked behind a boulder to talk.

"What in hell are we going to do?" he asked.

Jim later told me that I calmly lit a cigarette and replied, "We're all going to die, that's what we're going to do."

I guess I had to say it to get it out of the way. I'm glad I did. Life doesn't provide many opportunities to deliver a line like that. Anyway, the notion was not that far-fetched. The radio wouldn't work and we'd managed to get off without taking an extra battery. I restrained myself from throwing the radio down the mountain and satisfied myself with shouting into it, cursing and shaking it.

Eventually, by moving about from rock to ledge to chimney and bouncing our voices off the walls on the East Ridge, we found a place where we could shout out of the couloir and have some words heard and, we hoped, understood by Sterling and Doug. All we could tell them was to stay out of the couloir. What we wished to have been able to tell them was that we would be setting things up, up here, while they organized the equipment and men coming up from below. At some convenient moment, we would freeze all motion in the upper couloir while they set up belaying and lowering positions below us. Then we'd have a bucket brigade of various techniques, fixed ropes, maybe a litter or two, rappels, belays and so forth, depending on the terrain and condition of the members of the party. It could have been very elegant but it was not to be. Jim and I would just have to start moving the group down the mountain any way we could until we were back in communication with our teammates, or until they could see what was needed and we could see that they could see what was needed.

We started. There was a ledge big enough for the whole party below us but it was further than the two short pitches Jim and I could manage with the equipment available. Could Fenniman, the only one of the party who was reasonably ambulatory, help us? He'd have to. The fact that we had to use Fenniman in the shape he was in gave me a feeling like what I imagined the French Existentialist meant by the absurd. A little ironic repartee crept into the conversation between Jim and me, something of Hemingway, a bit of Camus' Stranger. Jim would lower one to me, I'd lower that one to Fenniman, he'd belay them to the ledge.

I had anchored Fenniman to a slab about thirty feet above the big ledge and gave him very precise instructions about what to do which I repeated several times. While doing so, my sense that things were absurd became a feeling that things were desperate. The entire operation had to funnel to and through this eighteen-year-old youngster just out of high school who was headed for Dartmouth. I'd once been a kid just out of high school headed for Dartmouth and couldn't imagine what I'd have been able to do if I were then in the position he was now in.

He had been there, within a stone's throw of this place, for two nights and now nearly three days. He was in what must have appeared to him as the most precarious position he'd been in during the entire nightmare. He was, in fact, quite securely anchored, but he had only my word for that. It would not be surprising if he had come to doubt the word of people who claimed to know better than he the position he was in. He might have been bound to a rock over an abyss by a strange god or demon for all the events of the past three days might have taught him.

It was no wonder that I wasn't quite sure if I was talking to the whole Fenniman or to a messenger the whole Fenniman had sent to hear me out. The messenger seemed reliable, even heroic. I felt that Fenniman would get the job done, but had the odd thought that I'd like to meet him some day. It occurred to me that he might untie himself from the anchor and step off the mountain. That had happened a few years before to a guide with a head injury on this same peak, three ridges to the south. I moved the knot tying him to the mountain around behind him, where it couldn't be reached accidentally as he tied and untied the people we sent down. I made my instructions simple, precise and routine and tried at the same time to speak to him as a peer who could of course do what we were asking of him.

It worked. He did it exactly as I instructed; exactly the same way everytime. When I had seen him swinging that coil mechanically back and forth when we'd asked for the upper belay some part of my mind had registered the potential in those precise movements and the potential in his, "I won't! I won't!" There must be a way that he could be made to say "I will! I will!" There was, but as the sequel was to show, something very different might have happened.

We first assumed that they could provide their own motive power and set the pace of the descent if we belayed them down a fixed rope. The least experienced of them would not have found the first pitch at all troublesome under normal circumstances. Now people were falling down on flat ledges, falling into a stream two feet wide and three inches deep and spending thirty seconds trying to figure out how to step over an eight-inch rock. Sometimes you see this in a beginners' rock-climbing class when the client is really frightened. There are ways to deal with it. But these people did not look frightened. What we were seeing on their faces and hearing in their voices wasn't fear but confusion, as if the problems of balance and motion were intellectual problems entirely. We had to give up trying to talk them through the moves. We were becoming exasperated at the ineffectiveness of our explanations and instructions and knew that our exasperation would only make things worse.

Tactfully at first, then less so, we relieved them of their autonomy. Staggering, slithering, stumbling, as long as they kept descending, they could pick their one way down. If they stopped too long, a tug, a nudge and finally steady, unrelenting pressure kept things moving as the sun got lower.

After the first of them had gone down the snow-covered ice, it was snow covered no longer and all the pretense of down-climbing was abandonded. They got soaked; sliding down the ice and water and I shivered for them. Speed was becoming imperative. Fenniman caught on. I overheard someone explaining to him that they had lost a foothold. To which Fenniman replied insistently, "They say you have to keep moving."

Speed under these circumstances is a relative term. We who were trying to imagine that we were in control of things were tying, untying, handling the rope with one hand, gesticulating with the other and talking and thinking as fast as possible. Those who were being controlled were rudely precipitated off a pitch, tied to an anchor and then left to a shivering halt of a half hour or more before it was their turn again.

Once down on the big ledge, things seemed better. Perhaps the ledge they'd spent so many uncomfortable but relatively safe hours on had been difficult to abandon. There was less of a feeling of us and them. There was some conversation. We found out all we could about what had happened as the opportunity arose. I began to learn their names and to take account of them as separate people. I noted that the Junes seemed to be holding together. That doesn't always happen to couples under stress in the mountains. I wondered if Germer was recalling warm summer days rock climbing in the Shawangunks. Janet was the wettest, coldest, seemed most out of place, but I was impressed by her endurance. I wondered if Mary Blade was worrying about Ellis, and if so would she be more concerned about his safety or the repercussions that seemed obviously destined to come to him. Kellogg appeared to be not badly off, something like a nice young man just recently embarked on a course of dissipation.

There was little time for these thoughts. Above all was the fact that we could make a mistake and kill one of them, or not make a mistake and still have one of them die. Lester Germer was the obvious candidate, the one everybody was worried about but there were others. And what of the missing three? We had to take Mary's word that they were in pretty good climbing shape, but what did 'pretty good' mean? The best we could hope for was that they would be spotted by Barry who was on the summit today. The trouble was, Barry would be down by now. Perhaps Doug and Ster already had news?

I chafed at our slow pace. My earlier route-finding mistake had cost us about two hours and that was going to make the difference between day and night in this gully, between warm sun and 32° granite, between pitches and icy pitches, between snow you could heel down and snow as hard as ice. My mistake had the appearance of meaning the difference between life or death for one or more of these people. Once you parade yourself in the world as a rescuer and once you take charge of the party, everything that happens after that is on your head.

We made another effort to communicate with Doug and Ster. We tried to impress on them the mass of equipment that would be needed and reiterated the point about them staying out of the gully. It was frustrating for them, and we could see that some of the guides had arrived too, to watch the shadow of the Grand move out over the valley at an increasing rate, while we appeared not to be moving at all. But the rock falls we were setting off were fairly convincing. The main thing we wanted to happen was to have the snowfield all set up for lowering so that as each of the party arrived at the top of the snowfield they could be lowered quickly from anchor to anchor.

Just before dark, Jim called down to me the news that two of the missing three were coming down from above. The significance of the fact that there were two, not three took hold slowly. I couldn't imagine how the third could be rescued. If we stopped everything to bring a litter and eight climbers up through us, I was sure somebody would die of exposure, there would be a rock fall both above and below and there'd be nobody left to help us get these seven down. I also found myself fervently hoping that I wouldn't have to go back up the mountain.

When Blade got to me I interrogated him fairly fiercely about the condition of the third. It was Smith and he was dead. I was in danger of feeling relieved and that made me ruder. Also, it was difficult to believe. "Are you sure he's dead, because if you're not, somebody has to go up. How did you check? How long did you wait before leaving him?" Blade told me that the body had started to get stiff. I didn't believe that but whether he was dead when they left him or not, he was certainly dead by now. I sized up Joyce. He was clearly in better shape than anyone else. It was a little startling to see a normal person apparently unaffected by this place.

I had pulled Blade aside to question him. I could imagine what the impact of the news that the strongest member of the party had died of exposure might do to their will to survive. Furthermore, if someone else was going to die it was unlikely that they'd do it quickly and allow us to go on. I had a horrible image of being immobilized there in that gully helplessly watching a slow chain reaction of dying. I ordered Blade not to talk about it.

He moved across the ledge and gathered everybody there around and made a little speech about how we were trying to help them and they'd have to cooperate with us. I found that astonishing and a little amusing as I tried to imagine how they could not cooperate with us. Then I had an awful insight.

What from their point of view would we be doing if we were not try-ing to save them but kill them? I was a little ashamed of my rough treatment of Blade. I had my own mistakes to worry about.

Janet got soaked again. She lost her footing while being lowered, swung into a waterfall and was too stiff and cold to roll out of it without help. I began to feel that she might not make it and I had to do something person-ally to give her heart. The distance the rescuer maintains between himself and the victims makes stepping out of it a more effective gesture.

I made her squeeze in behind a flake which would not only protect her modesty if that was necessary but mainly protected her a little from the cold evening westerly pouring down on us from the snowfields above. I made her take off her Levis, lectured her about the fact that denim was the worst possible material to wear in the mountains and wrung the water out of them as much as I could. They were new and stiff. I imagined that she'd bought them down in Jackson, in honor of her visit to the West. I gave her some food I'd been saving for someone it might make the difference to, including possibly myself. Then I took my favorite sweater out of my pack and made her put it on. I tried a little levity. I told her that it was a twenty-five dollar sweater and she'd better not get it dirty! She took me seriously—so much for levity. What-ever was going to happen was going to happen without interference from me.

There were shouts from below. They were coming up and we were to be careful about rocks. It was worth being a climber to feel the camaraderie that I felt then, an emotion that embraces much more than mere bullshitting around a table in a tavern.

First to arrive were Pete Lev and Al Read. Lev is the picture of earnest strength. Read is a man in command of himself. Witty, quick to perceive the ludicrous as the ironic, he is a natural leader and an unobtrusive one. Lev is very compassionate and was taken aback by what he saw, including me and Jim. Jim and I were emotionally numb by this point and I saw concern in their faces. But suddenly it seemed possible that most of us might escape from this place. Suddenly the mountain seemed covered with people who knew what they were doing. Herb Swedlund was down there, Swedlung who would joke with the Devil. I couldn't wait to get down to hear him say something like, "Sinclair, you're quaking like a dog passing peach pits." Rick Horn was down there, probably performing great feats of strength and daring while screaming, "The world is contrived to drive us insane."

The next pitch below ended in the middle of a slab which bulged out from the base of the couloir. Every rock that came down the couloir had to hit that slab. Jake Breitenbach was at the anchor. When I got to him, I was afraid for him, a fear that seemed familiar. Then I recalled the boulder in the great ice gully on McKinley that seemed to pursue us. He, however, was ebullient, as he was most of the time in the mountains. For him, this was what it was all about. How often do you get to have fun like this, up here in an interesting part of the mountain with practically all your climbing and guiding buddies? He was good for the people we were rescuing too. He told them, as he prepared to send them down the vertical slab below, "We always arrange to have the rescues at night so you won't know what you're stepping off of." He picked them up and kept them going. For one or more of them it is likely that Jake made the difference.

The man I was most eagerly waiting to get to was Sterling, because once I got to him and passed below, he would take charge.

I asked Pete and Al if they'd set up the snowfield. They hadn't. It turned out that the guides, Jake Breitenbach, Al Read, Pete Lev, Fred Wright, Dave Dornan and Herb Swedlund, Mike Ermarth and Rick Horn of the rescue team and Dr. Walker from Jackson had arrived at the base of the couloir just minutes after Jim and I reached the top of the couloir. Even if the radio had worked, the word that we needed masses of gear would have gone out too late. Again, the critical two hours I had lost. There went my hopes that things would soon speed up. It had taken Jim and me five hours to get the party down five pitches. It was another seven hours to two A.M. when the last victim was to reach the top of the snowfield. Just two more ropes would have cut that seven hours nearly in half.

Al and Pete tactfully suggested that Jim and I go down to the snowfield, they could handle matters up here. They received no heroic protests from us.

My last image of the gully is of Horn working on the pitch exiting the couloir. I was rappelling down a steep slab and Horn came racing up by me, foot over hand it seemed, to help someone who'd gotten hung up on a ledge. He was muttering to himself and lunged to the ledge just as I realized that he was climbing unroped. I asked him if he thought that was wise. He didn't, but there weren't any more ropes.

At the top of the snowfield, a huge platform was being cut, large enough to hold all the rescued and some of the rescuers. I described the situation above as best I could to Sterling after telling him he looked good enough to me to kiss. I told him that it wasn't at all clear they all were going to make it. Lester Germer had expressed a sentiment to be left alone to die. I'd be tempted to let him and was glad it was out of my hands. Actually the fact that Germer had the whole party dedicated to keeping him alive certainly gave them a badly needed focus for survival. Germer was, I believe, in some degree conscious of this because, as we later found out, he had spotted the rescue team coming up Teepe's Snowfield and had said nothing to his companions.

Jim and I stood around on the ledge until the first victim arrived on it. There was some debate about whether to set up a series of anchors down the snowfield a rope-length apart or fewer super anchors to which we would just add ropes. I tried to join in the discussion and realized that I couldn't think very well and that it was no longer our show. Jim and I decided to go down.

I got as scared as I've ever been descending that snowfield. We were without ice axes and crampons. The surface was so hard that we couldn't kick steps deeper than half an inch. The rock hammer and pitons we had to stop a fall weren't convincing. I couldn't judge the surface either by sight or touch. I had difficulty keeping my body balanced over the pitiful footholds we were kicking because there was no elasticity left in my legs. At any time I could have moved on a marginal hold to a place where I quickly needed a good hold to find that I was on water ice and that would be it. All the way down my thought was, "And I said we wouldn't need crampons. You stupid son of a bitch, if you fall you'll deserve it."

In those circumstances we paid little attention to the commotion going on above us except cynically to remark that we hoped our mates didn't bomb us with one of the victims.

At this point we shall leave Pete Sinclair for a while and let Al Read take up the story:

Pete Lev and I had climbed up several leads in the late afternoon and were the first to meet Pete Sinclair and Jim Greig who were coming down from the Otter Body Snowfield lowering the helpless people, all suffering from hypothermia. We did not reach them until late afternoon or dusk as I recall. Pete and I were quickly joined by other rescuers and we all participated in the lowering process down the rock wall to the top of Teepe's Glacier. We were all wearing headlamps and the shadows of the victims and the rescuers against the walls were quite dramatic. I remember Jake Breitenbach (killed on Everest the next year) strapping one man on his back and rapelling down. Some were in very bad shape and two, it seemed at the time, rather near death. Anyway, there was no time to wait for litters because it was still snowing and all the victims were absolutely soaked through.

A crew lower down at the top of Teepe's Glacier had hacked out a large platform just below the rock walls and were receiving the Appies as we lowered them or brought them down on our backs. All finally were sitting on the snow tied to a number of ice axes driven in to the hilt just above the platform. The snow was extremely steep and quite hard. A slip would have meant a 2,000-foot slide down the glacier (really more of a steep snowfield but technically a glacier) into the rocks of the moraine below and certain death.

We all were very concerned we would have more hypothermia deaths unless we got the people down to the rescue group waiting at the bottom of the glacier with medical attention, soup, sleeping bags, etc., and the helicopters which would be there at dawn (no chance of pickup at the top glacier). We decided to lower everyone—really just slide them—down the glacier from our top stance to a lower stance several hundred feet below. Here we decided to make another platform from which a final lower could be made to where the angle of the snow eased and the Appies could be carried or dragged to the edge of the glacier and assistance. Herb Swedland and Jake went down to make the lower stance—perhaps 500 feet down. Meanwhile, Peter Lev, Sterling Neale, Rick Horn and I tied five loops in a climbing rope and placed five Appies in them. Each victim was tied about ten feet apart. We belayed this expeditious arrangement from two ice axes driven into the floor of our platform. I stood on one and let out the rope while Sterling watched the system and prepared to add additional ropes. Pete Lev (wearing crampons) descended to assist the Appies as they were being lowered. We slid the victims one by one off the platform and began lowering. They were heavy and I wished we had had a better belay.

Suddenly Pete yelled up to stop. He said there was an empty loop. There were only four people on the rope. Obviously one had fallen out of his waistloop. Dead, we thought! But after yelling down to Herb and Jake, nobody had seen or heard a body whirling by. Because everyone was working in the fall line, obviously the person *would* have been noticed. Pete then saw someone in his light about fifty feet to the right. He yelled at him. No response. He ran over to him and told him to return to the rope and safety. Pete immediately began to cut a platform as the person was wearing no crampons—only his mountain boots. Of course he had no ice axe. Pete told him to follow him back to the rope. The victim, John Fenniman, said nothing but looked as if he understood. Pete began cutting steps back to the rope, which we had had now stopped lowering. Rick Horn was preparing another climbing rope to throw down to Pete, so he could tie in the victim. We all knew he could come off at any minute.

As Pete began cutting steps back to the rope, Fenniman ignored him and went the other way instead. Pete stopped and climbed back to him. Pete insisted he follow him. Then Fenniman suddenly grabbed Pete's ice axe and they began grappling and struggling. Pete yelled up to us for help.

Pete Horn, also wearing crampons, who had by then readied a climbing rope, quickly lowered himself down and diverted Fenniman's attention. Pete scampered away, still retaining his ice axe. From behind, Rick managed to tie a quick bowline around Fenniman's waist and get away. He quickly returned to our ledge and put a belay on Fenniman. We all looked at him with our headlamps. He began slowly to climb up towards our stance. I was still holding the remaining four Appies on belay through the two ice axes.

As Fenniman approached our platform his eyes were bulged out. He was ashen and looked as if he had gone mad. He had! He said very slowly, "You are the Devil. You are taking me to Hell"—or words to that effect. I could hardly believe what I was seeing and hearing. All at once he jumped up on our ledge and began hitting us. We believed he was trying to reach the several ice axes still stuck in the snow behind us. I remember thinking, as his fists were banging into my face, that I might have let go of the belay to keep myself from being thrown off the platform or hit by an axe if he ever got hold of one. I remember yelling to Rick, "Kill him if you have to!" One of the Appie victims still on the platform yelled back, "No, no, don't kill him!" It was all quite incredible.

Rick finally managed to give Fenniman a shove and he went over the edge, but was caught at the lip by the belay, secured by Rick, who yelled we were only trying to help him. But when he continued to resist, Rick had to knock him out with a kick to the side of the head. The frontpoints of his crampons missed by a fraction. Fenniman went limp, Rick dragged him over to the rope, tied him in, and sat on him. The lowering was renewed.

Coming up from below, Jack Turner describes the scene as first seeing four people being lowered out of the darkness—limp and facing every direction, some upside down. Suddenly he saw a victim being ridden by Rick. Rick was hitting him with his fists and gagging! What was happening was every time Fenniman showed signs of coming round, Rick had to put him out again without actually killing him, and the tension and desperation of the experience had nauseated him. According to Turner this remains as one of the most amazing scenes he has ever witnessed.

The rest of the victims were lowered without incident and all fully recovered. I saw Fenniman later that morning being carried in a litter down to the helicopter landing site. He remembered nothing and could not have been nicer or more thankful. He simply had momentarily lost his mind and was trying to protect himself. I rather imagine he had thought he was dead or dying and that we indeed were trying to take him to Hell.

Pete Sinclair and Jim Greig had spent twenty-two nonstop grueling hours on their vital first part of the rescue. But the next day something had to be done about Steve Smith's body. Pete Sinclair takes up the story again:

We didn't want to bring the body down. The Chief Ranger, Russ Dickenson, and the superintendent contacted Smith's parents and asked for permission to bury Smith on the mountain. I don't know how they found the words to ask them and I don't know how the Smiths found words to grant it, but they did. I felt awful about it, as if we were violating the code that Achilles violated in refusing to allow Priam to give Hector a proper burial. Achilles relented, we didn't. I knew the Smiths would probably recall that Steve had loved the mountains and might wish to be buried there. That might have been his wish had he died in the heat of action. But life had not ended in glorious action for Steve Smith, it had oozed out of him, sapped from him by an insidious worm of self-doubt that had gotten lodged in his soul, giving him no opportunity even to struggle.

On Monday, Rick, Jim and I were transported to the Lower Saddle by helicopter. The weather looked lousy. Soon it started to snow. We stayed in the guide's hut, lounging on several layers of sleeping pads and drinking tea, chocolate and soup. Rick told us about his adventures with Fenniman. He still hadn't quite recovered from that experience and obviously didn't relish the task at hand. Our plan was to go up the Owen-Spaulding Route, cross over the top of the mountain just south of the summit and descend the snowfield to the shoulder of the Otter Body where Smith's body lay, bury him, and descend the route taken by Joyce, Blade and Smith and then on down the evacuation route, cleaning up as much of the debris as we could. The snowstorm was not an auspicious beginning. This was turning out to be one of the worst climbing seasons in memory. Jake used to say that the Owen-Spaulding is both the easiest and most difficult route he had climbed on the Grand, easy under normal conditions, difficult under the conditions currently prevailing. That worried me some but that wasn't worrying Rick, much the strongest climber. Every hour or so Rick would inquire as discreetly as possible as to what we thought *he* would look like when we got to him. It dawned on Jim and me that this was to be Rick's first corpse, and I have to confess that we laid it on a little. We weren't unsympathetic but we knew that nobody can help you through that experience. The best you can do is to gain what distance you can by finding what humour you can, not laughing at the death but laughing at what your imagination is doing to you.

It snowed throughout Monday night and for much of Tuesday and then began to clear. We would leave for the summit before dawn on Wednesday morning and the whole upper part of the mountain was completely iced over. It might have been November. Jim and I climbed slowly and cautiously, protecting every high-angle pitch but Rick found that maddening. He seemed almost frantic to get to the summit ridge, out of the cold and into the sun.

Over the crest of the ridge we found a beautiful summer day in the mountains. Not hot of course because we were in fresh snow above 13,000 feet, but the sun opened our down jackets and eased into our tensed muscles. We called a halt for an early lunch. The partially mown hay field made squares of light green between the darker green willows along the Snake and the Gros Ventre rivers and the greenish-grey and light brown sagebrush flats of the valley. The snow was clean and too bright for unprotected eyes. We had passed from winter to summer in the space of a few moments and a few yards.

We moved at a normal pace now, picking out a route with caution in couloirs we had to cross to reach the snowfield and then descended with an occasional belay down the East Snowfield to the rock above the body. Some scrambling and a short rappel brought us to Steve Smith. Near him was an empty matchbook, the matches lay scattered about. Each one was tried, none had lit. Much later, we heard the story of how at Smith's death Charlie Joyce rebelled, took Blade by the shoulders and told him that they were going down, all the way down.

We took what personal effects we thought his family might like to have, tied a rope to the body and manoeuvred it over the moat between the base of the cliff and the Otter Body Snowfield. Getting it adequately protected was something of a problem. We looked for a place near at hand where the snow pack was thickest and least likely to bare the rock in eve the driest year. Rick was above anchoring the body. From a stance a few feet above the corpse I guided the rope to a position where it would drop directly down a small chimney to the debris at the base of the cliff. Jim straddled the rope at the body with his knife out.

"Well," said Jim, made the sign of the cross over Steve Smith and cut the rope. I had forgotten to bring a Bible. We covered the body first with small rocks, in case there were any carnivorous rodents up there, and then with larger boulders.

Part Two

Angels in Uniform:
Cops, Firemen, Emergency Services

Minute-by-Minute at the World Trade Center

From Inside 9-11: What Really Happened

BY THE REPORTERS, WRITERS AND EDITORS OF
DER SPIEGEL MAGAZINE

The German magazine *Der Spiegel* has provided coverage of the September 11 terrorist attacks that John Le Carre has called "deeply disturbing and comprehensive." This minute by minute reconstruction of the events of 9/11 tells the story from the point of view of both those trapped inside the towers and their would-be rescuers, including one firefighter whose own wife is one of those missing.

★   ★   ★   ★   ★

Battery Park City, Manhattan, 6:00 A.M.

Dan Potter hated the buzz of the alarm clock. Jean knew her husband's aversion, so every morning she was faster than the alarm clock and kissed him awake. In a year and a half of marriage the alarm clock had hardly ever caught them by surprise.

Jean worked on the 81st floor of the North Tower, in the offices of the Bank of America, where she was an assistant to the head of trading. Dan and Jean had met through an ad in the *New York Post*. His first marriage had broken up; his eighteen-year-old son had moved into Dan's small apartment after living with his mother became impossible.

Dan Potter had yet a third family: the New York Fire Department. He had been a firefighter for twenty-three years. He never complained, but he was beginning to feel that Manhattan was wearing him down. "You have to be young in Manhattan," he says. To carry one hundred pounds of gear up stairs,

72

sometimes as far the fiftieth floor, because a sprinkler had gotten set off by accident. "You feel like a cat chasing its tail."

The only thing worse than a false alarm is a real alarm. In an instant a skyscraper can be transformed into a huge, blazing furnace or a labyrinth of black smoke from which you have to grope you way out. You damn well have to love your own city and the people in it to endure this kind of work. Potter is that kind of guy.

The catch: He's forty-four years old. That's why he decided to find himself an easier position—as a fireman in the Bronx. Working there is a picnic compared to Manhattan. The buildings are seldom taller than four stories, and, best of all, you rarely have to go in. You park the engine on the street and aim the hose full blast. "A great job," says Dan Potter. Even if it means going back to school.

That's why he left home on September 11 in civvies: jeans, knit shirt, penny loafers. A couple of weeks earlier he'd started his course work on Staten Island, and at the end of it all he'd be a lieutenant—in the Bronx.

Canal Street, Manhattan, 8:47 A.M.

Chief Joe Pfeiffer of the First Battalion was examining a leaky gas pipe when he saw a passenger plane hit the North Tower.

He radioed a dispatcher with words like "a direct hit" and "huge jet." In an instant, Pfeiffer set off a level-three alarm. A level-three alarm means that nineteen FDNY trucks are immediately set into motion.

Metro-Tech in Brooklyn also received an emergency message: "BLDG EXPLOSION." The case number for the event: 0727.

8:48:03 A.M.: "Caller states explosion at top of WTC," an employee at the emergency center typed into the computer.

8:48:07 A.M.: "Plane into top of building," a caller states.

8:50:12 A.M.: "Male caller states: Plane just flew into WTC—possibly commercial airplane."

8:50:22 A.M.: "Female caller states: WTC exploded."

8:52:53 A.M.: "Female caller states big hole in right side."

8:53:28 A.M.: "Male caller states someone falling off building."

At 8:55 A.M. a 10–60 alarm was announced, signaling a larger disaster.

At 8:59 A.M. a level-five alarm was declared, the maximum level of alarm provided for in New York City emergency regulations.

American Airlines Flight 11 hit the World Trade Center just as New York's firefighting units were in the middle of changing shifts. Throughout the city's firehouses, men from the day shift were arriving to take over. Firefighters from both shifts stood together drinking coffee while mechanics cleaned equipment. Within thirty minutes of the first alarm, more than one hundred fire trucks had raced to Lower Manhattan.

Many thought a private plane had flown into the tower. Some probably had in the back of their minds the accident of July 28, 1945, when a twelve-ton American B-25 bomber crashed into the Empire State Building. The collision occurred shortly before 10 A.M. in a dense fog, between the 78th and 79th floors, at a height of about eight hundred feet. The plane had been going about 200 mph and tore a hole roughly twenty feet wide and eighteen feet high into the front of the building. The B-25 was carrying about eight hundred gallons of gasoline. The firefighters were able to take the elevators up to the 60th floor, and the fire was extinguished within thirty-five minutes. Putting out the fire in the Empire State Building had since become part of the training for all New York City firefighters in leading positions.

The dimensions of the disaster of September 11, however, were on an altogether different order: the Boeing 767 weighed more than 120 tons and was carrying close to nine thousand gallons of jet fuel, not gasoline.

A fire was now raging that would soon reach a temperature of over 2,000° Fahrenheit. The thin layer of fireproofing on the steel trusses of the stories that were hit had been jarred loose. These trusses were now exposed, without protection, to enormous heat.

The core of the building was considered a fireproof zone, with emergency stairwells and hydrants. Fireproof doors, sprinklers, and the firewalls between the floors were supposed to contain any fire until firefighters arrived. Building materials and fire protection measures had been so conceived that the World Trade Center would hold up for at least three hours—enough time to evacuate everyone from the towers.

Nobody considered the possibility that a plane might discharge several tons of jet fuel into the building.

The fire was further nourished by an enormous quantity of paper from the offices. Worse, apparently none of the fire extinguishing systems worked: sprinkler heads were ripped off by plane wreckage, and water pipes in the core of the building were destroyed.

Training Center for Firefighters, Staten Island

Dan Potter was working on the sixty questions of a test when the cell phone of the person sitting next to him rang. For a split second Dan was annoyed. Then his neighbor shouted, "A plan flew into the World Trade Center." Dan ran to a window. It was true. Thick black smoke was pouring out of the north tower. *I have to call my wife*, he thought and looked for a pay phone. He dialed her office number. Her phone rang. He heard her voice: "This is Jean Potter. I am not at my desk right now. Please leave a message."

"Are you there? Please answer."

Nothing. Potter ran to his car and hit the accelerator—70 to 75 mph in the left lane, wheel in one hand, FDNY badge in the other. He could have skipped the badge. The streets were empty.

World Trade Center, North Tower, 81st Floor, Bank of America Offices

To many American men, Jean Potter might be considered a trophy wife: a cascade of red hair fit for a shampoo ad, the figure of a model, dazzling brown eyes. Jean could have married a lawyer or a doctor. She wasn't interested. She didn't want an egomaniac with high-flying career plans; she wanted someone she could rely on; someone who would protect her against life's uncertainties and imponderables; someone who wouldn't discard her when five years later another trophy walked past the glass door of his office.

Dan had thought over the idea of using the personals for a long time. Firefighters usually meet their wives in a bar, or while saving lives in a burning building, or at another fireman's wedding, or at baptisms or barbecues. A sister, a cousin, the sister-in-law of a fellow firefighter—this was acceptable, but not someone from a want ad. Ads were for the vulnerable, the shy, those who get blown through life like leaves. Problem was: Dan Potter was the shy type.

Jean was the first to respond to the ad. The two made plans to get together at a pub in Greenwich Village, met a few times, and realized before too long that they were in love. Not the way young people are when they dance the night away at Jimmy's Bronx Café or some other "in" spot, but in a quiet, more touching way.

Since then, Jean had worn a silver chain around her neck engraved with 10617, the number on Dan's badge. It had been a Christmas present. They were more than a couple; they were a team that didn't need an alarm clock when they woke up mornings in Jean's apartment in Battery Park City. The first thing Jean used to see every morning as she got out of bed was the Twin Towers.

Jean never particularly cared for the World Trade Center, and on September 11 it was no different. She hated the elevator that in a matter of seconds catapulted her to the 78th floor, where she had to switch to a small elevator for the ride to her office on the 81st. Nor was she thrilled by the view of the Brooklyn Bridge and Manhattan Bridge. It unsettled her to look down instead of up at passing helicopters. On September 11, she was wearing a lavender pants suit and black shoes with flat heels.

Highway 278, Heading Toward Manhattan

Driving across the Verrazano Bridge, which connects Staten Island with Brooklyn, Dan started to count the floors. Did the plane hit below Jean or above? Her phone line was still working. She wasn't in the thick of it. He was driving 75 mph. He counted, messed up, counted again from the beginning. It was torture. Dan, who was supposed to protect his wife for the rest of his life, was taking a class while she burned to death! He counted again and thought about what he always preached about emergencies: "Take the stairs down, never the elevator. In case you're above it, take the stairs up. Wait on the roof until the helicopter arrives."

He counted again. The result: his wife was above the fire. He felt some relief as he raced across the Verrazano Bridge. He believed his wife was waiting for the helicopters on the roof of the North Tower.

FDNY Emergency Message Center

8:56:44 A.M.: "Male caller states he is on the 87th floor: Says four persons with him."

8:56:57 A.M.: "Female caller on 47th floor states: Building shaking, gas odors."

8:57:26 A.M.: "People screaming in background—caller states cannot breathe—smoke coming through door—103rd floor—possibly trapped."

8:59:17 A.M.: "Male caller: the 86th floor collapsing."

World Trade Center, Base of the North Tower

Fireman John Ottrando was one of the first to park his truck in front of the North Tower, at the corner of Vesey and West streets. Ottrando was the driver for Engine Company 24's five-man team. They came from a Greenwich Village firehouse at Houston Street and Sixth Avenue.

Ottrando, forty-four, is an Italian American who lives on Staten Island. When the first alarm sounded, Ottrando was standing in the garage raving about the New York Giants. His day shift was supposed to begin at 9 A.M. His buddy Louie Arena had brought in his broken lawn mower. They were counting on a quiet day, the kind of day on which you repair lawn mowers in the firehouse garage.

Ottrando's Greenwich Village firehouse was responsible for the World Trade Center, and no one was particularly thrilled about the assignment. There was always something: a broken sprinkler, a nicotine addict. The men from Greenwich Village always raced off, lights flashing, one hundred pounds of equipment on their backs. Every time they came home miffed. The World Trade Center was grating. So it was no surprise that Ottrando did not even look up at the glistening facades when he shot onto Sixth Avenue with his truck at 8:56 A.M.

When Ottrando got out, he saw the giant hole and the thick black smoke pouring out. "Holy shit!" he cried. An engine company specializes in entering a burning building to extinguish the fire. The parts of an engine company are: the man who holds the hose that spouts five hundred gallons of water a minute—about equal to the power of a wild horse, which is why a backup man has to stand directly behind the hose man in order to control the water pressure; a so-called control man, who counts and adds up the length of the hoses; the officer, who directs the whole scene; and the driver, who stays down on the street and works the pumps. For Engine 24 the driver was John Ottrando.

Every engine company teams up with a ladder company, a second fire truck. The men from the ladder company are not supposed to extinguish fires; they break open doors and windows, fight the smoke, and take care of the victims.

Ottrando followed the four men of Engine 24 and the eight men of Ladder 5 into the lobby of the North Tower. He climbed over pieces of marble and steel supports; he saw people pouring out of stairwells and smoke blowing out of elevator shafts. Ottrando had heard nothing about a passenger plane, or about nine thousand gallons of jet fuel. He didn't know that the plane had cut the steel cables of some elevators when it plowed through the tower, causing the cabins to plunge to the ground. But he saw what happened to the people who must have been standing in those elevators. They were charred and lying on the marble floor—nothing but burnt flesh, hair, clothes, scorched by flames and hurled out of the crashing cabins. Ottrando ran back to his truck to get covers for the burned.

His buddies rammed their axes through the windows to let out smoke. Then they got going, toward the 90th floor, while Ottrando stayed down with the hoses. Ladder 5 took Stairwell C, Engine 24 disappeared into Stairwell B.

Marcel Claes was Engine 24's backup hose man. Claes is the son of a Belgian immigrant. The father of three, he once worked as a nurse and had been with FDNY for eleven years. His biggest fire ever had been the one six years before at the empty St. George Hotel. Back then, ten stories had fallen and not a single person was killed.

Fear is something firefighters train themselves out of, and that's why Claes climbed the stairs, step by step. It was his job to climb up ninety flights to help others. After a dozen flights Claes struggled for air. He had to stop a minute. In addition to his heavy boots, helmet, and bunker gear, he was carrying an oxygen tank that weighted more than thirty pounds and a hose that weighed nearly as much. An orderly procession of office workers streamed past him in the opposite direction. Some patted him on the shoulder, some cheered him on, some offered him a blessing. Claes saw burnt hands and faces, bleeding heads. He moved on.

North Tower, 60th Floor

By now exhaustion had overtaken Jean Potter's legs, but still they went down step by step. People were trying to maintain order among the lines of the fleeing. Nobody thought it conceivable that the tower might collapse. People were in a hurry but they didn't push. As soon as the first tower shook it had smelled like a gas station. For a fraction of a second, Jean had been confused. Then somebody grabbed her by the hand. It was Ben, from the next desk over.

"We're going down the stairwell," he said. "Now."

Jean was fire warden for the 81st floor. They had regularly practiced for this kind of situation, and actually she was supposed to call the security desk to ask for instructions. She did nothing of the kind. Jean had no idea what had happened; she knew only that there had been a disaster. She looked down the stairs and prayed. Two things consoled her on her way down: one, that her husband was not on duty at his home firehouse on Liberty Street opposite the World Trade Center; and two, that she was wearing shoes with flat heels.

Base of the North Tower, 9:03 A.M.

Downstairs in front of the World Trade Center, firefighter Ottrando bent over the hose he was supposed to connect. While crouching on the ground, he saw a gigantic fireball falling from the sky. United Airlines Flight 175, with Marwan al-Shehhi in the cockpit, had smashed into the South Tower. He had to get the stupid hose from the hydrant to the truck and from there to the North Tower. The World Trade Center was supposed to have connections for hoses on every floor, but on what could you count on a day like this?

More and bigger pieces of steel and glass were crashing onto the street. Some things that fell were still moving. It took Ottrando a while to realize that these were people. He did not want to look but he had to—in order not to be killed. They were falling at a crazy speed; the ties of the men seemed to stand straight up in the air.

FDNY Emergency Message Center

9:03:11 A.M.: "Male caller. Wants to know how to get out of the building."

9:04:14 A.M.: "Male caller states: People trapped on 104th floor, back room, 35 to 40 people."

9:04:24 A.M.: "Male caller states: Trapped on 22nd floor—hole in the floor—smoke coming in, can't breathe—male caller states he will smash window."

9:04:50 A.M.: "Male caller states 103rd floor: Can't get out—floor on fire—people getting sick."

9:05:03 A.M.: "Police helicopter reports: Air Sea No. 14—people falling out of building."

9:06:41 A.M.: "Air Sea No. 14—not possible to land on roof."

9:07:40 A.M.: "Call from 103rd floor, Room 130—about 30 people—lots of smoke—female caller is pregnant."

9:07:51 A.M.: "Second plane hit second building . . . unknown extent of injuries."

9:08:02 A.M.: "Female caller, screaming."

9:08:15 A.M.: "Female caller states WTC in flames—states fire department has to put it out."

9:08:22 A.M.: "Elevator stuck on 104th floor—people in elevator."

9:09:14 A.M.: "Male caller states from the second tower that people are jumping out a huge hole in the side of the building—probably no one catching them."

9:09:43 A.M.: "104th floor—male caller states that his wife is stuck on the 91st floor—all stairwells blocked—says he is concerned about his wife."

9:11:30 A.M.: "Female caller states woman presumably in wheelchair on the 68th floor, possibly by herself."

9:12:18 A.M.: "Male caller states on 106th floor about one hundred people in room—needs directions on how to stay alive."

World Trade Center, North Tower Lobby, 9:12 A.M.

More and more fire companies had arrived at the World Trade Center over the last fifteen minutes. Peter Hayden, commander of the first division, had set up a central command station in the lobby of the North Tower. Hayden and the other FDNY officials believed there was no way to extinguish this fire. He and his colleagues hoped it would burn out in the upper stories, but they were afraid that these might collapse after a couple of hours. The most important thing now was to free the people trapped on cut-off floors, as well as anyone trapped in the ninety-seven passenger elevators or the eight freight elevators.

Every firefighter in the North Tower was getting his or her orders from Hayden, including Ottrando and Claes, the men from Engine 24, as well as Rick Picciotto, FDNY Battalion Commander.

Once he saw the second plane crash into the South Tower, Rick Picciotto could no longer bear staying at headquarters. Picciotto had been with the fire department twenty-eight years. He had a warm smile and a large gap between his teeth. He was also in shape. Every day, he rode thirty miles on his bicycle or sweated an hour on his StairMaster; he had brought the exercise equipment to the firehouse. Picciotto was smart and ambitious, and had gradually risen through FDNY hierarchy. In his wallet he was carrying graduation pictures of his son and daughter.

As soon as he entered the North Tower lobby with his crew, Picciotto headed straight for Hayden.

"Pete, how can I help?" he asked.

"Employees are trapped on the 21ˢᵗ and on the 25ᵗʰ," Hayden replied. "Go up and see what you can do."

Picciotto saw the destruction in the lobby. The burned bodies. Steel struts were crashing onto the plaza. But he switched off his sense of horror as if clicking a remote. He was here to help, not have the jitters. He had to get to the trapped people, then go up to the 90ᵗʰ. Thanks to his exercise on the Stair-Master, he should be up there in about a half hour, he guessed. One hour of StairMaster was the equivalent of 220 floors—the two towers of the World Trade Center combined.

FDNY Emergency Message Center

9:14:52 A.M.: "Female caller states from the 100ᵗʰ floor—unable to speak."

9:15:34 A.M.: "Several people jump from windows of the WTC."

9:17:20 A.M.: "Male caller states he can't get out."

9:17:39 A.M.: "Male caller states on 105ᵗʰ floor . . . stairs collapse."

9:21:31 A.M.: "Female caller states they are in Stairwell C on 82ⁿᵈ floor. Doors are locked. Caller states they need someone to open doors."

9:23:05 A.M.: "Male caller states he is on the 84ᵗʰ floor, Tower Number 2, can't breathe—call cut off."

9:24:54 A.M.: "Male caller states stairwell on 105ᵗʰ floor collapsing."

World Trade Center, North Tower Lobby, 9:24 A.M.

Hayden heard over his radio that a third plane was approaching the WTC. He ordered his people to evacuate, also by radio. The equipment malfunctioned. Nobody would hear him. He stayed in the lobby.

FDNY Emergency Message Center

9:25:28 A.M.: "Male caller states that he is locked in on the 105th floor. States doors are hot."

Shortly before 9:30 A.M. the last call came from Windows on the World. Within the next minutes 206 people died. Pastry chef Norberto Hernandez was photographed jumping from the 106th floor. Hernandez was the father of three daughters and grandfather of two.

9:36:33 A.M.: "Female caller states they are trapped in elevator . . . explains they are dying."

9:39:40 A.M.: "Female caller states floor is very hot—no doors—states she will die—still on phone—would like to call mother."

9:40:45 A.M.: "Male caller states people passing out."

9:42:04 A.M.: "People still jumping from tower."

World Trade Center, North Tower, 24th Floor, 9:25 A.M.

From her office on the 81st floor, Jean Potter had gotten to a floor in the twenties. She prayed. And gave thanks again to her flat-heeled shoes. She ran into firemen going the other way. She recognized some of them—they were buddies of her husband. Jean Potter did not know whether she should be happy or sad. On the 6th floor, daylight streamed into the stairwell. She'd made it. Then, suddenly, everything came to a halt. People were pressing against her. She felt squeezed in. Jean Potter did the forbidden: She shouted out hysterically, "Let's go." Nothing moved.

Manhattan, West Street

To Dan Potter it felt like evening. The streets of Lower Manhattan lay in deep shadow as he parked his silver pickup on West Street; black clouds of smoke darkened the sun. He ran across the street to the firehouse where his bunker gear was hanging. He had to get his wife off the roof, and you couldn't do that in penny loafers. There was an ambulance, and a few EMS workers were standing around. A Japanese man lay on the ground with a broken leg. Potter put on his suit and saw a familiar face next to him. It belonged to Peter Bielfield, an old friend of his from the Bronx.

"Hey, Pete, how's it going?"

Pete pulled up his pants and answered, "We're going into the burning towers, Dan. What else?"

Dan put on his helmet. He was about the leave with Pete when he realized that he needed to get his ax and crowbar.

"I'll just go now," said Pete.

Dan would never see him again.

World Trade Center, North Tower, 10th Floor

"Stay calm," said a voice from the loudspeaker. "Stay inside. It is now safer inside than outside."

Mark Oettinger went to the window. He saw three bodies fall on the grass directly in front of him.

"Let's go," he said to his five coworkers. "We'll take the passage through the basement to the South Tower." He knew his way around the World Trade Center. He was proud of that.

Mark Oettinger is a carpenter. He builds furniture and sets up panels and desks. He had already worked in the famous Dakota apartment building, in huge buildings on Times Square, and often in the World Trade Center. He loves wood and old stone. On September 11 he and his five coworkers were supposed to remodel floors and to expand work areas at the Bank of America.

Now, in the hour of disaster, Oettinger was afraid, of course, but he also felt something else, something exciting. He was needed. He was young, only thirty-five, and in good shape. Whatever was happening out there was dangerous, but he knew what he was doing. He knew about dangers, about bombs and explosions. Before he'd become a carpenter he'd been in the army. To be honest, he'd never seen combat, only been on maneuvers. This here was for real.

They were all depending on him, he thought. Not just his coworkers, but the bank employees too. First he needed to get a hold on the situation. The women first—he had to help the women. He hurried the people down ten stories. That part wasn't so difficult: His charges were pretty calm. Except when they were in the lobby and in front of them lay a figure, broken glass, blood everywhere. She was dead.

Ruins everywhere. More dead bodies. The explosion had hurled them from high above. They didn't look like the dead bodies you saw on TV. On TV when someone plunges from a roof he just lies there with a little blood around him. These looked exploded, thought Oettinger, exploded on impact.

There was a dull odor, a little like ammonia, and it left an unsettling taste that stayed in your mouth. A hospital smell that can't be erased no matter how much you try to get rid of it. The smell of death.

Oettinger believed he knew some of the dead. He had worked for lots on companies in the building. It wasn't unlikely one of them was someone he spoke with yesterday or the day before. He knew lots of people, and lots of people knew him. Often somebody would slap him on the shoulder. "Hey, remember me? You redid my office." He thought of Chris, Pat, Brian, of people from his shop who were on a job somewhere higher up in the tower. *Don't think now. Keep going.*

It was hard to get the women past the bloodbath. They wouldn't move.

"Don't look down and don't look to the side," he said. "Look over there at the exit sign. It's beautiful outside. Get out."

He sent them out onto Cortlandt Street, then went back in, climbed up past the 10th floor this time, looking for more women to get out.

They needed water. On TV you always see people with wet towels over their faces when there's a fire. He needed little towels, but there were only paper towels. He tore them off, wet them, and handed them to the women, who were having trouble breathing.

"Take deep breaths—but not constantly or the towel will go dry." He must have been on the 17th floor—no, 18th. He found more scared people.

"Come on. I'll get you out."

He came out of the stairwell with four women.

"We'll take it from here," he heard a fireman tell him. "We'll take over now."

He couldn't leave. As if mesmerized, he drifted about in the lobby looking for people to save, guiding them to the exits, constantly perking up his ears for someone crying somewhere—that sound told him where he had to go.

Finally he left the North Tower. For a minute he sat down in a small park. No birds. No people. He sat on some steps and cried.

North Tower, 44th Floor, Inside the Stairwell

"Don't worry, the fire's far above you," Jan Khan heard the firemen say. He squeezed against the wall to let them pass. They took up a lot of room with all their heavy equipment. They were sweating, panting.

"I still see their faces as they climbed past," says Khan.

Khan was sweating too. The stairwell was narrow and hot and in his legs he already felt the thirty-seven flights they'd come down. With him were Larissa and Chris, colleagues from the New York Metropolitan Transportation Council, an agency whose main responsibility was traffic routing.

Jan Khan has black hair, a black beard, a full face. He emigrated in 1992 from what was once British Guyana to the United States. He is a calm, thoughtful man not prone to big talk. He was born a Muslim but doesn't have much of a connection to religion.

His office in the World Trade Center was on the 82nd floor. His first thought on hearing the detonation at 8:45 A.M. was "a rocket." The second thought: "Get out."

His took his briefcase because his cell phone was in it. He ran to the office entrance, about fifty feet away. A dozen or so people were already there, but they didn't leave. The hallway was nothing but dark, thick black smoke. Khan heard screams for a second time. Here he was standing around with his fellow employees. How were they supposed to find the staircase in all this smoke?

His colleague Tony said he would go look. He groped his way out and was immediately swallowed up by smoke. The others looked at each other in silence. *I want to go home,* thought Khan. *I have to go home, my family's at home, that's where I belong.* On the outside he was calm. Then came Tony's voice.

"I've found the stairwell. Come on, follow my voice. Over here, over here, over here, over here."

Khan felt his way ahead, reached the staircase after a few steps, and started the descent.

Ever since the firefighters had started up the stairwell there'd been continual tie-ups. Sometimes Khan waited on a step for two, three minutes. He talked reassuringly to Larissa. Her husband worked in the South Tower and she knew that a plane had also exploded into it. She was crying. Khan said her husband was probably fine. *I want to go home, home, home,* he thought.

He took the cell phone from his briefcase and tried to call his wife but didn't get through. He saw cracks in the stairwell walls.

After the 10th floor things proceeded more smoothly. The air improved. Then the exit: Khan left the stairwell.

I will get home, he thought. *I'll get there soon.*

FDNY Emergency Message Center

9:47:15 A.M.: "Female caller states 2 World Trade Center—Floor 105-states floor underneath her—collapse."

9:47:23 A.M.: "Man waving jacket—man just jumped."

9:49:21 A.M.: "Twenty people on top waving—they are alive—please send help."

9:54:36 A.M.: "Male caller hears people crying."

9:55:28 A.M.: "2 World Trade Center—106th and 105th floors collapsing."

World Trade Center, North Tower, Ground Floor, 10:00 A.M.

Jan Khan had arrived on the concourse, the underground level that connected the two towers. This was also home to the Twin Towers' shopping center. Sprinklers were spraying water from the ceilings. Immediately Khan was soaking wet. He waded through and walked through a revolving door and past Banana Republic. Chris and Larissa were still with him.

All of a sudden as he was passing a coffee cart he heard a loud crash. "The sound of a gigantic explosion, as if something was collapsing behind us." Khan spun round to see the revolving door he had just used being folded top to bottom like an accordion. Same with the elevator doors. Entrance doors and shop windows burst from their frames and came flying toward them. Next a strong wind blasted through the shopping passage "like a hurricane."

"We'll die now," Khan said to Chris and Larissa, and reached out for their hands. The wind pushed Khan and Larissa to their knees, into the water and onto the broken glass. Chris threw his arms around a column and held on.

The gust of wind picked up Khan and Larissa and swept them across the ground. They came to rest in front of a pile of rubble. *I won't die, I can't die, I've got to go home, home, home.*

Suddenly all was quiet. All sounds, all wind, had ceased. Khan had lost his glasses. He was very worried he couldn't see anything anymore, everything around him was dark and black. Khan thought that maybe he'd been blinded. He was hardly able to breathe. He felt as if the air were a solid mass. He did not know that the South Tower had just collapsed.

"Larissa?"

"I'm okay," said Larissa.

"Chris?"

"I'm okay." Chris was still holding on to the column.

"I can't see anything anymore," Khan called out.

"Me neither," Chris replied.

"Me neither," said Larissa.

Khan knew now that he was not blind. It was the dust that had made everything so black.

"Over here, over here, over here, over here," Chris called. Larissa and Khan tapped their way toward him. Other voices rose out of the darkness. Soon, ten to twelve people had gathered. Khan was afraid "for the first time in my life." *I'll die after all,* he thought. And next: *No, I'll go home, I have to go home, that's where my family is.*

Liberty Street Firehouse

Dan Potter was still in the firehouse, a few minutes from the World Trade Center, when he heard a noise as though a freight train were coming straight at him. He saw a man standing at the front of the station house, his arms open wide, exclaiming, "Holy shit, it's coming down."

Glass, dust, and steel flew into the firehouse as if whipped by a dark tornado. Dan believed he would suffocate. "It felt as if someone was stuffing your body with black cotton balls."

World Trade Center, Base of the North Tower

Jean Potter had the descent behind her and had been running through the lobby of the North Tower, wet through and through from the sprinklers, when something rumbled behind her. She turned around and saw the South Tower, 110 floors, nearly one third of a mile of glass and steel, falling toward her. People were screaming. The black cloud descended, Jean surrendered. She had walked for an hour, and this was the end. There was no point trying to run. The black colossus would bury her.

A policeman grabbed her and dragged her down into a subway entrance. The colossus was coming after them. They went further down, as if into their own grave. *Thank God Dan's attending class on Staten Island,* she thought. *I have to call him. He will think that I am dead.*

North Tower, 35th Floor

Rick Picciotto stopped for a moment in the stairwell of the North Tower when he heard a sound such as he had never before heard, despite twenty-eight years as a firefighter. "As if a tractor trailer was rolling through your living room," is how Marcel Claes, the backup man for Engine 24, would later describe it. Picciotto thought than an elevator's cables might have been severed and shot down the shaft. It took fifteen seconds. Then there was nothing, nothing but silence. Just like after an earthquake. "Deafening silence," Picciotto says.

His firefighters looked at him. "What was that?" Picciotto radioed. Nothing but static on his unit's channel.

A few seconds later Picciotto learned from another channel that the South Tower had collapsed. Piciotto held his two-way radio and bellowed into it over and over, "What tower? What tower? What tower?"

No answer. He started to scream. "The TV antenna on the North Tower, a water tower, what tower?"

The response was full of static but clear: "The entire South Tower."

Picciotto could not grasp it. Nobody could grasp it, not on the 35th floor and not outside either, where John Ottrando, the driver for Engine 24, was running for his life, just like his colleagues from FDNY, the NYPD, and the Port Authority Police. Ottrando sprang after a jeep and was completely covered by a cloud of steel, glass, dust, and concrete. But he survived. Every firefighter heading up the stairs of the South Tower was dead.

Nobody in FDNY had expected that either of the monumental towers might completely collapse. Not so soon—less than one hour after the attack.

The South Tower was hit second but collapsed first. The point of collision was lower and thus a bigger load was pressing down on supporting columns that had also been damaged on the floors that were hit. Experts also think it possible that the core of the South Tower suffered more serious damage than that of the North Tower.

Steel columns bear their burden only when supported from the side. The columns in the tower cores, as well as those on the outside, received support exclusively from the floor trusses. These consisted of steel rods slightly over an inch in diameter holding a steel plate covered with four to five inches of reinforced concrete. The narrowly spaced steel columns on the four aluminum faces of each tower lost their side support once the floor connections broke and the first stories crashed down, taking one or two others down with them. The steel columns buckled under the load of the higher floors.

According to another theory, the light steel rods of the floor trusses heated up first. During the twenty to thirty minutes after impact, the floors between the inner and outer support columns began to sag. Without the support of these cross connections and softened by the heat, the outer columns buckled or broke like matches under the weight of the floors above the area of impact—an estimated 45,000 tons in the North Tower and about 110,000 tons in the South Tower. As soon as the fire-stressed outer columns lost their support from the cross trusses, the tower was doomed: The complete top of the building crashed down upon the flooring structure and the vertical impact continued, like dominoes, downward.

The uppermost floors crashed to the ground with an estimated speed of about 125 mph, close to the speed of free fall. In no more than fifteen seconds the whole building was down.

After the South Tower's collapse the firefighters' task changed radically. FDNY works under extremely risky conditions, but there has to be at least a slim chance for rescue. None now existed. FDNY is not a club for forlorn suicidal types, nor was Picciotto any such man. Trying to get from the 35th to the 92nd floor at this point would have been committing suicide.

New York firefighters are in a league of their own, a brotherhood with its own laws, its own code of honor, and its own history. Irish and Italian immigrants who couldn't get a job anywhere else in the New World devoted their lives to putting out fires. It was their chance to become part of the American dream, to find a home in the land of the "free and brave," their chance to move from worker to hero.

New York City has more tall buildings than any other city of the world, and the stairwells are like endless tubes. Whoever dares enter these burning traps day in and day out is revered. Even in a fast and tough city like New York. If for that reason alone, New York's firemen have earned the title "New York's Bravest."

Grandmothers wave when they pass. Wall Street bankers salute with red cheeks. Preschoolers learn their songs. Pretty girls push for dates. Not bad for a group whose average entry-level salary is $29,973 a year.

Liberty Street Firehouse

Not long after 10 A.M. the smoke in front of Dan Potter's firehouse lifted. From his distant corner he could see that the rest of the building had collapsed. No firefighters were to be seen. Potter decided to make his way to command headquarters on West Street, at the north end of the World Trade Center. On his way: debris, burning cars, and fire trucks. No people. It seemed to him as if he were the only survivor on the streets of New York. Since debris and bodies were still pouring down, Potter decided to make his way through buildings that were still intact.

He walked through the emptied halls of a branch of Deutsche Bank. Drawings by four-year-olds were hanging on the walls of a kindergarten. He remained the only survivor in New York.

He looked out a window and up. He saw no World Trade Center anymore, only blue sky. *Holy shit, the South Tower is gone.* Then he looked north. Okay, it was still standing. Up there on the roof, Jean was waiting. *Dan, you've got to get her down from there, the helicopter is not going to come.*

Church Street

Better to die up there than down here. Jean Potter turned around and left the subway station the policeman had pulled her into when the South Tower collapsed. Aboveground, the cloud had lightened some. Silence. As she walked along the street, whitewashed figures called out to her to cover her mouth with a handkerchief. The cloud was toxic. Wet and covered in dust, Jean Potter could only make out shapes. She walked like a robot, north, looking for some piece of peace amid this inferno. Other people might look for a church under these circumstances, but Jean Potter was searching for a firehouse. Maybe one of Dan's buddies could explain why the world had come to an end on a sunny Tuesday morning in September.

World Trade Center, North Tower, Lobby

The group around Jan Khan was debating how to get out from under all this rubble. They stood there talking. "We were too afraid to move," says Khan. Most of all they were afraid of falling into subway tunnels through holes in the ground.

They could not stay where they were, however. They couldn't see anything, but they could hear the building groaning and crunching.

"Let's form a human chain," someone said. They agreed this was a good idea. Chris went first, followed by Larissa, then Khan, then another woman. They clung to each other, Chris testing the ground with his feet. The building grumbled. They knew a subway station had to be close by. They groped their way over to it but soon realized nothing was left of it. They proceeded at a snail's pace, a caravan of fear. They had been on the move for about twenty minutes when they heard a voice from a great distance: "Somebody there?"

"Yes!" Khan and the others called back. "Who's there?"

"I'm a firefighter. Can you see the flashlight?"

"No. Please keep calling. We'll follow your voice."

"Over here, over here, over here, over here, over here, over here."

Soon Khan recognized the beam of a flashlight, then the firefighter himself. The man led the group to other firefighters. They suggested sending the group out through the station. "No fucking way!" said the first firefighter. He led them on, until suddenly they saw a ray of light. It grew bigger and stronger until they found themselves on Vesey Street, north of the World Trade Center.

"Don't look up! Don't look back!" policemen were screaming. "Run for it, run for it, run for it!"

Khan ran as fast as he could, past destroyed cars, past debris, across Vesey Street, onto Church Street, north. After two blocks he stopped and turned around. He had reached safety. He started to cry.

North Tower, 35th Floor

Nearly all civilians below the area of impact on the 96th floor had left the tower. Hundreds of firefighters, however, were still in the stairwells. *High time to get the guys out*, thought Rick Picciotto. Without waiting for word from higher up, he took his bullhorn and shouted, "Time to evacuate, drop everything, get out!"

The backup man from Engine 24, Marcel Claes, threw down his hose and started to run down the stairs. He kept his oxygen tank—you never knew.

Dozens followed him. Last was Picciotto, who checked every floor. Over and over again he kept yelling the same two words into the bullhorn: "Get out!"

The evacuation ran smoothly until the 16th floor, where there was a traffic jam. Rubble from the South Tower had destroyed parts of Stairwells A and C in the North Tower. Picciotto ordered his men to use only Stairwell B.

Down they went, floor by floor, until Picciotto opened a door on the 12th floor and saw some fifty to seventy people sitting in an office. He stood there. He couldn't believe his eyes. What were they doing here?

"Come on guys, let's go!"

Only then did he see the crutches and wheelchairs. Picciotto ordered his men to help the handicapped.

Marcel Claes reached the lobby and ran through a broken window to freedom. Seconds later, Picciotto once more heard the piercing rumble, the horrifying clamor. Picciotto was on the 5th floor and if the North Tower collapsed as quickly as the South Tower had, he would have exactly twelve more second to live.

Dear Lord, Piciotto thought, *do me one favor and let me die quick.* Picciotto thought of his wife, of his children in their graduation hats. Then he said a prayer.

The North Tower collapsed in an almost absurdly controlled way, as if following a master plan for its demolition. The first thing Picciotto noticed about the stories collapsing above him was the wind—not a wind so much as a hurricane, hurling him down the steps and turning day to night.

Picciotto saw nothing. He couldn't tell whether he was dead or alive, dreaming or thinking, trapped somewhere in Lower Manhattan or on his way to the other world. Minutes passed until Picciotto heard a cough, then he heard another one. Whichever pile of dirt he was in, Picciotto did what he had learned to do when civilization had still existed. He introduced himself.

Base of the North Tower, 10:40 A.M.

Shortly before the second freight train bore down upon Dan Potter he met a friend he had last seen twenty years ago—Fire Marshall Mel Hazel. Potter prepared himself to die. "You can be lucky once, but not twice." He was consoled by the thought that he did not have to be alone at the end of his life. His friend Mel Hazel crouched next to him, pressed against the wall, hands folded over his head. *If we have to go, at least we go together,* Potter said to himself.

For several minutes the two men were lying buried in dust and debris, unharmed. Potter tried to switch on his flashlight, but it was useless: he was too weak, he was trembling. The two crawled like blind beetles through the debris, until Potter said, "Mel, I think we're on the street."

"Nonsense," answered Mel.

"But look," Potter said and dug into the debris until he hit something that looked like pavement. He got up.

"My wife," he said, "was on the 81st floor. She went to the roof. I have to find her."

Church Street

Jean Potter did not turn around when the second tower collapsed, carrying with it her desk and handbag from the 81st floor. She continued marching on in her lavender pants suit. It must have looked as if her own ghost were walking through Lower Manhattan, a dead person on vacation. People handed her water, a cell phone. She moved on and stopped only about a mile north of the disaster site in front of Firehouse Engine 9, Ladder 6, on Canal Street. The men were down at the towers. Replacements from Long Island were filling in as best they could. Jean Potter walked through the raised door into the garage.

"Hello," she said. "I'm Jean Potter, wife of a firefighter. Have you got work for me?"

The guys pointed to a phone that was ringing without interruption. "Great if you could take care of it."

For over an hour, Jean Potter answered phone calls, doing her best to console those on the other end of the line. Mothers, wives, sons, daughters looking for the men. Three hundred and forty-three firefighters lost their lives.

Peter Langone. Forty-one, he had promised his daughters a trip to Disney World.

Joseph Leavy. Forty-five, an aficionado of skyscrapers, one of the first firefighters to arrive at the World Trade Center.

Ronnie Gies. Forty-three, a firefighter for twenty-five years. His children later saw him for the last time on an amateur videotape that showed him entering the towers.

James Amato. Forty-three, a captain who during the last big blaze had called his men back from a burning building seconds before the explosion. "Timing is everything," was all he would say later.

Vincent Giammona. He had planned to celebrate his fortieth birthday the night of September 11.

Terrence McShane. Thirty-seven, one of the few whose remains could be found.

Nearly all the men in leading positions in the New York City Fire Department were dead: Bill Feehan, first deputy commissioner; Peter Ganci, department chief; Terry Hatton, forty-one, chief of Rescue Squad 1.

Jean Potter had no inkling that her husband might well have been number 344.

World Trade Center, Within the Rubble of the North Tower

In the middle of the devil's chaos something like a heavenly counterattack took place. What else can you call it when 110 stories collapse within seconds into a mountain of steel and concrete—yet somehow create a cave of debris within which eleven people miraculously survive?

After the thunder of the destruction had died away, voices could be heard at about the level where the 4th floor of Stairwell B had once been. They belonged to men announcing themselves back into life. They belonged to firefighters Mike Meldrum, Matt Komorowski, Bill Butler, Tom Falco, Sal D'Agostino, and Captain Jay Jonas, all members of Ladder 6. They were from the Canal Street firehouse where Jean Potter was at that moment trying to calm their next of kin. Another voice belonged to David Lim, member of the New York Port Authority Police. The voices of Bacon and Cross, two firefighters, joined in the chorus. And then there were the slightly higher tones of a woman's voice. It belonged to Josephine Harris, an office worker with the Port Authority.

Josephine Harris had been sitting at her desk on the 73rd floor when the plane hit. She immediately started down. The problem was that the fifty-nine-year-old grandmother was not very steady on her feet. She had had to rest after nearly every step because of the pain in her legs.

She was on the 14th floor and at the end of her rope when she finally came upon help—Captain Jay Jonas and his men from Ladder 6. They had just dashed down the stairs from the 27th floor; the South Tower had collapsed and Jonas had given orders to evacuate.

"That's it, boys, let's get out of here. If one goes, the next won't be far behind."

They were running down the stairs when suddenly there in front of them stood Josephine Harris. In Jonas's head, the seconds were ticking away as loud as church bells. *Out of here, quick—but not without this lady.* Even if she weighs as much as a washing machine. David Lim, the policeman who had joined Jonas's unit along the way, and firefighter Bill Butler held Josephine Harris between them and carried her down until Jonas decided to make their work easier by looking inside offices and hallways for a chair to carry the "old lady."

That's when the North Tower crashed to the ground, as if someone had pushed the fast-forward button of a videotape.

Lim threw himself over Josephine to protect her but Butler was faster and so they both landed on top of her. The force of the tremor threw them down the stairwell like bales of hay. Captain Jonas, 240 pounds and a former football player, was able to save himself when the tower began to shake by taking a leap into the more stable stairwell.

It took some time before the survivors of the crash were able to see again. Dust and soot ate into their eyes like pepper spray. In the semidark the buried could hear the coughs and signs of their companions. Nobody had been seriously hurt—a dislocated shoulder, a broken rib, a concussion maybe, nothing more.

When Jonas sat up on the 4th floor and brushed the garbage from his clothes, a voice was whispering from his radio. The voice belonged to Mike Warchola.

"Mayday," said Warchola. "We're trapped on the 12th floor of the North Tower. We're seriously injured. Help."

Warchola was a close friend of Jonas. Today was his last day of work before retiring. He belonged to Ladder 5 in Greenwich Village. Jonas got up and climbed over rubble and broken steps to go find Warchola. The 5th floor was a dead end. Steel and rubble had formed an impenetrable wall. Over the next five minutes Warchola twice radioed Mayday. Then nothing. He and four of his men were found two days later, lying peacefully, dead.

About three steps below the 5th floor was a hole in the stairwell about the size of a small window. Jonas looked through it. Here, too, nothing but steel and smoke. It appeared mere chance that these lowest floors in Stairwell B had remained intact. But what if they were totally enclosed in tons of steel? How long would it take the rescue team to dig their way through to them? Two days? Two weeks? Would anybody still be breathing?

Jonas is forty-four years old. After college, instead of a career with a six-figure salary, he opted for the New York Fire Department and had been putting out fires with passion for more than twenty-two years.

Picking his way through the remains of the stairwell he found a black firefighter's boot. And a bullhorn. It was the bullhorn of Rick Picciotto who, up in the 35th floor, had given orders to his firefighters to evacuate. The hurricane had reached him on the 5th floor and hurled him down two flights, where

he was now. It was just after 10:30 when he heard the coughing and introduced himself.

Jonas and Picciotto assumed joint command of the group of survivors.
Were they the luckiest guys in the world or members of a club of the damned?
they wondered. Sure, they were alive, but for how much longer? The radio
transmitters registered the last words of fellow firefighters: "Tell my wife that I
love her." And the whispering voice of their battalion commander, Richard
Prunty: "I'm not going to be able to make it out of here."

World Trade Center, Inside the Ruins of the North Tower

The people around Rick Picciotto and Captain Jonas steeled themselves for a long stay in their stairwell prison. No one grumbled when Jonas
told them to turn off flashlights and radios in order to save power.

The men started to explore the stairwell. In addition to the filth that
clogged their eyes and lungs was the smell of gasoline. A match lit in the dark
or even a spark could mean the end.

During their search for an exit the men discovered a door on the 2nd
floor. They opened it. Nothing but rubble and debris.

On the 3rd floor, another door. Again they opened it. Again nothing
but rubble and debris.

On the 4th floor they discovered two sprinklers. At least now they had
water. A little farther they found a toilet. And an elevator shaft that went down.
It was black, no end. Picciotto decided it was too much of a risk. If no help arrived in a few days, they might try again.

The men were exhausted. David Lim, the policeman, went searching
for his bomb-sniffing dog.

"Stop it," said Captain Jonas. "Your dog doesn't matter now. People are
dying all around us."

At about noon, Jonas was again talking into his radio.

"Mayday. Mayday. This is Captain Jonas of Ladder Six. We are trapped
in Stairwell B in the North Tower, floors two, three, four and five. Come get us."

In response, Jonas heard a hoarse voice come out of the transmitter:
"North Tower? The North Tower doesn't exist anymore!" Jonas's spirits sank.
Until that moment they had hoped that only part of the building had collapsed. How many square feet of steel were on top of them? There was no one
to answer the question. And no longer anyone in charge of the rescue mission
either. Many of the highest ranks were dead, their command centers demol-
ished. Hayden was attempting to direct the chaos from West Street in the midst
of the ruins; his office was the roof of a fire truck.

The only things they could do were wait, radio, and wait some more. Adrenaline dissipated, the pain of injuries grew. It was 1 P.M., 2 P.M.

Then Captain Jonas thought he was seeing things: It was starting to get light. It seemed to him as if the sun were shining directly into the stairwell. He followed the beams, step by step, and ended up back on the 5th floor. He looked through the window-sized hole. He saw steel and smoke, mountains of devastation, and a bit of blue sky. The remnants of Stairwell B were not buried in the rubble but rising out of it.

Picciotto joined him, Lim on his heels.

"Oh, my God," said Lim, softly. "How lucky can you get? How often you think this kind of thing happens?"

"Once in a billion."

A trench about ten feet deep and one hundred feet wide lay between them and freedom. It looked like a glacier from hell: sharp steel, endlessly deep crevices, blazing fires, no end in sight.

Minutes later, on top of the smoking pile of rubble, they could make out firefighters from Ladder 43.

Rick Picciotto was the first to be brought by rope across the treacherous abyss; then came the men from Ladder 6—Mike Meldrum, Matt Komorowski, Bill Butler, Tom Falco, Sal D'Agostino—then firefighters Bacon and Cross; policeman David Lim; and finally Josephine Harris. Only then did Captain Jay Jonas take his turn. It was 3 P.M. when his men lowered him down onto West Street. There he saw one of the most beautiful sights of his life: All his men had escaped death, along with Josephine Harris.

For twenty-two years, when people asked what kind of work he did, Jonas always replied, "We go in, rescue people, put out the fire, and go home." This time the fire was stronger. But Jonas and his men did rescue a woman. And went home.

Jonas went over to Hayden's "office." They had last seen each other that morning at 9:03 when the second plane hit the South Tower and Hayden ordered him and his men into the World Trade Center. Hayden nearly wept.

"Jay, good to see you," he called out.

Jonas as well could barely hold back the tears. "Reporting in again, Chief. It's sure nice to be among the living."

Next the ambulance staff were fussing over Jonas's men. Only Jonas himself escaped treatment. He walked back to the firehouse on Canal Street.

Slowly it dawned on him that he owed his life to a tired lady. Everybody on the floors above and below was dead. "We all thought that Josephine was walking much too slow," Jonas would later say. "But really she was the one with the perfect timing. God gave us the courage to help her, and that's how we ourselves were saved."

Later the firefighters gave Josephine Harris, mother and grandmother and office worker from the 73rd floor, a Ladder 6 firefighter's jacket decorated with a green dragon—symbol of their station home in Chinatown. Below it was embroidered the following inscription: "Josephine—Our Guardian Angel."

Pennsylvania, Home of Jean Potter's Mother, 9:00 P.M.

Dan and Jean Potter looked for refuge at the home of Jean Potter's mother. Dust from the collapsed towers had made their own apartment uninhabitable, funereal. Jean's mother lived in Pennsylvania.

At around noon, after the collapse of the North Tower, Dan Potter had called his father, sobbing.

"Dad, Jean is dead."

"Nonsense," his father said. "She's on telephone assignment at the Canal Street firehouse."

Potter ran to his car and jumped in. He found her. Dust stuck to the two of them like cement, but when they lay sobbing in each other's arms the fear started to fall away. They wanted to get out of the city. When they stopped at a gas station on their way to Pennsylvania, people stared at them in silence. As if Jean and Dan Potter had not just survived but been resurrected.

Rescue in the Bronx

From *Report from Engine Co. 82*

BY DENNIS SMITH

Dennis Smith's 1972 memoir *Report from Engine Co. 82* is by now considered an American firefighting classic, providing as it does a searing vision of urban America through the eyes of the author, then a New York City firefighter stationed in the South Bronx.

★　★　★　★　★

Benny and I sit on our heels in the hallway. Artie Merritt comes crawling out of the apartment above the fire. He has a halligan tool in one hand and an ax in the other. It was his job to search the apartment thoroughly.

"It's clean," he says. "The walls are a little warm, but I don't think the fire has extended." Kevin and Cosmo have arrived, breathing easily in their masks. There is nothing for them to do but to join us in sitting on their heels.

The Chief from the Seventeenth Battalion passes by us. He disappears in the apartment for a short while. Upon reappearing, he says, "Take up, Eighty-two." The fire is out. Engine 50 saved us a lot of effort.

We drag the hose back down the stairs, and begin to fold it onto Engine 50's pumper. It is easy work, and we are all silently satisfied that the line wasn't charged, and there is no water to drain. I am not paying much attention to what I am doing, for I keep thinking of Louie Minelli. His eyes, heavy and watered, staring at me through the lifting poison. Tired and blank. "I got the first two rooms." His body robbed of energy, he barely mustered the strength to turn his head. "Mike Roberti will get the rest." His words, though barely audible, were filled with pride. Engine 50 can do the job. Engine 50 can put out any fire. I want to yell as I pass the limp, empty hose forward, "But Louis, the goddam building is vacant. We should let it burn." We won't let it burn through. I know that, and Louie knows. We have a tradition in this department of going where the fire is. And we know that two or three fires will be set in this building every week, until the city tears it down.

There are five Fire Department vehicles parked on 166th Street. The engines are running, and the radio volumes are at their highest. The rigs sing like a chorus as the dispatcher asks: *"Engine Eighty-two. Ladder Thirty-one. Are you available?"*

Jim Stacks is sitting in the cab of the pumper. He yells over to Lieutenant Collins, "We're available. Huh, Lou?"

Benny lays the nozzle over the hose, and Lieutenant Collins nods to Jim. We can hear Jim's voice blare over the radio as we run to our pumper: *"Engine Eighty-two is available."*

The dispatcher replies: *"All right Eighty-two. Ladder Thirty-one?"*

The Chief of the Seventeenth Battalion answers: *"Ladder Thirty-one is in the process of taking up. They will be slightly delayed."*

"Ten-four Battalion Seventeen. Engine Eighty-two, respond to phone arm Box 2509. Location, 1335. Intervale Avenue. Did you receive, Engine Eighty-two?"

Jim comes over the air: *"Engine Eighty-two, ten-four."*

The fire engine races and wails away from Louie Minelli and the smoldering abandoned building. 1335 Intervale Avenue is right up the street from the firehouse. We could have been there in thirty seconds. Now, it will take us three or four minutes.

We can see the smoke five blocks away. Our boots are up, and we are ready. Finally, we pass the firehouse and the sizzling hamburgers. The doors are open, and the house is empty. I look over the side of the pumper, and I see the men of Engine 85 stretching into a five-story tenement house. They are not assigned at this location, and they must have been special-called since we were operating elsewhere.

The fire is roaring out of two windows on the ground floor. Benny and I, and Kevin and Cosmo are off the pumper and running before Jim Stack brings the rig to a stop. This would be an ordinary fire, except that the fire escapes are a circus of people yelling desperately at every level. There is no ladder company at the scene, and we all know without speaking that we have to think about life. Engine 85 will think about fire.

"Aqui, aqui," the people cry fearfully. The drop ladder on the fire escape has been let down, but it is not secured well, and it shakes. I make a quick wish, as I climb the thin, narrow bars, that a ladder company will get in soon. Benny is before me; the others behind. There is a man yelling in wild frenzy on the third floor, and we are trying to reach him. But the fire escapes are crowded with fleeing people. Please hurry. Hold the handrails. Watch your step. Let us by. Let us by.

The man on the third floor is holding an infant out of the window. His arms are outstretched, and it seems he is offering the baby, as even Abraham offered his son. Benny nests the child in his arms. It is in its first month of life, and cries the high violent cry peculiar to its size. The man turns and bends down to the floor. He picks up another infant, and hands it to Benny. It is the sixteen-inch twin of the first. Benny cradles it in his other arm, and begins to descend the fire escape. There is a light mist of smoke in the apartment, and a little girl coughs. She is about three years old, and she wraps her small arms around my neck as her father hands her to me. I start down the fire escape, followed by the barefooted, shirtless man.

Cosmo and Kevin have carried children down from the second floor. In the street again, the children are delivered into the warm arms of neighbors. The fire whips around the center hall of the ground floor, and the men of Engine 85 have moved out to the vestibule. George Hiegman must be having trouble with the hydrant. Did someone hacksaw off the controlling stem for a quarter's worth of brass, or shove beer cans or soda bottles down the casing?

I look expectantly for Ladder 31, but they haven't arrived yet. Benny has returned to the fire escape, and I follow quickly. The people on the street shout about children being left behind on the fourth floor. Benny goes in one window, and I go in another. The smoke is heavy now throughout the building. I am in a living room. A cheap print framed in plastic hangs on the wall. It looks like a western sunset. I look under the vinyl-covered furniture. There are two bedrooms, and I look under the beds, and in the closets. My eyes are wet, and my nose is running, but the kitchen and the bathroom are clear—there are no unconscious bodies, or frightened whimpering children.

I return to the fire escape. I am not sure now if I should continue to search the building, or go down to the street and stretch a second line to the floor above the fire. The decision is made for me as I see Ladder 31 careening up Intervale Avenue. Ladder 48 is right behind them. The "truckies" will now search and ventilate the building. I head down the fire escape thinking again about fire. It was going good, and the chances are that it has probably gotten through to the floor above. As I reach the top of the drop-ladder I hear Benny's voice calling for me. He is coming down the fire escape with a small girl in his arms. I meet him between the first and second landing. "Take her down for me, Dennis," he says. "I found her in her crib. I'm going back up." His face is black with smoke, and a heavy cylinder of mucus hangs from his nose. The child is crying, which is a good sign.

There is a woman waiting at the bottom of the ladder. She is shrieking hysterically "Maria, Maria." Another woman holds her shoulders as she takes the baby from me. I can see through her tears the happiness in her simple, unadorned eyes—that true happiness that is unique in a mother's love for her child. She doesn't know Benny, and I wonder if she will ever think of him, pray for him.

Lieutenant Collins, Cosmo, and Kevin are in the street taking orders from Chief Niebrock. The Chief's walkie-talkie is blaring and squawking, and the transmission is broken up. The only words that are understandable are *"roof,"* and *"the bulkhead door."* The Chief speaks into the transmitter in his slow, confident way, *"Please repeat your message. You are coming in broken up."* And the radio just squeals in reply.

The Chief looks at Lieutenant Collins and the rest of us. Engine 45 has already started a second line to the floor above, and Chief Niebrock orders us to help them with the stretch. The second line should have been ours, but we have all been thinking about other things. Lieutenant Collins, Cosmo, and Kevin helped carry people down the fire escapes, and they searched the apartments on the lower floors. Now, we will have to help Engine 45 stretch its line without getting a real piece of the action. We'll just squat in the hall as Engine 45 fights its way in with the nozzle.

Engine 85 is making good progress with its line. Marty Hannon and Jim Barrett are on the nozzle. They are in the apartment, but they haven't made the front room yet, and the fire is still pushing out of the windows. Bill Robbie is right behind them with a mask, but Marty and Jim won't take a blow. Captain Konak is beside them yelling the traditional words of confidence. "Beautiful, Marty, you got it. Move in a little more. Give us some more line Robbie."

Benny has gone into an apartment on the fifth floor. He makes a careful search, but the apartment is empty. He opens the hall door, and he is hit with a hard wind of heat. He drops to the floor, and the heat passes over him. The smoke is thicker than he has ever experienced it, and he coughs almost uncontrollably. His first impulse is to get back out to the fire escape and air, but he puts his nose to the linoleum floor and tries to relax. As his coughing stops he can hear soft moaning coming from the hall. He listens carefully for the direction, and it seems to be coming from the landing between the top floor and the roof. He crawls on his stomach through the hall, and up the stairs. The heat is unbearable and he feels that all energy has been drained from his body. He reaches the landing, and sees before him an incredible mess of human beings. They are piled on top of one another, and some are thinking the last conscious thoughts of life while exhaling the sighs of death.

The landing is an inferno. There are seven people—five adults and two children—lying there. They tried to flee the burning building and they went to the roof door. But the roof door was chained closed to keep the drug addicts from entering from the roof, and the heat from a fire five floors beneath them had nowhere to go. And seven human beings lay there with the heat, before a chained bulkhead door.

Benny can hear the desperate thump of the axhead hitting the halligan tool as he grabs for the nearest body. A two-inch hole was cut into the bulkhead brick and into the steel-covered door, and the chair was run through both holes, bound by a lock on the inside. The links are heavy, and the firemen on the roof cannot break them. They work instead on the hinges.

Benny has a two-year-old girl in his arms again, but this one isn't breathing. He carries her down into a fifth-floor apartment. He closes the door behind to keep out the smoke, and lays the girl gently on the kitchen floor. He wants to give her mouth-to-mouth resuscitation, but he has to think also of the others on the landing. He blows two hard, hopeful puffs of breath into the girl's mouth, and returns to the landing. There is a large woman there, made even larger with a pregnancy. He grabs her under the arms and pulls, but she is heavy and Benny is sweating a last resurgence of power. He is pulling hard, but it is of no consequence. He is close to collapse, and gasping with the heat and smoke. Then, like a *deus ex machina* redemption, he feels an arm swing around him, grabbing the woman's arm. Artie Merritt has vented from the roof, and seeing the door chained he came down the fire escape from the roof to search the floor. He and Benny drag the woman down the stairs. She is still breathing, but badly burned. They leave her next to the baby in the kitchen and return to the landing. Artie cannot control a coughing seizure, but he partially lifts a man, and drags him down the stairs. As Benny lifts the other child the bulkhead door swings open, and hangs down, caught by the chain. The heat and smoke rush out to the midday air, and the firemen fight their way down the stairs. Benny and Artie know now that the worst is over, and they minister to the people whose lives were worth more than their own.

Engine 45 is in the apartment extinguishing the fire that has come up through the walls. We are waiting in the hall, but we know that the men of Engine 45 won't need us to relieve them. Kevin, Cosmo, and I follow Lieutenant Collins to the street, where he confers with Chief Niebrock. The chief wants us to make a secondary search of all the apartments in the building.

As we re-enter the building a man stumbles out. He is burned on the face, and bleeding heavily from the mouth. A large black man, he is wearing a light cotton shirt that is now red with blood, and he has only one shoe. He falls in front of us, and I catch him before he hits the ground. The others go in the building, and I stay with the man.

About fifteen minutes have gone by, and I have tried to clean the man as best I could. I used my handkerchief until Oscar Beutin, one of the men of Engine 85, brought me a wet towel. The inside of his mouth is gashed. He must have fallen down the stairs. I have loosened his belt, and placed my boot under his head as a pillow. The man is not in any real danger, at least as far as I can tell, and I try to make him as comfortable as possible. A call has been put in for ambulances, and they should be here soon.

A large crowd has gathered in front of the building. One man is agitated, and he shouts, "Why don't you put that man in a fire engine and take him to the hospital?" He speaks clearly, without any trace of the black dialect or the ghetto localisms. I ignore him, because I know that he doesn't understand the workings of an emergency service. We don't take people to the hospital because it ties us up. We deal in seconds and minutes. Seconds and minutes determine life and death in our business. But this man doesn't know that. He only knows that a man is bleeding on the street and there are no ambulances to take him to the hospital. He yells again. "You motherfuckers don't care about black people. If that man was white you'd have him in a hospital soon enough." Many in the crowd nod in agreement, and others stare with interest. I look at the man on the ground, and then look at the intruder. I would like to tell him about the kind of work foremen do. I would like to tell him about people in this very neighborhood who are enjoying life only because of the actions of firemen. But it won't make any sense. This man doesn't want to like me. Not here. Not now. Another time, perhaps. I can tell this man that I care as much as he about the bleeding man at my feet. Even more important, I can ask him why he thinks I don't care.

Four ambulances turn the corner at Intervale Avenue—the disaster unit from Bronx-Lebanon Hospital. The Chief radios the word into the building, and firemen begin to carry the victims out. They are in chairs, or on stretchers. An attendant brings a wheel chair to me, and we lift the bleeding man into it. The attendant rolls the chair to the ambulance, and the driver assists us as we lift the chair into the antiseptic confines of the truck.

★　★　★　★　★

No one ate hamburgers in the firehouse today. They were ruined, but even if they were not burnt and dried out I don't think anyone would have felt like eating. It is after six now, and I'm sitting on a bed by my locker, putting on a clean pair of socks. The Chief called the hospital, and they told him that three of the victims were dead on arrival. The large woman was dead. She was eight months with child. Two men were dead, but Benny puffed life into the baby.

And now Benny is lying in a bed in the men's ward of Bronx Hospital. He collapsed finally, after bringing the small, breathing girl to the ambulance. The men's ward at Bronx is a dingy place, and I've seen many firemen recoup there after they brutalized their bodies in the course of their work. There are sixteen beds in the square, dim-gray room, and lying next to Benny is Joe Mazillo who was one of the men who fought his way down from the roof. And next to Joe is Lieutenant Connell who supervised the roof operation. The department medical officer has told us they will remain in the hospital for at least three days, for rest, blood tests, and X-rays. But Jim Stack will have to stay a little longer. He is across the hall in the intensive care unit, suffering dangerously high blood pressure and nerve palpitations. He felt a shocking pain as he helped George Heigman connect the pumper to the hydrant. And Artie Merritt has been transferred to the Manhattan Eye and Ear Hospital where he will spend the night. He cut the cornea of his eye as he hit a table corner while crawling through the smoke. Three human beings are dead, and ten are hospitalized for a fire that should have been routine.

I wonder what all this means. Is it ontological proof—that what God gives, He also takes away? Or does it mean that if there were no drug addicts in New York City people wouldn't have to put chains on roof doors?

To Save a Life

From *The Fire Inside: Firefighters Talk About Their Lives*

BY STEVE DELSOHN

How does it feel to save a life? Steve Delsohn's oral history of American fire-fighters tells us, in their own voices.

★   ★   ★   ★   ★

On the morning of Halloween night, our shift had just started at 7:30 A.M. Forty-five minutes later we got an alert. A four-family dwelling was on fire.

I was working on Engine 21 at the time, with a good friend of mine whose name is George Orzezh. As we rolled up on this place—a small apartment building—we saw a man and woman on the lawn. The father was bleeding. He was in his underwear. The mother was in her nightgown. They were jumping up and down, screaming that their two kids were still in there.

The fire was on George's side of the street, so he got off the rig and ran inside. I got off the rig, ran around the rig and came in behind him. The building was a four-flat, with two dwellings downstairs and two dwellings upstairs. The fire was in the downstairs, on the right side. The kids were supposed to be in the back of that apartment.

We worked our way through the living room and the dining room. There were still pieces of furniture burning there, but mostly there was heat without a whole lot of flame, because the fire had already used up all the oxygen.

It was smoldering now, like the white, hot coals in a barbecue pit.

As I came down the hall toward the back of the apartment, George came running back out the other way with a seven-year-old boy held in his arms. I continued forward, down the hall and into the back bedroom. The smoke was so heavy in there, I couldn't see. So I did our normal technique when looking for people in smoky conditions: I felt around for the bed, found it, and gave it a push to see if I'd get a bounce. If there's anyone on a bed, their body will bounce.

The first bed, I got nothing. The second one I felt a bounce, so I ran my hand across it real quick. I felt a little girl, about three years old.

I grabbed her, and I got her in my arms, but in my haste and excitement to find her, I had lost track of where the door was. Fortunately, by now, my sergeant was standing outside the bedroom door. I heard him calling my name from out in the hallway.

I said, "Yeah! Which way is the door?"

He said, "This way. Come to my voice."

I got to his voice and out to the hall. We were going to try and egress the same way that we came in—through the living room and the dining room. But at that same exact moment, the firemen outside were doing their ventilation. It happened very suddenly. They broke the windows out, more oxygen came in, and this superheated room burst into flames again.

The guys doing ventilation had done the right thing. We have a policy here in Detroit: you don't ventilate until you have water in the hose line. Because as soon as you ventilate, you are going to make the fire worse. That's one of the purposes of ventilation—to feed the fire, so it will show itself. Then as soon as it lights up, you open the hose and you put it out.

So those guys used proper procedure. They waited until there was water in the hose. Then they ventilated. The mistake that got made was by the guys on the hose line. When they stretched the line, they should've brought it through the front door of the building; the same door we came in. But they stretched to the side of the building and came inside a door there. In those few seconds they lost, the room ignited again and there was no water. It was just a bad call. I don't blame anyone. We've all made our own bad calls.

We were halfway through the dining room when everything lit up. Furniture, carpet, walls—it was like someone took lighter fluid and squeezed it into the pit. The heat was so strong it drove me to my knees. My sergeant hit his knees also. It was a pretty bad scene. I have a three-year-old kid in my arms, she is unconscious, and we are in a room that's suddenly on fire. A second ago it was smoldering. Now it's raw flame.

I pulled the girl as close to me as I could, and while I was doing that, I looked up and saw the front door through all the fire. I'm not gonna say I found it because I have so much experience, or because I'm so good at what I do. I found it because it wasn't my day to die.

I jumped off my knees when I saw the door. My sergeant must have seen it at the same time. He jumped back up, too. We didn't speak. We just looked at each other like, *There's the door! Let's get the hell out of here!*

Just as we got through the door, more flames mushroomed out the apartment behind us. By then, there were plenty of firemen out in the hallway. They said they could not believe what we just came though. It looked like a wall of flame.

Out on the lawn, I snatched off my mask to see what condition the kid was in. Her forehead was burned. So was most of the hair on the top of her head. Otherwise, considering, she looked good. And I still remember that moment vividly. It was cool outside. Late October air. We released so much heat into this cool air, the steam was rising off the three of us. The little girl, my sergeant, and myself.

They took all three of us to the hospital. The little girl lived. As a matter of fact, she had a full recovery. The blessing, I believe, was that she was so young.

My neck was burned and I missed a month of work. It took two weeks for my burns to heal, and then about two more weeks for the skin to grow back. Until it grew back, they wouldn't *let* me return. The skin on my neck was too tender. I couldn't put anything on it, like my mask.

Several months later, I was privileged to receive the Medal of Valor, the highest award for bravery that year. They also gave one to George, for pulling out that seven-year-old boy. It was the first time in the history of the Detroit Fire Department that they gave the Medal of Valor to two people.

I always love it when we save someone. I always love it when we win. But that was singularly, to date, the moment I am most proud of on this job.

How It Feels to Save a Life

It is the ultimate high. Nothing else comes close.

I remember my first night out of the training academy. Watching all the firemen, I felt like I wasn't one of them. Even though I *was* one, I felt like an observer.

After I made my rescue, that feeling changed. I distinctly remember feeling, *I'm one of these firemen now.*

It's real weird stuff, saving somebody's life. Hard to articulate, because it's a *feeling*. I don't really know what else to compare it to, other than your first love, or maybe your first child being born. You get these butterflies in your stomach, and you get all welled up and you want to cry.

A lot of it is luck. And you'll hear that a lot when someone's pulled out of a fire. "Geez, I was lucky. I happened to stumble on them."

They're telling the truth; it's not just being modest. With the smoke and the heat, you can't always tell what's what. Children, for example, are notorious for going under beds, or behind beds, or in closets, because they feel that's where they'll be safe. So one firefighter will look in all those places, and end up saving a kid. Another firefighter will pull out a doll. I've seen it happen. Both firefighters searched in all the right places. One guy had the luck.

Many times, rescues are made where the people aren't in much danger. They're hanging out of windows, but they're hanging out where the fire is not gonna spread. But they don't realize that, and they may jump. So we have to take the risk and go and get them. Basically, we're saving them from themselves.

I've been on a couple CPR calls where the person was dead when we walked in their home, and they were up and talking to us by the time we pulled up to the hospital. That's not the doctor that saved them. That's us that saved them. It's the best feeling in the world—the one that you stole back from the grim reaper. He had his rig backed up with the doors open, and we reached in and plucked someone back. Of course, he's probably a little pissed at us right now, and he'll come one day for us, but this one we denied him.

Unfortunately, it doesn't happen that often. It's not like that TV show, *Rescue 911*, where everybody they save comes to the fire station and meets the fire guys. That's a load of shit, because nobody on that program ever dies. It's a fantasyland fire department. They save *everyone*.

But every once in a while in real life, you do get to save someone, and that's all it takes. Making the difference in one child's life—or any person's life—will get you through years of shit.

I had an elderly gentleman once who was having an aneurysm.

The large vessel in his brain was about to burst. There didn't seem any way that he would live, but we brought him back to life in the back of our ambulance. We rushed him to the emergency room. ER took him up to surgery. A few hours later, we went back there on another call. So I checked on the old man. The guy was awake and talking and doing pretty good. I can't tell you how great that felt.

Ultimately, he died about one week later. But it didn't take away from the feeling I had had. See, I have these three rules. One is, You don't spit on the floor of my ambulance. Two is, You don't get sick and throw up back there. The third rule is, You don't die in my ambulance when I am back there with you.

That's how I see it. If I know I've done everything I can do, and that patient is still alive when I deliver them to the emergency room—not only alive, but in better condition than when I first got to them—I feel good.

For me, the best incident is what we call a live rescue. They're not only alive when you get them out, they stay alive. The very best is saving a kid. Kids who perish in a fire had no chance at life. So to give back to a little kid his chance to have a life? That's hard to top.

I've worked in different places, and for me it's especially nice if you're working in a small town. Usually, in a big city, you don't hear from them again. I guess it's just . . . life goes on. But in smaller towns, you can see the kid walking to school, or you might know their uncle, or you might see the kid's name in the sports section. Maybe he scored ten points in a basketball game.

You don't tell anyone, "Hey, I saved that boy's life." You just sit back and smile.

We pulled out this little girl whose name is Shamika. After the fire she could barely walk. Her hands were all swelled up and burned severely. Now she's come a long way. After six or seven operations, she's able to use her hands and she's walking properly. She's a very nice little girl, tough little girl. In all honesty, I can't imagine going through what she went through.

I just talked to her the other day. She's doing well. She keeps telling me she's getting straight A's, so I think she really is. You know, she and I come from totally different backgrounds. She's black, I'm white. She's from the city, I'm not. But I think we'll have a bond the rest of our lives.

Working as a team with other firefighters, to save a person's life, I don't know how to describe it. It's rewarding. It's refreshing. It's heart-wrenching. It brings tears to your eyes. And then you get credit, of course, and anyone who says they don't like credit, I don't think is telling you the truth. Everyone is smacking you on the back—people out on the street, fellow firefighters—and everyone is saying you did a great thing. It's absolutely fabulous. It's a great job. It's the best profession in the world!

When one of us makes a successful rescue, our chief goes on our radio to report it to dispatch. The chief gets on there and he's giving his size-up: two story wood frame. The fire started on the second floor, extended throughout. We used so much hose, we used so many ladders. Three victims were rescued by firefighters. First victim was rescued by . . . and he says your name over the radio.

That, for me, was a super rush of pride. All over the city, you know everyone's hearing it. Because it isn't just firefighters. Everybody in scannerland hears that report. Every person, every old lady, every newsroom in the city—anyone who has a scanner will hear that you rescued someone.

In my case, when I saved a woman, I thought that was pretty much it. I never knew it would turn into such a big deal. I thought it would be the usual thing: Put the hose back on the rig, go back to the fire station, clean up and then cook lunch. That's not what happened. Shortly after we got back from the fire, the news people came to the station. Then these other firefighters were calling me, even some guys I didn't know, saying, "Way to go, beautiful job." That afternoon, for lunch, we went to the Broadway Market to pick up meat. This little woman came up and said a prayer for me. She had seen me on the news and said, "You're the guy!"

When I got home from work, I had a ton of messages on my machine. The woman's mother called, too, and I called her back. When I asked how her daughter was, I noticed that she didn't sound optimistic. But she thanked me for going in there. She thanked me for giving her time, so she could go in and say good-bye to her daughter. That's what she appreciated the most. Having the time to say good-bye.

All the medals I have, except for one, are for dragging other firefighters out. I've rescued seven brothers in my career, and I've never gotten a thank you from any of them! In their heart, you know they're grateful. But firemen aren't real big on paying each other compliments. And saving one another is part of the job.

It does get pretty dramatic when it happens. I mean, your adrenaline pumps when anyone is trapped. But when one of the brothers goes down, man, the whole place goes crazy. One of the signals we have is a helmet thrown out a window. That means a brother is trapped. Which means it's more than a life. Now there is a family member in there, and you just kind of go berserk. You dig deeper inside yourself than you ever have before. Nothing else will suffice. You gotta get in there.

I've been on the Boston Fire Department for twenty-five years. In that period, I've experience quite a few gruesome deaths and real bad accidents. In time, you get over it. Maybe you go out after work that night and have a few beers.

It stiffens your lip a little. In the months and years to come, you learn to let it go.

That's usually how it works, but not every time. We had a tragedy here this June I'll never forget. We lost one of our own, and I was involved in that. In fact, I had gotten lost in the building myself.

It was a warehouse on top of a pier in the Charlestown section of Boston. A little after midnight, we received a call for a building fire there. I happened to be driving Rescue 1 that night. Going over the top of the North Washington State Bridge, I could see we had a small fire at the end of a pier. I said to myself: *Oh. We'll be out of here in fifteen or twenty minutes. It's no big deal.*

So we got out of the truck and grabbed our tools and masks. Engine 8 and Ladder 1 were already there. As they started to stretch a line inside the warehouse, we followed them in. Even though we knew we had a fire, from that vantage point we still saw no indication. We were standing right in the middle of the warehouse. It was as clear as my kitchen.

Without any warning whatsoever, this whole place turned to thick black smoke. The smoke came down from the ceiling. It was so thick you couldn't see the hand in front of your face. I dropped to the floor, trying to get on my face piece. I got it on and turned on my air supply. Otherwise, I'd be choking.

It was so dark you couldn't see anyone now. Nobody from the Ladder, the Engine, the Rescue. There was probably thirteen of us, but you couldn't even see one. All you could hear was mumbling and grumbling and groaning. I was still down on my hands and knees. When I looked underneath me, I saw the fire coming up from the floorboards. That was when we determined to leave the building. Anything that turns sour that fast, there is something definitely wrong.

When I turned around and yelled for the rest of them, they were gone. I got no reply at all. Everybody was already on their way out.

Normally, your training and experience always tell you: If you bring a hose into the building, you follow that hose line right back out the door you came in. So I started scrambling around the floor, searching for the hose. I knew it was off to my right, but I didn't know where. So I go off to the right and, geez, there's the line. I start to follow it back, and meantime this place is really turning rotten. The fire is up through the floor, and I'm following the hose, and suddenly it hits me: I'm going in circles.

I thought, *I'm in real trouble here. I should be going in a straight line, and I'm going round in a circle.*

Then I thought, *Stop! Get your head together and try something else.*

So I got another plan. I'd follow the hose line the other way, back to the nozzle, and start all over again. But in the next split second, I realized that I had no time to do this. I didn't know how far back the nozzle was, and this place was burning up. That's when I got worried I might get trapped. Because I still couldn't find anyone.

I thought, *I'm lost. I'm trapped in here. I'm gonna die in this place. All the rotten, lousy, friggin' vacant warehouses there are, I'm gonna die in here.*

That was the last thing I remember going through my mind. Then one of the fellows I work with grabbed my shoulder.

He said, "Come on, you stupid son of a bitch. You're going the wrong way."

We turned around, hand in hand, followed the line, and went out the front door. Outside the building, I turned around and looked back and started shaking my head. I couldn't believe it took off the way it did. Even to this day, they haven't found the cause. But I think it still seems suspicious. How does a pier take off like that, at midnight, if there aren't any combustibles involved?

Assuming now that everybody was out, we went back to the Rescue to get the K-12 saws. We had seen an overhead door, and thought we could make another entry there. But as I went to start the saw, the deputy chief's driver came running up to us. He said the deputy chief wanted us right away. Two men from Engine 8 were reported missing.

Once we got the order to go back in, we put down our saws and grabbed our steel cables. They have hooks on the end, for hooking to outsides of buildings. You use them for guidelines when you go inside. You keep your hand on the cable and never let go. That way, if you gotta leave, you know you're coming back out.

The cables are about fifty feet in length; I think we grabbed a couple hundred feet of them. A building this deep in size, we figured we needed that much. Then we went back to make another entry. The entire pier, not just the warehouse, was burning at this point. Underneath the pier, also, was fully involved. It had gotten some wind, and that wind was like gasoline. It just went up like, *poof.*

We didn't know what to expect once we got inside. We didn't know if the fire had penetrated the floor entirely. But we were going in there anyway.

We had to make an attempt to find the two guys. Anybody on this fire department would do it. This is a ballsy department in my opinion.

Five of us went inside from the Rescue Company, but there was an instant problem. The fire was overlapping the door we just came in. An engine company tried to knock it down, but there was too much fire. So now we had fire behind us, and we knew we'd soon have heavy fire in front. It was determined that we could not stay inside.

We were informed outside that both men from Engine 8 had just been found. They were located in another part of the building. Both men were still alive and on their way to the hospital.

We were also informed at this time about Lieutenant Minehan. They said he was missing. His entire company, Ladder 15, had gone in the same door we had, to look for the two missing members of Engine 8. Like us, they had encountered great fire and heat and determined they had to leave. But as they turned to go, the lieutenant got separated from his crew. And he got lost in there.

I looked at the warehouse burning. I prayed he wasn't inside. Maybe he'd gotten out some way we didn't know.

Then they asked our Rescue if we could get in there again.

If they got a couple of lines in the front door, we said we would give it our best shot.

So they got some lines in there, and they started hitting the fire and knocking some of it down. We took the cables again and in we went. But we were not able to penetrate very deep. The fire by then had burned right through the floor. For the third time that night, we were driven out of the building. That's when I looked at the water.

I said, "Maybe he was able to get out a window. Maybe he jumped in the harbor. He could be hanging on to a pier. A piling or something."

Right away, we had divers in the water. It was probably 2:00 A.M., but with that amount of fire beneath the pier, the water was all lit up. You could see pretty well. There was no sign of Stevie Minehan.

We ended up there until first daylight. By then, it had already been determined that he was lost. But then, around 7:00 A.M., the commissioner asked if we could get in there again. So we went in again and took a look. Most of the fire was pretty much knocked down, but the walls had collapsed. Sections of the roof had dropped on top of the pier. Parts of the pier had dropped into the water. There was scattered debris all over, pieces of roofs and walls. We lifted the debris, looking everywhere. We were in there two hours when one of the Rescue members hollered to me.

He said, "Hey, I found him."

I went over and looked and there was Stevie. He was the farthest point in the warehouse that you could possibly be. It meant that we would never have found him anyway. That made us feel a little bit better. If we had found him right inside the front door, we would have felt terrible. This way at least we didn't miss him, you know?

Before we had gone in to find him, we had been told not to touch him if we did. Because if Stevie's own company wanted to remove him, with our assistance, they would have that option. Only if they didn't feel up to it, would we bring him out ourselves.

The commissioner and the chaplain came in. The chaplain gave Stevie his last rites. Then the commission called in Ladder 15.

He said, "You guys want to take him out?"

They said, "Yeah, we do."

So they took him out and we gave them a hand. He was later pronounced dead.

It turned into a very big story. Not only in the city of Boston, but in all the surrounding cities and towns. His funeral was carried on all the TV stations here, and the public was extremely sympathetic. They raised quite a bit of money for his family. The outpouring was unbelievable. I think it was because of the way he died. If Stevie was inside there to save a civilian, or if he died because his fire truck flipped, it wouldn't have been the same. But he died trying to save two other firemen. He knew they needed help and he went in.

Stevie's death hit close to home for me. We are a very tight family in this department. Even to this day, if we go on a rescue call and run into Ladder 15, I stand there and look at their truck. I look at the front seat. I still think, *Where's Stevie? He should be there.*

It was a Sunday morning. It was summertime, so we had our windows open. I was sleeping at home, about to wake up and go in to the firehouse. A few minutes before six, I heard someone screaming outside our bedroom window.

I recognized the voice and stuck my head out the window. My next-door neighbor was yelling to me for help.

There was a fire in her house and her mom was in there. I knew her mom and she was eighty years old.

I yelled, "I'm coming down!"

I didn't have a shirt on, but I had slept that night in some cut-off sweats. So I bolted out of the room, told my wife to call 911, threw on my work shoes and ran downstairs. By the time I got outside, I could see smoke seeping out their windows.

I asked her, "Where's your mother's bedroom at?"

She said it was in the front part of the house. I asked if the front door was open. She said yes, so I ran to the front door. It all happened fast. I didn't think about getting hurt. I just ran into the building. I know how fire is and time is a major factor.

Smoke was starting to push out the front doorway, so I got in the crawl position and crawled inside the front entrance. Then I crawled up five or six steps to their first-floor apartment. Once I crawled in their door, I could feel the heat and smoke building up.

About eight feet inside their apartment, I saw another doorway. That's where the fire was concentrated at. As I went through that doorway, I kind of stood halfway up.

All I could see was the woman on the bed. Even though she was unconscious, I new she was alive. I could see her body twitching, still reacting to the flame.

As I made my way toward her, the flames were already starting to jump up the sides of her mattress. She was right in the center, so at first I tried to put my arms around her, in a bear hug position, and pull her off the bed that way. But with the flames now coming through the mattress, my hands and arms were starting to burn. She was slipping out of my hands, because my skin was melting.

So I tried something different. I pulled her arms toward me and got a lock on her wrists. With that grip, I started dragging her off the bed. At one point she slipped from my hands and we both fell into the curtains. They were on fire, and I felt the burning sensation right on my buttocks. When I stood back up, I started feeling woozy from the heat. It was almost as if I was in a drunken state. But I wasn't going to stop. We were already halfway out.

I grabbed her wrists again. I kept dragging her body across the floor. The room was becoming more involved in flames, but there was more fire than smoke, so I could see enough to spot her bedroom door. Just before we got there, her hip hit a chair that was sitting by the door. She got jammed between the chair and the doorway. The doorway, by that time, was on fire, and that did some damage to me. I got burned on my back, my upper arm and my shoulder.

I pried loose the chair and untangled the woman, then I continued dragging her through the apartment. I was close to passing out when I got through her front door, so I just took her out to the hallway steps, jumped over her body and ran downstairs. By then, there were people assembled down there.

I said, "Come on! Help me get her down the stairs!" No one came up, so I went back up myself. I dragged her down the steps, then a couple guys helped me drag her out to the lawn.

First, I opened her airway. Her breathing was barely there, and I didn't want it to stop. Her tongue was black from smoke. I mean black like shoe polish. Then I did some compressions on her chest, a couple of respirations into her mouth. She started breathing at more of a normal pace. Then my wife ran up with the woman who lived below us. Together, they started peeling off her burnt clothing. By that point she was breathing on her own, even though she was unconscious. That was a good sign. Firefighters were already showing up, and I thought she could hold on until paramedics arrived.

I stood up at this point and walked back and forth. That's when I started feeling extremely hot. I actually felt like I was on fire, so I asked my next-door neighbor to hose me down. But when my neighbor hit me with his garden hose, I screamed for him to stop. The water was hitting my burns and it hurt like hell. So I yelled out to my wife. I told her to run upstairs and call 911 again.

I said, "Tell them we're going to need a second ambulance."

While we waited for the ambulance to come, I realized that I was in pretty bad shape. The adrenaline had worn off and the pain was sinking in. My body started shaking uncontrollably. I was going into shock.

The firemen told me to sit down on the sidewalk. Once I did, I saw the damage I'd done. The skin on my left arm was hanging off and melted. On my left hand, the skin melted there had fused together my fingers. My fingernails had also fallen off.

I thought that was pretty much it—I thought my left arm and hand were burned up. But it turned out I had burns over 30 percent of my body. Actually, I had burns almost everywhere, but only 30 percent were third-degree. Most of that was sustained by my upper body, because I went into there without a shirt.

The first thing they did at the hospital was put in a catheter. Then they tried hooking me up to the IV, but my arms were so burnt they couldn't get into the veins. Instead, they stuck two IVs into my femoral artery. So I had these two big needles going in next to my groin.

They then proceeded to take me into the scrub room, which is just a steel bed with hoses all around it. They started washing and scrubbing off my burnt skin, probably the worst thing I've ever felt in my life. I think I can take most pain pretty well, but I screamed at the top of my lungs when they took me in there. Everybody screamed. You could hear each person they brought in. You have to scream. You have to let it out.

After I was scrubbed, they rubbed this cream called Silvadine all over me. Over the cream, they wrapped me up like a mummy. They told me I would swell up, and I swelled up like a balloon. One eye was completely shut. The other one, I could barely see out of. The swelling came from the burns, and also all that intravenous fluid.

They listed me in critical condition.

For the next three days, they did their scrubbings two or three times a day. After my fourth day there, they took me in for my skin graft operation. The doctor said since I was young and in real good shape, they would try and do the whole thing in one operation. It lasted somewhere between eight and twelve hours. They stripped the good skin off my legs and lower back, and they grafted in onto the places where I had third-degree burns. Then they stapled the skin so it would remain in place. When I came out of surgery the next morning, I had about fifteen hundred staples on my left side.

When I woke up from that, the guys I work with were there. So was my wife. I couldn't talk with this tube going in my throat, so I just scribbled notes. I told them I was fine, but I wanted to know when this doctor was taking this tube from my throat. I really wasn't fine, though. There were areas on my left arm where the skin grafts didn't take. Those areas had formed large open wounds. I couldn't sleep that night or several nights after. Not only from the burns, but all the sweating you do when you're all bandaged up. I have to tell you, some nights it felt like torture. There were some moments, you know, I wished I was dead.

I was also dealing with the psychological thing. I mean about my burns, the way I looked. I kept thinking about that day when they'd let my children see me. Our oldest daughter was nine, our son was almost five, and our little girl was two. I had already dropped about forty pounds, and I had been gone three weeks. I was afraid our two-year-old wouldn't know me. All that stuff was playing on my mind.

Finally, about three or four days before I got released, they let the children come. My smallest child ran right up to me. I picked her up and she knew it was her dad. Wow, did that feel great.

At first, with those open wounds, it didn't look like I'd be going home too quickly. The doctor said he was guessing about six weeks. I couldn't wait that long. After twenty-two days, I said, "I want to go home. I've shown you people that I can walk. I can exercise. I can handle it. Let me go home."

So they gave my wife some lessons on how to treat me at home. She was just wonderful. She would change my bandages and bathe me. She would help me eat. We hung in there together, but it got hard sometimes for both of us. I was off work for nine months—a real up-and-down time, emotionally. I was still self-conscious about my looks. There were times I doubted why my wife was with me. I didn't want her to be with me out of pity. When you get burned like that, all these crazy things go through your mind.

It took awhile for my head to get straight. Sometimes out of frustration, I'd go off the deep end and punch a wall. It was pretty bad, but my wife just stuck with me the whole way through. I needed that from her. I needed that sense of security.

The rescue effort I made was actually successful: the elderly woman survived. She stayed in the hospital for about six months, then her family put her in a nursing home. Unfortunately, she died in the nursing home about four months later. This entire time, there was never a knock at our door from her daughter and son. They never said one word. Never even, "Is everything okay?"

At first, that was hard to deal with. Especially for my wife. She saw her husband get burned, and this family was so cold.

I told my wife, "I understand how you feel, but you should stop being upset. I don't regret what I did."

I never have regretted it. It doesn't matter who was inside that building, how old the person was, or how the family was afterwards. What I did was right. I took the extra step. I'll always be proud of that.

For that particular rescue, I wound up winning several big awards. I got first prize that year from *Firehouse* magazine. I received the Lambert Tree Award, the highest award from the city of Chicago. There were state awards and national awards, and an international award from the International Association of Fire Chiefs. For that ceremony, they flew my wife and myself to California. They took us to Disneyland and Universal Studios. They put us up at a nice hotel.

It was great. All of that kind of recognition was. We have a real good fire department here in Chicago. I felt honored to carry on that tradition.

"Under the Rubble: Two Cops Learn About Life"

From *The Daily News*

BY JIM NOLAN AND NICOLE WEISENSEE EGAN

There has never been a crisis that has called for more heroism from uniformed professionals than 9/11. The following article from The New York *Daily News* describes in stirring detail the saga of two cops buried under tons of twisted steel—and how, incredibly, they were rescued.

★　★　★　★　★

Will Jimeno could barely move.

The Port Authority police officer was buried 20 feet under the concrete, glass and steel of what used to be the World Trade Center, his left leg pinned by a collapsed wall, his right foot wedged under rebar and cinderblocks.

Some 15 feet down in the same hole, enveloped in darkness, was Port Authority Sgt. John McLoughlin—crushed from the hips down by a concrete slab. He was on the verge of passing out from pain.

"It was like the gates of hell had opened up and swallowed them," said Port Authority Sgt. Mark O'Neill, a friend of both men.

In the anxious hours that followed the Sept. 11 terror attack, Jimeno and McLoughlin didn't know whether they would live to see Sept. 12, much less Jan. 1, 2002.

The two cops are celebrating the holidays with their families now. But they came within a miracle or two of being statistics that tragic day in New York.

Twists of fate and twists of steel, the random heroism of strangers and the random collapse of concrete saved them—two of the last survivors of barely a dozen rescued from the rubble of the Trade Center towers.

The account of their harrowing ordeal is a reminder of just how narrow the divide was that day between life and death, triumph and sorrow.

"None of us were taught how to fight a war," said John McLoughlin. "That's what we faced that day."

They are survivors, heroes, living miracles.

Or as McLoughlin's brother, Paddy, said: "The hope of the world."

They just kept jumping

Jimeno heard Sgt. McLoughlin's voice above the chaos.

"We need three volunteers!"

Jimeno, Antonio Rodrigues and Dominic Pezzulo—all rookies and police academy classmates just six months on the job—stepped forward.

"Before you knew it, we were running in," said Jimeno, 33, remembering the scene at the World Trade Center near the southern tip of Manhattan.

A Boeing 767—American Airlines Flight 11 en route from Boston to Los Angeles and loaded with fuel—had just flown into the Trade Center's North Tower.

The plane struck the 110-story building at the 86th floor, exploding into a huge fireball and sending chunks of building and aircraft showering down on people below.

"We looked up, and all of a sudden there are people jumping out of the building," the 33-year-old Jimeno recalled, tears welling.

"They looked like little rag dolls. Everyone was frantic. They just kept jumping.

"One guy—I felt as if my eyes had a zoom. I saw his blond hair, a pink shirt, pants what looked like to be Dockers, and he's jumping," Jimeno said. "He was going straight down and he just disappeared. It was crazy."

Within minutes, squads of Port Authority Bus Terminal cops were barreling down Ninth Avenue toward Ground Zero in a commandeered city bus.

McLoughlin, 48, an Emergency Services Unit cop who had worked at the Twin Towers for 12 years before being promoted to sergeant, led the men to an equipment room in the Trade Center complex.

They met up with Chris Amoroso, a former bus terminal cop who had been transferred into the rotating pool of Port Authority officers working at the Trade Center.

"We just hugged each other," said Jimeno.

Before the group left, McLoughlin's wife, Donna, called her husband at the Trade Center police precinct.

"He's busy right now. Is this an emergency?" asked the cop who answered the phone. "No," she said, hanging up.

The cops took a freight elevator down to the main concourse below ground level, where retail stores were.

They headed toward rescue stations to pick up some more equipment. Air packs only last 30 minutes. Any rescue on the fiery and smoky upper floors would take longer.

Rodrigues was pushing a laundry cart with the equipment but was falling behind, so Jimeno went to help.

At that moment a thunderous roar began to shake the entire complex. At fist, McLoughlin thought it was a car bomb, similar to the one that damaged the Trade Center in the 1993 terrorist attack.

"I had no idea the building was coming down," said McLoughlin, speaking for the first time about that day in an exclusive interview with the *Daily News*.

"A brown wall of destruction was rolling toward us. The lobby was just being churned up and coming right at us," he added.

"Run to the freight elevators!" McLoughlin told his men. He knew it was the safest place structurally, thanks to extra steel supports around the shafts.

"We were getting bombarded, hit with concrete—boom, boom, boom," said Jimeno. "It seemed like forever."

The cops fell to the ground. Then silence. And darkness, save for a small hole just over Jimeno's shoulder, where a stream of light filtered through.

"Sound off!" McLoughlin yelled.

"Jimeno!"

"Pezzulo!"

Then nothing.

"Sarge, I just hear three people," said Jimeno.

"A-Rod? Amoroso? A-Rod, Amoroso?" he yelled.

"Sarge, they're not answering," said Jimeno. "I don't think they made it."

"Will," said Pezzulo calmly, "they're in a better place."

Bracing for death

Thirty feet underground, in the elongated void that contained the three Port Authority cops, Pezzulo managed to free himself from the rubble.

Jimeno could only get slight movement in his left leg. McLoughlin couldn't move his legs at all.

"I need somebody to relieve this pressure on me," McLoughlin called out from the darkness.

Pezzulo found room in the crawl space to stand.

"I'm not going to leave you, Will," he told Jimeno. "If I get out, I'm coming back."

"Dominic, do not leave," came McLoughlin's voice. "You've got to get Will out. Then you and Will can get me out."

Pezzulo began working feverishly to free Jimeno.

"That's when you just heard this horrible, horrible noise." Jimeno remembered.

It was about 10:30. The North Tower was coming down.

"It sounded like some horror movie, when some big monster makes a huge roar," he said.

"I braced myself for death. I thought we were done."

When the roar ended, Jimeno looked up to see Pezzulo slumped over in a seated position. Something had dislodged, striking him on the back and head.

"Dom, are you all right?" asked Jimeno.

"I'm hurt. I'm in pain," Pezzulo responded sluggishly.

"Dom, are you all right?" Jimeno asked again.

"Willie, I'm dying."

"Dom, don't die."

"Willie?" asked Pezzulo, struggling. "I love you."

"I love you, too," said Jimeno.

"Please don't forget that I died trying to save you guys."

"Dominic, we'll never forget that. We'll never forget you," said Jimeno.

Jimeno looked away for a moment. When he looked back, he saw Pezzulo raising his service pistol and pointing it toward the small hole where light entered the void.

Pezzulo fired a round into the opening, a last-ditch effort, perhaps, to tell someone that his brother officers were still alive. Then he collapsed and died.

Jimeno stared down at his fallen friend, the father of two young children.

"Sarge," an emotional Jimeno cried out. "Dominic just died. He's gone."

"I know," said McLoughlin, remaining calm. "I know."

Just two hours earlier, five Port Authority cops had entered the gates of hell to save lives. Now only two were still breathing.

Anxious hours

McLoughlin and Jimeno were buried in the middle of a vast, unstable debris field, ringed with fire and fogged by dust and thick, black smoke.

They were getting closer to the two small holes above Jimeno, pinned on his back and side.

He arched his neck and yelled at the top of his lungs.

"10–13! 10–13!" the police code for an officer who needs assistance.

"McLoughlin, Jimeno, PAPD. We need help! We need help!"

Then, incredibly, Jimeno heard a voice.

"He said, 'Is so-and-so down there?' " Jimeno recalled.

"No, but Jimeno and McLoughlin, PAPD, are down here," Jimeno yelled back desperately. "Don't leave here. I got a 4-year-old daughter."

"Then he said, 'Are you sure so-and-so is not there?' " Jimeno added.

"No, but we're down here. Don't leave us!"

The voice disappeared.

"He's gone," Jimeno yelled down to McLoughlin.

McLoughlin, battling pain that was close to making him pass out, knew that they were on their own. "They're backing out, Will."

"The guy could have been in shock—maybe he was looking for a loved one," Jimeno reasoned later. "Or he could have been a cop or a firefighter looking for his buddy, which I know how I would feel.

"Or he could have just died."

A name and a prayer

Back at her home in Clifton, NJ, Allison Jimeno was trying to convince herself that her husband was OK, that he was simply directing traffic or something.

Finally, about 6 P.M., surrounded by family, she got up the nerve to call the Port Authority Bus Terminal.

Yes, cops told her. Willie had gone in—and he was missing.

"It was not what I wanted to hear," said Allison, then seven months pregnant— suddenly forced to face the possibility of life without a husband for her, and a father for the couple's four-year-old daughter, Bianca, and unborn baby girl. The couple hadn't even settled on a name for the baby. Allison wanted Olivia Marie, but Willie didn't like it.

For Jimeno, hours passed by without hope. He thought about death and started to pray.

He prayed that his wife would be able to go on without him and that his daughter would remember him.

And he asked his sergeant for a favor—to get on the police radio and say that Jimeno wanted his unborn baby to be named Olivia Marie.

McLoughlin knew the radio didn't work outside of the Bus Terminal, but he did it anyway for his rookie.

Allison Jimeno was glad she had seen her husband off to work earlier that day. "I thought about kissing him that morning and my daughter kissing him and saying goodbye," she recalled, dabbing at tears in her eyes.

"I thank God we kissed him."

Pact with a brother

Donna McLoughlin knew where her husband was. A cop's wife for 22 years, she had steeled herself not to worry as much as others.

Just like she knew the sex of her four children before they were born, she knew her husband was alive.

"He is always prepared, he always thinks things through," she thought to herself.

"She has a lot of hope," said John McLoughlin. At the time, however, the cop wasn't as confident.

"The pain was so severe I didn't know how much longer I could put up with it," he said. McLoughlin also was unable to urinate and worried that his kidneys would fail and he would poison himself.

"There was a desperate need to see my family again. And then sometimes you'd get a hopeless feeling and realize this is where you are going to die," he recalled. "Then you'd come back and say, 'I'm going to survive this somehow.' It kept switching."

Donna McLoughlin knew that John McLoughlin had a pact with his brother, Paddy, a recently retired Port Authority police officer who spent most of his career at the bus terminal.

If something ever happened to either of them on the job, it fell to the other brother to tell the wife.

She decided not to listen to the messages on her answering machine. She wouldn't watch TV. She would wait for her husband.

As the hours of Sept. 11 went from late morning to early evening without a call, Paddy learned his brother was considered missing. He drove upstate to the family's home in Goshen to fulfill his pact.

He was barely out of his car when Donna appeared outside her door. If it had been good news, she figured, Paddy would have simply called.

"Are you here to tell me something?" she asked, on the verge of tears. "Don't you come here!"

Paddy hugged her and they went inside.

We need to go in there

Accounting is what Dave Karnes does for a living. But being a Marine is his life.

When Karnes' sister Joy called him at work at Deloitte & Touche in Wilton, Conn., to tell him a plane had just struck the World Trade Center, Karnes—a staff sergeant with 23 years' experience in the Marine Corps infantry and active reserves until 1998—knew he couldn't stay behind his desk.

"I don't know if you guys know it yet," the banking and securities auditor told co-workers. "But this country is at war."

Karnes hopped into the 1974 Porsche Targa he had just bought and gave it a road test—driving south on I-95 at 110 mph.

He stopped in Valley Stream, Long Island, to pick up his old Marine gear. Then he headed to his family's church, Bible Baptist in Elmont, and asked the Rev. James Barker to pray with him.

"We asked that the Lord would lead me to a survivor," Karnes explained in a recent interview. "And I asked that he please pray for me."

It was about 6 when Karnes parked his car just over the Brooklyn Bridge, near City Hall. He unloaded his rescue and rappelling gear—rope, canteens, flashlight and 9-inch knife—and headed toward the disaster area.

Hundreds of rescuers were already at the crash site. Before the collapse of the Twin Towers, police and firefighters had managed to evacuate an estimated 25,000 people.

Thousands were still buried—most of them dead, or dying, including McLoughlin and Jimeno.

Above the hole, fires raged. Black smoke and dust created an artificial night. Vast piles of shifting, jagged wreckage stacked five stories above street level. Another building, 7 World Trade Center, had caved in and crashed to the ground about 5:30.

By the time Karnes arrived, nearly all of the rescuers had retreated to safer ground along Vesey and Church streets. Off to the side he spotted a Marine sergeant, whose namepatch said "Thomas."

"Hey, devil dog," he yelled to Thomas. "We need to go in there."

"Aye, aye staff sergeant," Thomas responded.

"Once we cross this street, there's no going back," Karnes said, gesturing toward the pile. "If anyone tells us to stop, we keep going. We don't hear them."

Thomas nodded, and the pair started off, disappearing into the smoke.

Fire and bullets

Things were heating up inside the hole. Small fires scorched the air that the dehydrated men were forced to breathe.

"We were scared we were going to be burned to death," said McLoughlin.

Suddenly a fireball shot through one of the openings above Jimeno. The heat, Jimeno believes, had been building for hours on the gun of Pezzulo, who had died about nine hours earlier.

Pezzulo's unattended Glock began spewing its 15 rounds, one by one. The bullets ricocheted throughout the tiny crawl space.

Bing! Bing! Bing! Pop! Pop!

The scare had a strange effect on Jimeno. Instead of creating more despair, the burly cop got angry.

"We're getting out of here, Sarge. We're getting out of this thing," he said to McLoughlin.

With renewed energy, Jimeno began banging on a section of steel pipe above him.

"10–13! 10–13! McLoughin and Jimeno, PAPD. We're here! We're here!"

"Will, keep doing that," McLoughlin encouraged.

"I've got a big mouth," Jimeno later admitted, "I just kept yelling."

Jimeno took out his own gun and tried to chip away at his concrete prison. He started scraping at the debris with his handcuffs—a $20 pair purchased seven years before when he worked a security job at a Toys 'R' Us store in North Jersey.

He had kept his cuffs through three other jobs, including one at Steinbach's department store in Bergen County—the place where he met his wife.

Karnes and Thomas picked their way through the fires, thick smoke and debris, stepping carefully to avoid the shifting cement and steel made red hot by the fire.

"U.S. Marines," they called out in the blackness. "If you can hear us, yell or clap."

They repeated the call every 10 meters or so. The only light available came from Karnes' flashlight.

Then, about an hour into the search, Karnes saw a depression in the debris about 200 yards in, toward the center of the plaza.

As the Marines moved closer, Karnes thought he heard a muffled sound, but he wasn't sure. Years as a mortar section leader in the infantry had taken their toll.

"U.S. Marines! If you can hear us, yell or clap!"

That's when they heard Jimeno.

"10–13! 10–13! McLoughlin and Jimeno, PAPD. We're here! We're here!"

Karnes and Thomas followed Jimeno's voice for about 40 meters and stopped above a hole.

"All I saw was a dark void, full of smoke," Karnes recalled. "I could see some fires down there. There were fires several feet away from them."

Karnes shined his flashlight into the hole, and finally caught sight of Jimeno's outstretched hand. He sent Thomas for help.

"Please don't leave us," Jimeno begged.

"I'm not leaving you, buddy," Karnes reassured. "You're coming out." It was 8 P.M.

Don't die on us now

McLoughlin and Jimeno had been found, but no one quite knew how to get them out.

Within minutes, firefighter Tom Asher arrived on the scene. He had come to Ground Zero after work in the Bronx to search for the missing brother of his captain.

Paramedic Chuck Sereika also came upon Karnes standing over the hole. The former city EMT had donned his old medic's shirt and hitched a ride in an ambulance to Ground Zero, where he began searching on his own.

Emergency Services Unit veteran Scott Strauss leaped head-first into the tiny hole, roughly 2 feet square. He crawled 20 feet down with only his flashlight.

Strauss found Pezzulo's body slumped against the wall next to elevator doors that had been twisted open.

About 10 feet to the left of the elevator shaft and 6 feet up on the other side of the void lay Jimeno.

"All you could see was his face, his right arm and part of his right leg," said Strauss. "The rest of him was buried."

McLoughlin lay another 15 feet down in the hole in total darkness, not making a sound.

Sereika took Jimeno's blood pressure. Karnes was on one side, Strauss on the other. ESU cop Paddy McGee threw debris down the open elevator shaft.

"We were just using our fingers, our hands, handcuffs," Strauss said, recalling how rescuers worked to free the men. "We had no room for equipment."

Karnes passed his canteen to Jimeno. Asher opened a fire extinguisher to give the dehydrated cop more water. Jimeno began to hyperventilate.

"Don't die on us now," Karnes said.

McGee was also concerned about McLoughlin. By coincidence the cops knew him from joint EDU training with the Port Authority. McLoughlin was considered a top authority on emergency response in high-rises.

For a time, the cops thought he had died.

"Hey, Irish eyes, speak to me. Where are you?"

"I'm buried further in. I'm hurt," came a voice from the darkness. "I don't want to lose my legs."

"Hang on, Irish eyes," said McGee. "We'll get to you."

First they had to free Jimeno. They removed his airpack and tried wrapping his chest in nylon and using hooks to pull him free, but he screamed in pain. His leg was still pinned.

Rescuers handed down a battery-operated Hurst "Jaws of Life" tool.

"It's either gonna happen and we'll get out of here, or it's not gonna happen and we'll both be buried," Strauss told him.

"Take my leg if you have to," Jimeno told him. "Just do it. I want to get out of here. I want to live."

Using rubble as a wedge, Strauss pried a piece of rebar upward and grabbed Jimeno's foot, freeing his leg.

After two hours, the exhausted cops pulled Jimeno out on his stomach and loaded him onto a rescue basket. A fresh team would be sent down to free McLoughlin.

Asher kissed his fellow rescuers on the forehead.

"Let's get the f—out of here," he said. All would be treated at the hospital—and return the next day to look for more survivors.

With danger above ground and McLoughlin's condition deteriorating, a doctor suggested amputation.

McGee told him directly: "He's keeping his legs."

'Where is everything?'

Jimeno made it to the surface about 10:30, roughly 13 hours after being trapped.

At one point, Jimeno lifted his head and looked around.

"Where is everything?" he asked.

"It's all gone, kid," someone said.

At Bellevue Hospital, Jimeno again was surprised by what he saw. Clusters of doctors and nurses, just standing around.

"Where are all the victims?" he asked.

"You're it," a doctor told him.

Allison Jimeno got to Bellevue shortly before midnight. She took her husband's hand in the emergency room.

"The only thing I could think of," she said, "was how was I going to tell our daughter that her daddy wasn't coming home."

Karnes followed Jimeno to Bellevue, and stayed with him until 3:30 in the morning. Cops found him a bed in the hospital's psychiatric ward.

Karnes lay awake most of the night in fresh hospital pajamas. His head pounded. He could barely breathe. "My lungs were on fire," he said. His whole body itched from fiberglass fibers.

His mind raced. He thought about John McLoughlin.

"He never once complained," recalled Karnes, who decided to re-enlist in the active reserves and asked to be posted on the front lines in the Middle East.

"He never said, 'What about me?' " Karnes added. "He forsook himself and thought about [Will] first."

It took nearly another eight hours before a team of Nassau County cops and firemen from Rescue 5 freed McLoughlin from the concrete that crushed his legs.

Medics had offered him morphine for his pain, but he refused and stayed conscious the whole time.

"I was getting very weak and I didn't want to be weakened any more," McLoughlin explained. "I thought it would suppress the pain and that would be it—I'd pass out and never come back again."

Genelle Guzman, a Port Authority office worker, would be pulled out two hours later. The last survivor.

That morning, police closed 42nd Street to all traffic to escort Donna and Paddy McLoughlin from the Times Square Bus Terminal to Bellevue.

Donna went to her husband's bed in the emergency room. She held his hand and kissed him.

"I stayed alive for you," he told her.

What's really important

McLoughlin underwent 27 operations over 11 weeks at Bellevue. He nearly died the first night and spent the next six weeks in a medically induced coma to cope with the pain.

Bellevue doctors coined a nickname: "Unkillable."

"I just take it as a miracle that all these coincidences fell into place for Will and I to be able to live and survive," said McLoughlin. "Because there were too many of them."

McLoughlin now relies on a wheelchair and a walker. He faces painful weeks ahead at a rehab hospital before going home. He still has no feeling in his feet, but the brave Port Authority cop expects a full recovery.

"I intend to be walking—my goal is to walk right back into the precinct doors," he said. "All it is is nerve endings. Right now it's wait and see."

There are some things that John McLoughlin isn't waiting for. On Sept. 11, he didn't think he was going to see the next day. On Christmas Day, his children woke him up at 5 A.M. to open gifts.

"I say 'I love you' more than I ever said in my life," he said. "It was always hard for me to express those things—now it's not hard. It comes real easy."

McLoughlin doesn't consider himself a hero.

"I just did my job," he said. "I'm not worthy of that."

But his survival has forever changed him. "I've got to be a better person," he said. "You look at so much death and destruction and realize how truly lucky you and your family are. You've got to give back the kindness you received."

Jimeno, too, is overjoyed to be home and eager to return to work. Outfitted with braces, he is learning how to reuse his damaged legs.

Like McLoughlin, he was hospitalized and unable to attend the funerals of Pezzulo, Rodrigues and Amoroso. Thirty-seven Port Authority cops died that day.

"On one level I didn't want to be alive—I felt guilty," Jimeno said. "I looked at the board of people who died and said, 'Why am I here?' "

But Sept. 11 has also given Jimeno's life additional purpose. One of his New Year's resolutions is to be a voice for his fallen friends. "To tell their sons and daughters how brave their fathers were," he said. "What true heroes they are."

Jimeno got his Christmas wish early. His second daughter, Olivia Marie, was born the week after Thanksgiving. In the new year, and for years to come, he will be a father to her, not just a memory.

"She's beautiful," Jimeno said, one living miracle to another.

Part Three
From a Watery Grave:
Rescue at Sea

Ready to Surface

From *The Terrible Hours*

BY PETER MAAS

In the spring of 1939, months before the advent of World War II, the United States Navy tested a new submarine, The USS *Squalus*. It was one of the first of the new, "fleet-type" torpedo boats: 310 feet long, twenty-seven feet wide, surface speed of 16 knots, shiny teakwood deck. But on a test dive off the coast of New Hampshire, something went terribly wrong and she plunged to the bottom of the North Atlantic. Miraculously, 33 of her crew members survived. Peter Maas's *The Terrible Hours* vividly recreates the story of how Charles "Swede" Momsen—Navy visionary and man of action—helped save these men with his new invention: the diving bell.

★ ★ ★ ★ ★

Near noon, the rescue chamber was hoisted off the *Falcon's* fantail. Newscaster Bob Trout would tell millions of radio listeners, "We reporters up here really don't know what to call it. Officially, it's a rescue chamber, but it sort of looks like a bell. All of us here know, however, that we are witnessing a historic event."

Momsen watched as it was hoisted out over the water with its two operators inside. For the first time, men in a sunken submarine were going to be returned to the surface alive—and from a depth once thought unreachable. Not even this bell, ten feet high and seven across at its widest, had ever gone so deep in rescue run-throughs.

Tethered to the *Falcon* by an up-haul cable, it floated some twenty feet away. Its lower compartment was not yet flooded, its main ballast tank and fourteen auxiliary cans filled just enough to provide positive buoyancy so that its gray top was visible. Beside the cable that would be used to retrieve the chamber in an emergency, two air hoses and electric lines for a telephone and interior lights ran from its top to the *Falcon*.

Two minutes after the chamber was in the ocean, one of the operators, Walt Harmon, reported to Momsen that he and his partner, John Mihalowski, were all set in the upper compartment.

"Go on down," Momsen ordered.

Harmon started the air motor and the reel began winding in the down-haul cable that Sibitsky had attached to the *Squalus*. The chamber crept along the surface like a huge water bug for perhaps fifty feet. Then, as ballast was blown and the lower compartment flooded, it sank from sight.

Inside his control room, Naquin listened to the *Penacook's* signal that the chamber was descending and that seven men were to make the first trip. Over the battle phone, he instructed Nichols that besides Harold Preble, he should pick five men whom he felt were in the worst physical shape. "You go, too, John," he said. "I want an officer up there in case any consultation is necessary."

Naquin said that he and the rest of the men in the control room would stay put until the first group was out of the boat. Moving to the forward torpedo room now would simply overcrowd it and create confusion. Nichols had a question. During the night, the *Wandank* had requested the removal of all confidential publications. What about this? Naquin told him to forget it. It wasn't worth the waste in energy.

Thirty minutes into the descent, at 150 feet, the rescue chamber halted. There was some trouble with the air vent lowering the pressure to maintain proper flooding and buoyancy. Three minutes later, flooding commenced again.

Harmon continued to sing out their progress until at last, peering through the chamber's porthole, he reported, "Submarine in sight."

The chamber slowly settled on the flat steel collar surrounding the escape hatch. Now the process of blowing ballast and flooding the lower compartment that had begun on the surface was reversed. The main ballast tank girdling the chamber was filled while the lower compartment was emptied.

The enormous force of the ocean then sealed the rubber gasket around the bottom of the chamber to the escape hatch.

Harmon reported, "Seal complete." Mihalowski opened the hatch in the chamber that divided its two compartments and dropped into the lower one where several inches of water remained. He attached four steel bolts to rings around the sub's hatch. Then he lifted the hatch cover.

On the *Falcon,* Momsen could hear it fall with a thud against the side of the chamber. But in his growing excitement, he suddenly froze. "Upper submarine hatch is open," Harmon told him, "but no answer from submarine." What happened was that Nichols had kept the hatch at the other end of the escape trunk closed until a drainage pipe siphoned off the excess water, about a barrelful, that had come from the chamber. That done, he ordered the lower hatch opened.

Mihalowski looked down in the faint light. He could barely distinguish the pale faces staring back up at him.

Momsen heard the magic words from Harmon. "Mihalowski sees them!"

"When I heard that," he wrote of the moment, "I experienced a thrill I cannot possibly describe and I wonder if any man ever could."

Mihalowski himself didn't know what to say. It was as if both he and the men below had been rendered speechless. "Well," he finally said, "we're here. I'm passing down soup, coffee and sandwiches."

That broke the ice. De Medeiros said, "What, no napkins?"

Mihalowski heard another voice say, "Where the hell have you guys been?"

Mihalowski laughed. "You should have seen the traffic," he said.

To accompany him and Preble on this first ascent, Nichols selected the last two men to flee the after battery, Isaacs and Roland Blanchard, who had been helping him in the galley when the dive began. Next were Gerry McLees and Charlie Yuhas, both of whom seemed particularly affected by the cold. The fifth man was Ted Jacobs, who continued to vomit following his exhausting assignment to hammer messages on the hull through the night.

One by one Mihalowski and Harmon helped them into the upper compartment of the chamber. After they were all seated, Mihalowski ran down an air hose and ventilated the forward torpedo room. After that, Harmon announced, "Submarine hatch closed. Ready to come up."

Momsen ordered a thousand pounds of ballast dumped from the auxiliary cans to compensate for the added weight of the seven passengers so that positive buoyancy would be maintained.

"Ballast blown," Harmon reported.

"Unbolt," Momsen said. "Flood lower compartment. Blow main ballast tank."

It took fourteen minutes. "Seal broken," Harmon said. "Coming up."

The chamber slowly rose, its air motor chugging away in reverse, the reel unwinding the cable attached to the hatch cover on the *Squalus.* On the *Falcon,* the up-haul cable was taken in.

The seven dazed survivors inside the chamber said little. None of them had been in one before, and finally Will Isaacs asked, "Are we being pulled up by the *Falcon*?"

"No," Harmon said. "That motor your hear runs a reel that takes us up and down."

"Oh," Isaacs said.

As the chamber neared the surface, it could be seen by correspondents in a half-dozen planes circling low over the sea. With about thirty feet to go, it looked to a New York *Daily News* reporter like "a great green blob." Then it broke through the slight swell, less than fifteen feet from the *Falcon*. Boat hooks quickly brought it alongside, and two sailors scrambled down to open the hatch.

Lieutenant Nichols was the first to stick his head up. Cheers erupted from the ships surrounding him. Nichols blinked in the sunlight and faltered briefly as he tried to climb out. Hands from the *Falcon* stretched out to help him on board.

Harold Preble followed him. As he stood unsteadily on deck, he spied Momsen, with whom he had been having the dispute about the accuracy of the stopwatches he had supplied the experimental diving unit. He hugged Momsen with a big grin. The first thing he said was, "Swede, I'll get some new watches to you right away."

Once all the others were on the Falcon, Commander Andrew McKee, an officer on Cole's staff who had been involved in some of Momsen's early experiments, looked at him in amazement. "Gosh, Swede," he said, "how can you be so calm at a time like this?"

Recounting this later in notes to himself, Momsen wrote, "Maybe I missed my calling. I didn't know I was such a good actor. Perhaps I tried to appear calm, but to me this was the most exciting moment in my life. Eleven years of preparation, combating skepticism and trying to anticipate all sorts of possible disasters—and then to have it all telescoped into this one moment. Who could stay calm?"

On the *Falcon's* deck under the glare of floodlights, the North Atlantic night sky moonless and starless, Momsen moved to meet a reversal all the more malevolent because it came just when everything appeared to be going so well, the ocean seemingly cheated of victims it had routinely claimed as a matter of course.

If anything, the rescue chamber's fourth descent was the smoothest yet. Exactly one hour after it had left the surface, Jim McDonald reported that the hatch of the *Squalus* was being opened to receive the final group of officers and crew. The men quickly entered it. As commanding officer, Naquin was the last to abandon the sub, dogging down the hatch himself. He noted the time, nine minutes to eight. To no one in particular, he said, "We're out of the boat." There was a tone of sadness in his voice.

Twenty minutes later, the seal was broken. With the main ballast being blown, the chamber started reeling itself up. At about 160 feet, it happened. The chamber stopped rising. Over the phone, Momsen heard McDonald say, "The wire is jammed on the reel."

Before Momsen could respond, McDonald reported more bad news. Under this unexpected stress, the air motor that operated the reel conked out. Desperately, McDonald and Mihalowski tried to coax it into starting again. But it wouldn't turn over.

"Increase buoyancy and try riding the brake," Momsen said.

The brake was normally used to control the chamber as it neared the surface. Increasing the buoyancy while braking might loosen the cable. For a second, it appeared to solve the problem. But after rising a few feet, the chamber would not budge another inch.

"Well, we're stuck," McDonald said, his voice flat and emotionless.

Momsen made a last stab at clearing the reel. A second cable, called the retrieving wire, ran from the top of the chamber to a winch on the *Falcon*. "Stand by," he informed McDonald. "We're going to heave on the retrieving wire." But that didn't work either. Loose turns on the down-haul cable had allowed it to jump the reel and table beyond repair.

It was useless to fool around with it anymore. The fouled down-haul cable had to be unshackled from the *Squalus*. To get some slack in it, Momsen ordered McDonald to flood his main ballast. At the same time he had the retrieving wire payed out. The chamber slowly sank. When it had reached to 210 feet, he instructed McDonald to hold it there.

A diver would have to descend into the black depths to finish the job. Momsen picked Chief Torpedoman Walter Squire, a powerfully built, two-hundred-pounder, to do it.

Just after nine o'clock, Squire went over the side. He slid down the same hawser that Sibitsky had traveled along that morning. Squire found himself in an eerie world. Off to one side as he landed on the sub, he could see the lights inside the chamber.

Never was the fact that the *Penacook* had hooked the *Squalus* so close to the forward escape hatch more crucial. Guided by a small battery-run light on his helmet, he bent to his task. He tried to unshackle the cabin from the ring on the hatch. And failed. He tried again in vain. Momsen could hear his labored breathing. "I can't unshackle the wire," Squire gasped. "It's too taut."

"Stay where you are," Momsen instructed. "We will send you wire cutters."

Once armed with the big shears, Squire groped for the cable and found it. Staving off nitrogen narcosis, he kept repeating, "I must cut the wire." On the surface, Momsen listened to him grunt with exertion. "I have the cutters around the wire," he was saying to himself. The seconds passed. Then, with his strength ebbing, Squire chopped through the cable. "I have cut the wire," he announced.

"That is fine," Momsen said. "We are bringing you up."

As Squire was lifted off the deck, he could see the chamber swinging free, actually brushing the side of the sub's conning tower.

On the *Falcon*, Momsen allowed himself his first easy breath since the reel had jammed. With the chamber unshackled, it could be hoisted to the surface on the retrieving-cable winch. From inside the chamber, McDonald sang out their progress, "We are at two hundred and ten feet. Going up smoothly."

The ascent continued at a steady five feet per minute.

On the crowded fantail of the *Falcon*, everyone watched as the cable came out of the sea. Suddenly, before their horrified eyes, its individual steel strands began to unravel. The strain was too great. Somewhere along the line, they had parted.

Momsen was dumbfounded. But unbeknownst to him, he was not working with a single length of cable. It had been too short and an extra piece had been spliced on. Overall, the cable still should have been strong enough, but it was actually made up of a bunch of separate strands that were wound together. Clamps used in the splicing had slipped, and this in turn produced an uneven pull on the strands. Under the tension they were now being subjected to, Momsen thought, they must have popped like firecrackers down below.

As soon as he spotted the cable unraveling, he issued a stop order for the winch hoisting the chamber. While he had been apprehensive about a breakdown of some sort, he had not counted on one mishap after another. But there was no time to spare fretting over this. McDonald had last placed the chamber at a depth of 195 feet. To save what was left of the cable, Momsen ordered him to flood his main ballast tank.

The chamber slowly dropped to the bottom.

"What's your depth?" Momsen asked.

"The gauge reads two hundred and thirty-two feet," McDonald replied.

Momsen and Allen McCann were in instant and absolute agreement as to the next step. A diver would have to go down to attach a new retrieving cable.

It was now nine-thirty. And the eight remaining survivors of the *Squalus* disaster, instead of being readied for their transfer back to Portsmouth, were right back where they started—on the ocean floor.

They sat in a tight circle on the auxiliary ballast cans. Besides the two officers, Naquin and Doyle, there were Charles Kuney, who had manned the control room battle phone, and Allen Bryson, the forward battery talker, neither of whom would ever forget the awful plea to surface they had heard from the after compartments. In the chamber with them were Donny Persico, the seaman who just missed being crushed by the dummy torpedo that went wild as the sub was sinking, and Carol Pierce, who had futilely sent thousands of pounds of pressurized air into the ballast tanks. There were, finally, Gene Cravens, who had fired off rocket after rocket during their long wait, and Charles Powell, the radioman whom Naquin had kept with him till the end in case additional hammered messages on the hull became necessary between rescue trips.

They were in no immediate physical danger. The chamber was unheated and they still suffered cruelly from the cold. But they had light and a continuous flow of fresh air, and communications with the *Falcon* were excellent.

Even signs of psychological stress were absent. All through the early phase of the ascent and the subsequent attempts to unsnarl the jammed reel, they had remained silent. Now, as they waited for deliverance from the bottom, Momsen caught snatches of banter.

When the chamber, free of the down-haul cable, bumped into the side of the conning tower, McDonald had said, "Hey, that's a Ripley Believe It or Not. A collision between a rescue chamber and a sub more than two hundred feet down. Can't beat that."

Mihalowski broke off pieces from a couple of chocolate bars he had and passed them around.

"How about a steak?" Kuney said.

"That's for topside. I'll call up your order. How do you want it?"

"Well done."

"I want mine rare," Pierce said.

"You got it," McDonald said. Then, to Momsen's amazement, he heard him lead them in a rendition of "Old MacDonald Had a Farm."

One Squire was back on board, another diver, Torpedoman First Class Jesse Duncan, was lowered into the pitch-black sea to hook up a new retrieving cable. But as he followed the stranded cable down, he ran into major trouble. When he was just above the chamber, the lines from it and his own became fouled. The effort to untangle himself took every ounce of energy he could muster. Every time he tried, the new cable he was clutching in his right hand would jerk him up. Now his whole arm seemed paralyzed.

"I have a problem," he said. Duncan was exhaling more carbon dioxide—"smoke," the divers called it—than the ventilating system in his helmet could handle.

"Talk to me," Momsen quietly said.

"I . . . I . . . I don't . . . I," he mumbled. On the verge of passing out, he had become incoherent.

He had to be hauled up—and fast. He was rushed into the *Falcon's* recompression chamber where he would be put under the same ocean pressure he faced below and then brought out of it in easy stages.

But first he managed to pass on hair-raising news. The break in the cable was worse than anyone imagined. All that remained intact was a single strand of steel about the thickness of ordinary string.

The prospect of sending down another diver who might end up the same way was harrowing. But the condition of the retrieving cable made it imperative. "We're just going to have to risk it," Momsen told Cole.

The assignment went to Metalsmith First Class Ed Clayton. To give him a fighting chance, Momsen ordered a thousand-watt underwater lamp lowered separately. During Clayton's descent, however, the lamp got caught in the stranded section of the old cable. He kept going down anyhow until he arrived on top of the rescue chamber. Time after time, he attempted to attach the new cable. There was light coming from the chamber's eyeports, but not enough to really see what he was doing.

Still, in an extraordinary display of determination, Clayton refused to give up. Squire, for instance, had spent a total of eight minutes on the bottom cutting the down-haul cable. Squire was down fifteen minutes trying to do what Clayton was now attempting. Finally, after thirty-three minutes, Clayton's own lines were tangling. His hands encased in rubberized canvas gloves were so cold that he had no feeling in them. The despair in his voice was increasingly evident. He spoke haltingly. Momsen sensed that he was near to blacking out.

"I'm bringing you up," he said.

For Momsen, to send down still a third diver was out of the question. As it was, there had been two dangerously close calls with men of matchless ability trying to connect a new cable. If they couldn't do it, nobody could. Yet somehow those cornered in the rescue chamber had to be saved. Nor was there any time to lose. There was a limit to what their nerves could withstand. The weather, while not getting worse, wasn't getting any better.

After discussing the foreboding situation with Cole and McCann, Momsen decided on a last-ditch, all-or-nothing strategy. "It's a gamble, but we don't have any choice," he told Cole. The plan he unfolded was breathtaking.

They could no longer use the *Falcon's* unyielding winch to hoist the chamber. A sudden swell that sent the ship rolling despite her five-point mooring could instantly snap that one remaining strand of wire. What had happened to the marker-buoy line was a stark reminder to them all. If that occurred again, the chamber with its human cargo and operators would be irretrievably lost.

So Momsen instead would direct the chamber's operators to blow ballast so that it remained ever so slightly below neutral buoyancy. That way, the strain on the cable would be minimal and, despite its damaged state, it could be used to haul the chamber up. The catch was that the hauling had to be done by hands sensitive to the *Falcon's* stability.

And it would require exquisite timing.

Once Cole's consent was obtained, Momsen got on the phone to McDonald. He explained the scenario and told him, "Whenever you get the word, I want you to blow ballast exactly as long as I tell you. If you gain positive buoyancy, let us know immediately."

It was, literally, down to the wire. Ten men took hold of the cable, Momsen in front, McCann right behind him. Tensely watching officers and sailors crowded the starboard side of the *Falcon*. Binoculars were at a premium aboard the cruiser *Brooklyn* and the other ships in the rescue fleet.

At precisely midnight, Momsen had the slack in the retrieving cable drawn tight. He ordered McDonald to blow ballast for fifteen seconds.

There was no response from the chamber.

He called for fifteen seconds more.

Still, there was nothing.

It was absolutely silent on the Falcon's deck save for the sound of Momsen's voice. His only guide was the strain on the cable that he felt through his fingers. If he miscalculated and the chamber blew too much ballast, it would hurtle to the surface with every likelihood of splitting itself wide open as it smashed into the hull of the *Falcon*. And if he did not lighten it sufficiently, the single strand holding the chamber would part, sending it tumbling back down, its fragile air hoses broken, the lives of the men inside snuffed out.

For the third time, Momsen told McDonald, "Blow ballast fifteen seconds." He knew he was edging perilously close to positive buoyancy. But the chamber still did not move when he ordered a tentative tug on the cable. Another fifteen seconds of blowing main ballast would leave it half-empty.

He ordered it. Afterward, the strain on the cable seemed to ease. At Momsen's command, everyone in the hauling crew braced himself on the deck and heaved up. The cable slowly came over the side. The chamber at last had begun to rise. One minute later, it had risen four feet. It was now off the bottom, suspended at 228 feet.

The silence within the chamber was punctuated only by McDonald's acknowledgment of each order from Momsen to blow ballast and then the rush of air as it was done. He and John Mihalowski, his usual broad grin gone, worked in swift, cool tandem in the cramped space of the chamber's upper compartment as they operated the levers controlling its buoyancy—and their fate.

After four minutes had gone by, McDonald reported, "Depth gauge reads two hundred feet."

"What's your buoyancy?" Momsen wanted to know.

"For some reason, we're a little heavy," McDonald said.

Momsen ordered ten seconds of blowing ballast.

On the surface the swells were running six feet. The men hauling in the cable always went with the motion of the *Falcon*, letting it out a bit whenever she rose, pulling in when she dipped. Foot by foot the chamber continued up.

It was bitingly cold on deck, but Momsen could feel the sweat trickling down his back as again and again he and his men brought in more cable.

Suddenly a rogue swell swept in. A lookout spotted it just in time. If the chamber had been connected to the winch, that would have been the end of everything.

"We are at seventy-five feet," McDonald reported.

Then the moment arrived that Momsen had been waiting for. Out of the ocean came the break in the cable, the water dripping from it glistening in the *Falcon's* floodlights. He watched it inch toward him. Squire had been right. Only a single strand of wire was left. The temptation to give one last yank, to get this all over with, was almost irresistible. And then at last it was over. A deckhand was able to get a clamp around the cable below the break.

The rest was simple. Steadily now they hauled the cable up and saw the chamber bob to the surface right next to the *Falcon*. The long journey home had been completed.

The time was 0038, May 25. Almost to the minute, it was thirty-nine hours since the *Squalus* had begun her test dive.

The last survivor of the disaster to climb out of the chamber was Naquin. Momsen stood by as he was helped onto the *Falcon's* deck.

"Welcome aboard, Oliver," Momsen delightedly said.

"I'm damned glad to be aboard, believe me," Naquin replied, shaking his hand.

Admiral Cole took Momsen aside and told him in an emotion-filled voice, "Swede, a 'well done' doesn't begin to express my feelings."

In Portsmouth, Hanson W. Baldwin, covering the story for the *New York Times*, filed his lead for the late city edition. An Annapolis graduate himself, Baldwin wrote, "Man won a victory from the sea early this morning."

All in a Day's Work

From *Heartbreak and Heroism*

BY JOHN MELADY

In the spring of 1975, during one of the worst storms ever to hit southern British Columbia, one pararescue jumper helped save 11 people stranded in turbulent waters over a 12 hour period. His unique story of bravery is chronicled by John Melady.

★   ★   ★   ★   ★

S hortly before midnight on Saturday, March 30, 1975, one of the worst storms in history lashed the coast of British Columbia. Before the gale blew itself out some twenty hours later, several people were dead, scores were injured, and property damage was in the millions. As well, untold numbers were inconvenienced in a myriad of ways, through such things as hydro interruptions, ferry cancellations, washed out roads and flooded basements.

At the height of the storm, winds were clocked at eighty to eighty-five miles per hour in several locations and the driving rain made travel of any kind virtually impossible. Throughout the lower mainland, from the coast to Kamloops, power lines were down, traffic lights were dark, and mature trees were twisted and torn from their roots. A heavy snowfall blanketed the Hope-Princeton highway.

In the Vancouver area, Stanley Park had to be closed, half a dozen ocean-going ferries dragged their anchors in English Bay, and fifteen light planes were either flipped over or badly damaged at the airport. Others would have been destroyed, had not their owners arrived to physically hold the machines down. A few were saved only because they were lashed to cars, trucks and steel fence posts embedded in concrete. A house under construction in Delta was flattened.

One of the large B.C. ferries, *Queen of Tsawwassen*, was tossed around during the gale and ended up with several gouges and dents in her hull, along with a bent propeller. The vessel had to be removed from service. At one point, all ferries between Vancouver and Vancouver Island were stopped, their cancellations resulting in hundreds of motorists lined up for boats that were not going to sail. Those in the vehicles spent hours in their cars, virtually marooned where they were. Fortunately, their plight was eased somewhat through the efforts of civil defense workers who brought them blankets and hot coffee.

Depending on the location, the storm was at its fiercest between 10:00 P.M. that Saturday and 2:00 A.M. the following day. In Victoria, the Armed Forces Rescue Co-ordination Centre received fifty-nine calls for help in those four hours alone. Most were from boaters in distress, who feared they were in danger of death, or at least imminent harm. In such cases, assistance was rendered as soon as conditions and available personnel permitted.

At Canadian Forces Base Comox, midway up the eastern coast of Vancouver Island and home of Search and Rescue Squadron 442, the first grey streaks of daylight were filtering over the mainland mountains as an Air Force Labrador helicopter was readied for work. Crew call-out had been at 5:10 A.M., and despite the high winds, the big chopper was in the air before 6:00. The pilots that morning were Captain Wilkinson and Major Carr-Hilton. In the back of the ship, the flight engineers were Master Corporals Kennedy and Meider. In 1975, only one Search and Rescue Technician was normally a part of the crew complement. On this day, it would be Master Corporal Bill Wacey, an Ottawa-born Para Rescue specialist who had come to the air force after three years in the army. He was 39 years old.

The Lab headed south, threading its way among the numerous islands that dot the Strait of Georgia. Just off tiny Ballenas, the anchored sailboat *Sly II* strained at her lines, both of which were being taxed beyond their capabilities. However, when Corporal Meider used a loud hailer to contact a couple who were on the yacht, they declined assistance, so the chopper moved on the Active Pass, a stretch of water between Galiano and Mayne Islands. "That was when our day *really* started," recalls Wacey. "We found four teenagers, two guys and two girls, all of them hanging onto a catamaran that was about to be smashed to smithereens against boulders along the shore. Those kids were wet, cold and scared."

The four had been in the wrong place at the wrong time. Several hours earlier, a coast guard hovercraft had been responding to a distress call, and because of the wild winds and rain, and the state of the sea at the time, it collided with the catamaran. The hovercraft was beached, and the young people had to fend for themselves.

"They were pretty happy to see us," Wacey says. "By the time we got there, they were pretty upset."

One of the flight engineers hooked himself into a safety harness and opened the door on the right side of the helicopter. The other cleared space in the back of the ship for passengers, while Wacey checked and rechecked his equipment, prior to going to the stricken vessel below them. He was already in a wetsuit.

"The winds must have been sixty or seventy miles an hour at that point," he says. "The chopper was bouncing all over the place, and the waves were really high. It was also raining."

Wacey was hooked onto the hoist cable and slowly winched down to the catamaran. The process took time, because the boat would rise to the top of a wave and then would immediately plunge into a trough. Often Wacey was almost on the deck only to be yanked into the sky when the boat dropped away under him. While all this was happening, the aircraft was being buffeted unmercifully as the pilots fought to remain in one place.

Finally, Wacey reached the boat and got a horsecollar rescue sling around one of the girls. He signaled to the hoist operator up above, and held on to the young woman as they were pulled to safety. Wacey then went back down—three more times—and got the others. On the final hoist, however, he had trouble.

"I had just put the harness on the last guy," Wacey explains, "when the boat went out from under us. The two of us went down under the hull and the waves threw us against it. I was wearing a hard hat, so when my head banged against the board, I was okay."

The young man was not so lucky.

"When he hit the hull, I heard a crack, and he broke his jaw, but I managed to hold onto him until the hoist operator got us up out of there. The boy was hurt and bleeding so we laid him down and worked on him until we got to the hospital in Victoria. The poor kid was okay until I rescued him," says Wacey with a twinkle in his eye. "But he had a real sense of humour. On the way to the hospital he was trying to talk to me, and at one point said, 'My mother is going to be *mad* at you.' I asked him why and he tried to laugh when he said, 'Because you don't know how much she's spent on my teeth.' Several of them were loosened."

Even before the Lab reached the helipad at Victoria, the crew was informed of another problem near the ferry terminal at Tsawwassen. The teenagers were quickly turned over to the hospital emergency people, and within five minutes the chopper was back in the air.

"It was another sailboat," recalled Wacey, "this time maybe twenty-five to thirty feet long, with lots of cables, gear, and ropes all over the deck."

On board were two adults and two children, both youngsters under six years of age. The boat was sinking fast, and although it was not too far from the ferry terminal, people watching from there were powerless to assist. The seas were much too rough.

"We swung around over them," says Wacey, but with all the gear on the deck down there, I knew I'd never be able to drop on it. I wondered then, and I still wonder today, why people don't toss stuff overboard when they're in real trouble. Making the boat lighter could keep them from sinking.

"Anyway, I talked things over with the engineers, and decided to have them put me in the water behind the boat and I would swim to it."

Corporal Kennedy hooked Wacey to the hoist, and he started down. The winds had slackened somewhat but the operation was far from easy. Just as the would-be rescuer touched the water, a swell pulled him under and dragged him, spitting and sputtering, away from the boat. Wacey got his bearings, then swung around and swam back towards it. As he grabbed a deck cable, another wave slammed him against the hull.

"Finally I was able to grab one of the kids," Wacey remembers, "but the little guy was so small, I was afraid he would flip out of the harness, so I just held onto him. We hoisted him over to the ferry dock and set him down. I told him to stay there and I would get his parents. He was crying through the whole thing."

On the dock itself, a spectator named John Garnham watched in awe as the operation took place. He would later describe the "hell of a courageous" helicopter crew for the March 31, 1975 *Vancouver Sun*.

"The chopper was having difficulty stabilizing itself about fifty feet above the boat," he said. "Finally they let a man down on a wire. He was swinging like a child on a swing and even fell into the water once. He harnessed up one of the kids and got him off, then the other. Then the chopper dropped the kids off on the causeway and went back for the parents."

"We got them all to safety," said Wacey, "but the boat was gone. Then we left."

In fact, a radio call directed Captain Wilkinson to pick up a very frightened woman from Saturna Island, midway between Vancouver and Victoria. "She had broken a leg trying to pull a sailboat in, but apart from that, was okay," says Wacey. "We dropped her off at the hospital in Victoria. She was also pretty worried about getting off the island, I guess," he adds. "She was hardly out of the helicopter when another call came in. This time we flew over to Mayne Island to pick up two girls."

This call would be even less pleasant than the ones that preceded it.

Two young women had been camping in a wooded area when the storm came up. At first, apparently, they felt it would pass and remained huddled in their tent as the rains swept over it. As the winds strengthened however, the tent was little protection for the two. A tall pine tree behind their shelter was ripped apart and it crashed onto the tent. The full weight of the trunk came down on 19-year-old Ottawa native Dierdre Jacques and crushed her skull. Her friend, Teresa Wojcihowicz, suffered serious back injuries in the incident.

"Both were in terrible shape when we got there," Bill Wacey explains. "The victim whose skull was crushed was unconscious, so I administered oxygen and used a syringe to help clear the blood out of her throat. The other woman was conscious at first and I looked after her as best I could."

Both the injured parties were placed in litters on the ground and hoisted into the chopper, which hovered just above the trees.

"They were alive when we got them into the helicopter," Wacey continues, "but I don't know to this day if either survived. I know I was awfully glad when we touched down at Vancouver General. I felt so bad for both of them. They never had a chance."

Several hours later, the hospital listed Teresa Wojcihowicz's condition as poor, but the injuries sustained by Dierdre Jacques had proven fatal.

"We got fuel sometime during the day," Wacey recalls, "and I grabbed a sandwich. I know I was still gulping it down when we got called again. A couple of boats had foundered just off Point Grey."

About 2:00 P.M., a nineteen-foot rented fishing boat carrying four males from Edmonton encountered choppy sea conditions at the mouth of the north arm of the Fraser River. As water sloshed into their craft, the occupants baled for their lives, but their efforts were in vain. The little vessel continued taking on water and within minutes slid beneath the waves. The four started swimming, but the cold, rough water was just too overpowering.

At about the same time, three people in an outboard who came to help ran into trouble. Their boat was tossed all over the place by the surf, and then it flipped upside down. Now several souls were fighting for their lives.

By the time the big Lab appeared overhead, two men from the second boat had struggled up onto a beach, where they huddled together in a futile attempt to get warm. Wacey was lowered to them—twice—and each was hoisted into the helicopter.

"Both were suffering from exposure," he said. "I treated them on board the aircraft, and I was sure they would pull though. Then one of the engineers noticed another guy in a lifejacket floating in the water, so I went down again.

"It was a young boy, 13 or 14 I supposed. He was still alive, but was unconscious so I had a bit of a struggle getting him up. I started mouth-to-mouth as soon as we got him into the chopper, and I continued on the way to the hospital, but he was dead when we got there."

The helicopter returned to Point Grey and located one of the men from the first boat. Wacey was lowered to him.

"By this time, I had been in and out of the water so many times, I was exhausted. I knew he was pretty bad so I started mouth-to-mouth as soon as I got down to the guy. I kept doing so until I noticed that he had sand in his mouth and I realized that I was giving mouth-to-mouth to a corpse. We turned him over to the Vancouver RCMP. When there was no sign of anyone else, we left."

But Bill Wacey's day was still not over. The man and woman on the *Sly II* who had refused help in the early morning now needed late-afternoon assistance.

"I think they tried to hold on as long as they could," Wacey says, with a touch of admiration in his tone, "but they finally found it impossible. When we got to them, they had only one line out, and they were on the top of the yacht, holding on for dear life. They also had their dog with them.

"I knew for sure they were coming up, and that the dog was as well when I saw the woman putting a coat on it, a scared little poodle.

"In the morning, I'd been reasonably sharp, but by the time of those last hoists, I was so tired I could hardly think, and I was careless. When hoisting from a boat where there are ropes and stuff on the deck, you always make sure none of them are around your feet or legs. As I was bringing the man up though, there was a cable around my foot and I didn't even notice. I was really lucky because I was able to shake it off partway up.

"Those folks were so pleasant, and they kept thanking me and the other guys. I really don't think they expected to survive. They were from Van Nuys, California. And even though we rarely hear from people we might have rescued, I did hear from them. We took them into Nanaimo."

It was dusk when the helicopter got back to Comox. The crew members disembarked and walked into the hangar. Wacey phoned his wife.

"I called Maureen to pick me up," he laughs, "but when she asked if I really needed a ride, I told her I guessed not. She had to have the car for something or other. I sure could have used a lift, but I didn't bother telling her that I had had a hard day. I walked home alone. Later on, when she heard what I had gone through since early morning, she felt bad."

In his report of his day's activities, for which he was later awarded the Star of Courage for bravery, Bill Wacey wrote: "We conducted 12 double hoists, 11 were survivors, 1 was dead. There were three stretcher patients, 2 critical. We recovered 2 bodies and also recovered 2 people alive (no hoists involved). We searched and refueled in between and took two Coast Guard members to hovercraft. We flew a total of 9.5 hours and I was in a wetsuit for 12 hours."

His conclusion was the ultimate in understatement: "Rather weary."

He didn't mention the poodle.

The Most Dangerous Occupation

From *Coming Back Alive*

The coastal waters of Alaska are probably among the worst places in the world to effect a sea rescue. Yet Spike Walker's *Coming Back Alive* tells of one such mission which has taken on legendary status over the years: how a US Coast Guard helicopter and rescue swimmer came to the aid of a father and his young son as they were about to be swept off a fishing boat into turbulent seas.

★ ★ ★ ★ ★

During the summer months, Jim Blades made a good living trolling commercially from the *Bluebird* for both king and coho salmon. During the rest of the year, whenever the weather permitted, he long-lined for bottom-feeders offshore, specifically codfish and red snapper.

The boat's trolling poles were twenty-five feet long and made of spruce wood. When the boat was underway, the poles were stored upright, tucked in tightly against the wheelhouse. When fishing, Jim lowered the poles, secured them, and extended them out on either side of the *Bluebird* at a forty-five-degree angle, providing stability to the small vessel, in much the same way a balancing pole aids a gymnast during a tightrope walk. Over the years, Blades had become so sensitive to the feel of his boat that, while trolling, he could often determine the weight of the salmon striking the lure by the trembling transmitted to the hull through the poles.

Jim Blades often took his son Clint on fishing excursions. Though only six years old at the time, the youngster could already be counted on to contribute to the work effort in a meaningful way.

Just before Christmas, while fishing for codfish near Cape Edgecumbe on the far edge of Sitka Sound, only a dozen or so wilderness miles from home, Blades and his son encountered the exceptional.

From the outset, the fishing that day had been excellent, and Clint and his father were quickly caught up in the excitement and steady action of pulling fish after fish aboard. They hooked, landed, cleaned, and iced some six hundred pounds of ling cod. At a $1.70 a pound, Blades would pocket about $1,000 for the day's work. With Christmas only two weeks away, such a profit would be a welcome boon.

It was only 3:00 P.M. when another long December's night in the far north fell upon them. The advancing darkness and the lucrative day of fishing set Jim Blades to figuring. I should run back in now, he thought. It was a judgment call, but with two intimidating reefs, Low Island and Vitskari Rocks, lying between him and home, he hesitated.

Smooth swells twenty to thirty feet high had been rolling through the area all day, but with no wave tops capping them, riding over them had been no problem.

Fatigued as he was, and with no working radar on board, he decided not to attempt the two-hour run back into town. He and Clint would catch up on their sleep and pick up where they left off on the fine fishing first thing the next morning.

I'll just ride it out here in the lee of St. Lazaria Island tonight, he decided finally.

Jim Blades radioed his wife and told her of his decision. He might have trouble with his anchor dragging on the rock bottom there, but he wanted to sit out the night behind St. Lazaria Island anyway and wait for dawn.

Jill wasn't exactly crazy about the idea but said she would leave the final decision in the matter to her husband.

"Okay, then, take care," she radioed. "Love ya! Talk to you in the morning," she added, signing off.

Jill switched off the radio, shut off the lights, and climbed up into the loft of their one-room A-frame cabin. Then, as her three-year-old son, Curt, quietly crayoned in his picture book on the bed beside her, she sat and read.

"Daddy will be home in the morning," she told him.

Blades would have been hard-pressed to pick a more picturesque spot. Located on the farthest edge of Sitka Sound, St. Lazaria Island is a bird sanctuary, the breeding ground of literally millions of seabirds and a National Wildlife Refuge since 1909. The protected anchorage behind it is a favorite of local fishermen.

As he dropped anchor in the lee of the island, countless gulls and murres and comical-looking tufted puffins looped noisily out from their cliff-side dwellings before returning again to their precarious perches. St. Lazaria is only a few miles from Cape Edgecumbe and the Fuji-like form of Mount Edgecumbe rising on the island of Kruzof.

Generally, Blades knew, there were telltale signs that warned a fisherman of an approaching storm as much as a day in advance. Usually, he would detect some cat's-paws, the strange moving islands of rippling water where gusts of wind touch down as if pawing at the ocean's surface. Under such circumstances, one might expect a storm by the following morning.

On this night, however, there was little evidence of approaching danger. It looked to be a decent night to lay up and ride it out. But several hours later, sudden thirty-mile-per-hour gusts of wind arrived without so much as a hint of warning. They, in turn, were followed by punishing gusts of thirty-five and then forty miles per hour. Within minutes, a blast of wind approaching seventy miles per hour came hurtling around the island's granite cliffs, roaring through the spruce trees and imprinting the water before whistling off through the *Bluebird's* rigging.

As the seas rose into breakers, the *Bluebird* began to shift restlessly at anchor. Jim Blades found himself surrounded by the close yellow glow of the ship's cabin light; beyond that lay a larger theater, a seamless curtain of impenetrable darkness.

Now the swirling wind began making bizarre course changes. Blinding volleys of jetting snow shot past them. Jim knew then that he'd been caught out in the open by an intense little storm cell, the type Alaskan meteorologists often refer to as "bombs."

This doesn't look good, he thought as the abrupt rock formations of St. Lazaria Island rose and fell before him. Then Blades turned to his son. "Clint, go put on your survival suit," he said.

Working the hydraulics from inside the *Bluebird*, he winched his anchor back aboard and got under way. He wanted to escape the gnarly breakers now surging up and down on the cliffs before him. Following his compass, he idled slowly past the cliffs and through the slapping seas in the lee of the island.

As the storm intensified, the craggy rock shoreline of the island in front of him disappeared altogether in the blinding blizzard. Amid the disorienting flurries, Jim Blades tried to calculate where the protruding rocks had been and to navigate accordingly.

Caught in outside waters, without radar, running in the blind, Jim Blades fixed his eyes on the only dependable navigation device he had left—the little red compass light mounted on the panel in front of him.

He was feathering the throttle, trying to maintain his course, going the way that he thought he should be going, when the pitching *Bluebird* crunched down on a pinnacle of rock. The pointed crown of the Volkswagen-sized boulder pierced the wooden hull of the boat. Then came the echoing crunch of wood rending, much like the sound of a sledgehammer striking a watermelon. Blades threw her into reverse and floored it. Pivoting, he bolted anew. Seconds later, seeking his escape through the vision-obliterating snow squall in the opposite direction, his beloved *Bluebird* plowed bow-first into the cliff face of St. Lazaria Island. Bringing the boat around once more, Blades once again reversed his course. He was now certain that he knew the way out. As he motored ahead, waves exploded against the cliffs on one side and roared in among upright pillars of rock on the other. Passing nervously by the rock upon which his boat had previously been impaled, Blades slipped gladly into deeper waters.

With the destructive sounds of the impact still echoing in his ears, Jim Blades didn't even bother going below for a closer inspection. He knew that the ship was sinking and that they had very little time. As if to reaffirm this belief, the automobile horn that he'd cleverly rigged to his bilge alarm sounded. He grabbed the wire and tore it free, silencing the blaring noise. Then he grabbed his radio mike and called for assistance.

"Mayday! Mayday!" he called. "This is the fishing vessel *Bluebird*! The fishing vessel *Bluebird*! Mayday! Mayday!"

"Fishing vessel *Bluebird*, this is the U.S. Coast Guard, Sitka," came the quick reply. "Sir, please give us your name, your location, and the condition of your vessel."

"Sitka Coast Guard, this is the fishing vessel *Bluebird*," he replied. "My name is Jim Blades, and you had better send someone out to get us, because I'm sinking fast here off St. Lazaria Island. I hit a rock pretty hard. I've got my six-year-old boy on board with me here. I don't know how long we'll be able to remain afloat. Over."

As the Coast Guard gathered information and rushed to prepare for the mission ahead, an anonymous voice of a fellow fisherman sounded over Jim Blades's CB radio.

"Hang in there, Jim!" encouraged the voice. "You're going to be all right. Just keep jockeying."

Blades found comfort in those words.

★   ★   ★   ★   ★

To rescue swimmer Jeff Tunks, on duty at the USCG base in Sitka at the time, the Mayday sounded urgent. The situation was obviously critical. Pilot John Whiddon informed Tunks that they would debrief while en route to the scene.

With thirteen years of aviator experience under his belt, Cmdr. John Whiddon would do the flying, while Lt. Greg Breithaupt would ride shotgun as his copilot. Tunks would go as the mission's rescue swimmer. Carl Saylor would run the hoist, and Mark Mylne would ride along as their avionics man.

It took Tunks and his crewmates just eighteen minutes to roll out the H-3 helo, fuel it up, load it up, and prepare for liftoff.

The model HH-3F "Pelican" helicopter (or just H-3, as most Coasties refer to it) is a large, powerful, and very dependable workhorse of an aircraft. It has two jet engines and a semiamphibious hull that can be used to land on water to facilitate a rescue, so long as the weather and conditions are relatively calm. If the rotor blades plow into a wave in heavy seas, however, the aircraft will flip over and fill with water as quickly as a capsized canoe.

That night, it was raining furiously outside. A building wind blowing in off the sound was driving the inch-an-hour rainfall horizontally. Sheets of it were inundating the area, tumbling across the airfield's apron and out across the ramp.

While the helicopter's jet engines were warming up, and before her main rotor blades were engaged, Tunks sat in the rear cabin, looking out through the side door of the H-3. From there, he could see the long rotor blades extending out from directly overhead. Now, in the gusting winds, the long, flat blades began leaping up and down like diving boards bouncing in the wind.

The blades of the helicopter had only just begun to turn, when a gust of wind rolled in off Sitka Sound, pounding against the metal sides of the hangar nearby and scooting the eleven-ton helicopter several yards across the runway.

"We've got a boat sinking off St. Lazaria Island," said Commander Whiddon, climbing into the pilot's seat and strapping himself in. "We're going to go out and see how we can help."

Sitka Sound in winter, Tunks knew, is a brutal place. The seas are often short, choppy, and unforgiving. Should a mechanical failure force them down on this night, there would be no backup. Of the three choppers stationed at the Sitka base, one was currently down for repairs, and another was on patrol well north of them, outside of Cordova. Only theirs remained.

They had hardly risen clear of the circular helicopter pad when their loran-C computer shut down. Whiddon rose to the standard altitude of three hundred feet, where, in the cooler atmosphere, he encountered a wall of swirling snow. He found it both disorienting and hypnotizing, and ultimately, blinding. Nevertheless, Whiddon continued on, closing determinedly on their destination. As he did so, he encountered fierce storm winds tearing around Cape Edgecumbe and accelerating down off the steep slopes of Mount Edgecumbe itself. They were closing on St. Lazaria Island when they were besieged by the battering nine-mile-per-hour gusts.

Under favorable conditions, a pilot might hover within fifty feet or so of the ocean's surface and those he hoped to rescue. But on this night, at an altitude of seventy-five feet, Whiddon found that he was being pelted not only with blowing snow but freezing sea spray, as well. Shortly, the face of the radar screen outside became so coated in ice, it ceased functioning altogether. Worse yet, the gale-force winds were driving into them with such velocity, and in such irregular bursts, Whiddon knew it would be impossible to maintain anything like a stationary hover. With his navigational equipment now dead and only his altimeter and horizon-leveler instruments to guide him, Whiddon flew on.

"*Bluebird!*" radioed John Whiddon as his eyes searched the inky void all around. "This is Coast Guard rescue helicopter one four eight six. Do you read me?"

"Yes, I hear you," replied Jim Blades.

Bluebird, I need you to key your mike and count backward for me from ten to one. And keep counting. As you do, we'll try to track you down using our DF [direction finding] equipment. Over."

"Roger that," said Blades. "Ten, nine, eight, seven, six, five, four . . . "

Glancing outside, Blades noticed seawater creeping up his back deck. This is not looking good, he thought.

"Well, guys—we're here. Where you at?" Blades radios finally.

"We're doing our best to find you," replied John Whiddon.

"Give me another DF count," Whiddon radioed.

Whiddon could tell by the interference—the amount of static caused by the surprising power of the storm cell—whether they were gaining or losing ground.

At first he sounded close, then he seemed to fade away.

Jim Blades knew that his always-dependable *Bluebird* was sinking. Dying partnership or not, he hated the idea of going back inside the ship's cabin, each time, to answer the radio; like any fisherman, he abhorred the idea of getting entombed inside the sinking hull.

Wind-whipped flurries of cascading snow were tumbling unabated out of the coal black night when Blades opened the back door and shined his handheld spotlight downwind of the boat.

"Do you see that?" he radioed Whiddon. "Do you see my light?"

With their visibility limited to just a few hundred feet, none of the searing eyes on board the helicopter could see a thing. Then Carl Saylor spotted a tiny glint of light shining through the swirling snowfall off to their right. But as he watched, it soon disappeared. Jim Blades's spotlight had shown itself as the founding *Bluebird* crested over a wave, but the seas were so large that each time it did, the F/V *Bluebird* would disappear entirely into the yawning pit of the wave troughs, taking the light with it.

"Pilot, this is the flight mech. I think I see a flashing light," radioed Saylor.

"I don't see it yet," shot back Whiddon. "Give me a heading."

As they drew closer, copilot Greg Breithaupt spotted it, too.

"We've spotted you, *Bluebird!*" said copilot Greg Breithaupt. "Yes, we see you!" he paused. "We'll be on scene in two minutes."

Using full power, Whiddon motored upwind toward the foundering vessel. Drawing nearer, he could see that she was riding low in the stern, with wave after wave pummeling her. The *Bluebird* was pitching wildly as she drifted up and over the long-rising swells. With her bow banked at a forty-five-degree angle and her stern constantly awash, Whiddon could see a man and a small child in orange survival suits snuggled in close to each other, clinging tenaciously to the back of the wheelhouse.

From the chopper's side door overhead, rescue swimmer Jeff Tunks could see that Jim and Clint Blades and their beloved *Bluebird* were getting the "hell beat out of them," as he put it. The fishing boat looked minuscule amid the burly storm waves lifting and tossing her. The waves themselves were covered with gray-white streaks of windblown foam, stretching in thin layers across the slate black surface. Yet wherever the chopper's floodlight touched down on the otherwise black face of the sea, it illuminated the world below in a brilliant circular swath of color and life—the green of the water glowing with an almost phosphorescent intensity.

Tunks could feel Whiddon fighting to maintain an even flight plain. Lowering the rescue basket from their wind-jousted helicopter onto the tiny gyrating rectangle of the *Bluebird's* back deck looked impossible.

The gusts were williwaw blasts of cold mountain air roaring down off the slopes of Mount Edgecumbe. Cooled well below freezing by the altitude, gathering tremendous energy and speed as they descended, the accelerating winds struck the helicopter and shook it to its rivets. At one point, the H-3 helicopter dipped so low that it nearly impaled itself on the twenty-five-foot-high cedar trolling poles that rose up on either side of the wheelhouse.

Whiddon, Tunks could tell, kept putting forward and up control commands into the flight stick, but the helo kept sliding back and down. Tipping as far as twenty degrees from side to side, they were often forced to hold on, as if riding a bucking bronco.

Then an exceptionally powerful gust of wind, well in excess of 110 miles per hour, struck the helicopter, driving them back. Whiddon fought to bring the nose down and regain control, using all the power the aircraft possessed.

"You're backing down!" shouted Carl Saylor.

As they plummeted toward the water, Whiddon and Breithaupt glanced over at each other, exchanging a look that said, This is it! Whiddon was certain that they were about to crash. It was one of those instinctive feelings. They were going in.

Yet John Whiddon felt too caught up in his duties to be scared. Oddly, a sense of peace and calm settled over him, and the message he internalized was one of acceptance, one that said, This is just the way it is.

Whiddon had three boys and a loving wife, to whom he was devoted, waiting at home just across the bay. They were all safely ashore now—a world apart. Then his mind seized upon the memory of his good friend and flying partner Pat Rivas. Pat was a superb pilot and a wonderful human being. Back in the early 1980s, they had flown alongside each other on a number of missions in Alaska. And they had made a difference. Their most notable effort was being part of the largest medivac operation in U.S. Coast Guard history. Working with their airborne comrades, they employed a relay system and were able to pluck more than five hundred survivors off the cruise ship M/V *Prinsendam* when it caught fire and began sinking far out in the Gulf of Alaska. Jut ten months later, Pat Rivas and his entire crew were killed in that infamous crash in Prince William Sound, when their tail rotor chipped a wave, toppling them from the sky.

So this is how it all ended for Pat, thought Whiddon as he, his crew, and the weather-beaten helicopter carrying them careened out of control.

Both Whiddon and Breithaupt were yanking up, pulling "full-collective," on the horizontal arms mounted on the sides of their seats. Waiting for the H-3 to respond was a painfully slow process. They were just fifteen feet from striking the water itself when the wind gust released them.

Heart in throat, Whiddon turned the Breithaupt. "Boy, let's never do *that* again," he said, forcing out a chuckle.

For the rest of the crew, Whiddon's comment proved to be an aptly timed tension breaker.

"Let's get back up there and get these guys," he told them.

"Damn straight!" replied Jeff Tunks from the rear cabin.

Now Whiddon found that he nearly had to max out the engine to move ahead at all. Slowly, however, flying into winds that fluctuated between 90 and 115 miles per hour, he inched the helicopter forward.

Hoist operator Carl Saylor worked to conn Whiddon back over the sinking *Bluebird*. "Forward and right three hundred," he said. "Forward and right two hundred. Forward and right one hundred. Hold."

The floodlights shining down on the *Bluebird* created an amphitheater effect. The boat was taking on water and riding ever lower; then as Jeff Tunks watched, a storm wave broke against the boat, sending up an almost dazzling light-filled spray over the *Bluebird's* entire length.

Jim Blades hurried back inside and grabbed his mike. "How do you want to do this?" he radioed.

"Sir," replied Breithaupt, "the only way we're going to be able to executive this SAR operation is if you get your son and get off the boat."

To Tunks, Jim Blades's voice sounded so concerned with saving his son's life that he was sure the man would have gladly eat a bucket of nails if that would have helped.

"Okay," said Blades.

"Hang on, Clint," Jim Blades told his son. "We're going to have to get in the water now."

The elder Blades found that he couldn't get the zipper on his survival suit to work properly. Some months before, he'd broken that very zipper and had gone to great effort to have it replaced. The person who had repaired it, however, had failed to put back the two-inch whistle that had always served as a handle and was normally attached to the tiny metal zipper flap itself. Now, wearing the suit's clumsy two-fingered Gumby gloves, Blades found that despite all his efforts to prepare for just such an emergency, he was unable to pull the zipper the entire way up and lock it into the all-essential position directly beneath his chin.

As Jeff Tunks watched from the side door of the helicopter above, Jim Blades gathered up his son and walked out onto the pitching back deck of his boat. Clipping his son's suit harness to his own, he then stepped off the vessel's stern and into the tossing sea.

Their predicament, Tunks could readily see, soon went from bad to worse. For although Jim Blades and his son had dutifully abandoned ship, the prevailing winds quickly blew them in against the hull of the *Bluebird*, pinning them there.

After a half-dozen more attempts, Whiddon became convinced that the plan to basket-hoist the pair from the water unassisted would not work. When their efforts to lower the basket failed once more, Whiddon turned to rescue swimmer Jeff Tunks, who was seated behind him in the rear cabin.

"Jeff, we're not going to be able to complete this rescue without you. Do you want to give it a go?"

"Yes, sir. I'll give it a try," replied Tunks without hesitation.

"Do you think that you can get them?"

"Yah, I think I can. Let's give it a shot."

"Okay, then, Jeff, why don't you go ahead and get ready."

Hardly a year old at the time, the Coast Guard's rescue-swimmer program was still in its infancy. A swimmer wore the basics: two fins, a mask, a snorkel, a wet suit, a harness, and a knife.

Tunks was still prepping for the into-the-water deployment at hand when the F/V *Bluebird*'s bow rose sharply into the air and slipped stern-first into the waiting sea. With little Clint Blades still riding on his chest, Jim Blades lay on his back and stroked urgently away from the boat and any possible entanglements.

Jeff Tunks followed the lights of the ship's cabin as it descended perhaps twenty, even thirty feet below the surface. It was, Tunks said, "Just blazing all the way down." Tunks found it quite dramatic, even touching, to see the Bladeses' entire living and everything they were about to sink out from under them.

Little Clint Blades had said nothing as his father carried him down the sloping deck and stepped off into the water. Clint's suit had arms but only a single mummylike compartment for his legs. He was lying on his back on top of his dad's chest, sea-otter-style, when the first breaking wave rolled in over them.

"Clint, keep your mouth closed and hold your breath!" Jim Blades yelled to his son. "Hold your breath until the wave passes!"

Then everything went black. Jim Blades felt the cold wash of the wave water stinging his face, and the invisible currents pulling at them. As they tumbled through the surging space, the elder Blades was certain that had he not strapped his son Clint to himself, he would surely have lost him.

Back on the surface again. Blades could feel the chilling sea water flooding in through the neck opening of his suit. He was quite aware of the advancing stages of hypothermia and the paralyzing immobility that ultimately accompanies it. Though he would not go down without a fight, Blades was certain that he had a limited amount of time. If the rescue team didn't get to them quickly, he'd soon be dead, and his son Clint would drown, too, strapped to him as he was.

Then, as he waited, he glanced to one side and caught sight of his boat careening down the face of a wave, white smoke trailing from her stack.

Jim Blades could already feel the cold robbing him of his strength and his ability to resist. He studied the chopper struggling overhead and soon realized that the erratic and unpredictable winds were making rescue virtually impossible. "God," he prayed, "could you please slow the winds down just a little. We're in a real jam here. I don't believe my son and I are going to survive this without your help."

After a quick but precise final run-through of the rescue swimmers' checklist, flight mechanic Carl Saylor signaled Tunks forward. Tunks took a seat in the doorway and snapped on his gunner's belt (safety strap) to keep him from tumbling out. Then he slid the four-inch-wide, four-foot-long loop strap down over his head, shoulders, and arms. Theoretically the strap would allow Tunks to extend his arms overhead and slip free of it whenever he chose. He then pulled his mask snugly into place and bit down on the snorkel's mouthpiece. With finned feet dangling out into space, he gathered himself for what looked to be a wild descent.

Barely three years prior to this, on a bitter cold night, during a driving winter storm off Cape Hatteras, North Carolina, thirty-six crew members were left to survive as best they could in the icy seas after being forced to abandon the sinking freighter *Marine Electric*.

When the pilot of an H-3 Pelican finally located them, he found the waves too high to attempt a landing on the water, and dozens of seamen scattered across the crowning seas. Though the flight mech was repeatedly able to place the rescue basket in close proximity to those struggling in the water, in the end, he and the others aboard the helicopter could only watch as, one by one, no less than thirty-three of the severely hypothermic survivors fell unconscious and died.

Ultimately, Alaska's own LCMD Kenneth Coffland (now retired) would play an instrumental role in helping wrestle something redeeming from the ruins of this tragedy and others. Subsequent hearings, investigations, and inquiries into this deadly incident explored the key shortcoming in the link between the Coast Guard crews in the air, and those imperiled souls in the water below.

As a result of the efforts of Coffland and many others, Jeff Tunks knew, just ten months before, the U.S. Coast Guard had gone "operational" with the rescue-swimmer program.

"Prepare to deploy the swimmer," ordered Whiddon.

"Okay, deploying the swimmer," replied Saylor.

Then came the token signal for which Jeff Tunks had so intensively trained—Carl Saylor's one tap on the chest. In response, Tunks released his gunner's belt and gave Saylor the standard response, a thumbs-up.

Jeff Tunks could feel the harness tighten under his arms as Saylor, working the hoist controls, lifted him into the air. As he swung out the door, Tunks heard the log-shredding power of the mammoth storm waves exploding along the shore of Kruzof Island, several thousand feet away.

"Swimmer going down," radioed Saylor.

"Swimmer going down," reiterated Whiddon.

Now Tunks took in the panoramic scene one hundred or so feet below him and saw precisely what he was "fixin' to get into."

He could see Jim and Clint almost directly beneath him, and he found himself thinking, This is going to be fairly simple. I'm going to disconnect, and then I'm going to gather them up and drag them to the basket and put them inside. Once they're safely aboard, they'll drop the basket down to me and I'll crawl in myself, and we'll be out of here.

But in what seemed no more than a snap of a finger, Tunks found himself being dragged backward through the waves as another gust swept the chopper downwind. With so much tension suddenly seizing him under his arms, he quickly discovered that he had no way of releasing himself from the harness strap now holding him fast.

Whiddon gunned the engines, bringing the reverse odyssey to a halt, but not before dragging Tunks close to a hundred yards from the Bladeses. Finally able to slip free of the body strap, he free-fell into the sea, submerged briefly, then resurfaced and glanced quickly around. The Bladeses were nowhere in sight.

Above him, Tunks took in the "magnificent" vision of the H-3 aircraft "exuding power" and the large black USCG letters stenciled across the helo's white belly. He could see that, for all her power, the H-3 was being buffeted—its nose up, then down—and was shimmying from side to side, as if its 22,000-pound weight was inconsequential.

Tunks tried to call out to the Bladeses, wherever they were, hoping that in spite of the roar of the helicopter above and the breaking seas, they would hear him. Strangely, however, he couldn't make a sound. Tunks had never experienced anything like this. Perhaps it was the tremendous surge of adrenaline coursing through his system. Regardless, Tunks was forced to accept that he was unable to express so much as a "single blessed word."

Tunks performed a frantic 360-degree turn, searching for the man and his son, but it was pitch-black out, and the waves rolling through the area were so high that he was unable to visually hit upon them.

From the uncertain position of the helicopter overhead, it was clear to Whiddon that Tunks had become disoriented and that he no longer had any idea where the Bladeses were. Then Whiddon struck on an idea. He swung the searchlight away from Tunks and shone it down on the Bladeses.

Tunks took in the powerful column of the aircraft's floodlight as it swung to point somewhere in the distance. The shaft of light seemed to imply that Jim Blades and his son were several hundred feet away. Though Tunks could not see them, or communicate with Whiddon, he was certain that the end of that light was where he needed to be, and he began to move in that direction.

It was not a previously choreographed signal. "He didn't know to do that," John Whiddon later recalled. "It was one of the miraculous things that happened that night."

Moving along, his head completely above the water, Tunks used his arms only to steer him and his flipperlike fins into the oncoming storm waves. He swam up to the top of one wave and down to the bottom of the next. En route, he was roughed up severely when several of the waves broke over him. Peering intently as he passed over the top of one wave, he saw the searchlight beam bang off the reflective tape as the Bladeses simultaneously crested over a distant wave.

Feeling both grateful and relieved, Tunks urgently sprinted ahead in order to prevent any possibility of losing them again. When he finally closed on them, he swam up behind the drifting pair, grasped Jim Blades by the back of his suit, and swung him around. And suddenly he found himself staring into the youthful face of six-year-old Clint Blades. The boy possessed a serenity that Tunks had not expected, a kind of grace under pressure, which, given the present set of circumstances, seemed inexplicable.

Tunks would forever remember the moment. The boy seemed very peaceful. Tunks had a little boy, too, and he realized that he had to do everything that he could to get the boy and his father out of there.

"How are you doing?" shouted Tunks.

"We're hanging in there," Jim Blades replied, even though he was certain that he wouldn't be able to get into the basket under his own power. "Do you think they're going to be able to get us out of here?"

"Not to worry. We do this all the time," replied Jeff Tunks reassuringly, stretching the truth more than a little.

"Okay, now," explained Tunks. "We're going to get the basket over here, we're going to put you in the basket, we're going to hoist you up into the aircraft, and everything's going to be fine."

Several minutes later, the rescue basket landed in the water, well off from them. Immediately, Tunks grabbed the Bladeses and started dragging them toward it. They were closing fast on it, when the helicopter struggling to hover overhead was abruptly blown back off the site. The basket sprang from the water and shot into the sky like a missile being launched.

For the next few minutes, each time Tunks saw the basket land in the water in anything like a stationary position, he'd immediately start hustling toward it towing the Bladeses along behind him.

Half a dozen similar attempts ensued before the gyrations of both basket and man finally coincided. Tunks could feel another sudden surge of adrenaline flooding his system. He grabbed Jim Blades by the back of his body harness, pulled the basket close with the other, and floated the Bladeses near. Then, just as he had been trained, he rolled them up and over his hip and set them down inside the basket in one seemingly effortless movement.

Tunks could see the hoist operator, Carl Saylor, crouched in the side doorway of the helo. He was waiting for Tunks to climb into the basket as well. There was no room left, however, so Tunks pushed the basket away, lifted his right arm, and gave Saylor the thumbs-up sign.

Jim and Clint Blades sprang from the water as if weightless as Carl Saylor "two-blocked" the hoist, bringing the basket up at top speed. As they rose, the Bladeses began swinging violently below the chopper. Tunks could see how commander Whiddon, climbing frantically in the H-3, was doing everything possible to make sure the precious cargo below cleared the wave tops. It turned out to be a beautiful hoist. Jim Blades and his son rose clear of the sea and ascended to the side door of the helicopter, untouched by further calamity.

As he watched them rise, Tunks was suddenly struck with a euphoric sense of accomplishment at having successfully completed one of the first high-seas rescue-swimmer operations in USCG history. "Yes!" he howled aloud.

And just as suddenly, he felt himself breaking free of the fears that had bound him. He had full confidence in his crewmates, and as Whiddon and his helicopter danced across the skies and Carl Saylor rushed to lower the basket to him again, Tunks experienced a resolute faith in the final outcome. They'll get me, he thought as he drifted alone over the pummeling seas and through the darkness. I'm going to be fine.

Inside the helicopter, Jim Blades still did not feel safe. The rattling, wind-battered machine that carried them felt no more substantial to him, he said, then "a bunch of spare parts all flying in formation." Furthermore, it was agonizing knowing that Jeff Tunks was still in the water and that they were having real trouble trying to fish him out.

As Tunks drifted in closer to the craggy, abrupt, sheer rock cliffs lining Kruzof Island, Whiddon flashed his floodlight along the shoreline. Even from the water, Tunks could see the ponderous storm waves gathering themselves in the shallows and crashing against the cliffs. He was certain that there was no way he could survive an attempt to reach shore through such a surf.

But Tunks also knew that with thirteen years of flying under his belt, Commander Whiddon was probably the finest stick-and-rudder pilot at the base in Sitka. With Lieutenant Breithaupt seated beside Whiddon as copilot, Tunks could not have imagined being caught in such a predicament with better people sitting up front. Nor could he think of more competent men than Carl Saylor on the hoist and Mark Milner on the radio.

After three or four more missed attempts to drop the rescue basket close to him, Jeff Tunks reached overhead and managed to snag it with an arm as it swung past. Sinking the basket with the weight of his body, he swam into it, wearing fins, snorkel, and all. He came to rest on his buttocks on the floor of the metal cage. Doubling over into a ball, he rose up only long enough to give Carl Saylor another thumbs-up before crouching back down again.

Abruptly, a gust of wind of a hundred miles per hour or better plowed into the hovering helicopter chopper and sent it reeling. Completely helpless to rise, barely able to keep the aircraft in the air, Whiddon struggled to regain a semblance of control.

In the mayhem that followed, the rescue basket was jerked from the water and launched into the sky like a recoiling paddle ball. With Jeff Tunks huddled down inside, the otherwise-hollow shell was jerked about on the end of the cable line like a knot on the end of a whiplash. Tunks was jerked around so violently that he nearly collided with the bottom of the helicopter itself.

As the accelerating chopper fled backward at more than sixty miles per hour, there was a "massive explosion" as the rescue basket collided with an oncoming wave. The water struck him from behind, knocking the wind from him and ripping both his mask and snorkel from his face. Tunks hadn't even seen it coming.

It was then that John Whiddon caught the unsettling vision of Jeff Tunks out his front window. His favorite rescue swimmer was being dragged along behind them. Both basket and man bounced across the water like a skipping rock, and wherever they touched down, white explosions of sea spray erupted.

Coming off the previous collision, Tunks and the basket would arch down and forward, flying through the broad wave troughs on the blunt end of a pendulum swing before hitting the crown of the next wave. Tunks plowed into three consecutive waves before Whiddon was able to instruct a climb. The third wave proved to be the culmination of his ride. Tunks hit so hard that Whiddon could actually feel the helicopter shudder.

"Oh my God! Did you see him hit that wave?" barked Carl Saylor.

I've killed him, thought Whiddon.

Jeff Tunks felt the basket start to capsize, so he clutched at the steel meshing of the floor to prevent himself from being tossed out.

"Bring him up!" screamed John Whiddon.

When Jeff Tunks was finally yanked aboard, he was choking on some saltwater he'd inadvertently inhaled.

"Swimmer's in the cabin, sir. Ready for forward flight," reported Saylor triumphantly.

Tunks crawled across the heaving floor and pulled himself up on to the troop seat. Then, looking over at Jim Blades and his son Clint, he once again gave the thumbs-up sign, which they returned.

"Jeff's all right," Carl Saylor told Whiddon. "He's swallowed a lot of water, and he's bruised, but otherwise, he's all right."

With the fishing boat *Bluebird* destroyed but her shivering survivors safely on board, Whiddon turned the H–3 toward home.

At the time Jim and Clint Blades were aboard the sinking *Bluebird*, Jill Blades and her son Curt were talking quietly. Then a freakish blast of wind rocked the house. Jill could hear the cables tethering the house to the shore cinch up tight and groan under the strain as the house swung out across the water.

Jill hurried down out of the loft and threw open one of the portholes her husband had so cleverly built into the living room walls. The wind and rain were blowing straight into her face, driving against the outside walls, pelting the windows, and sending a stream of seawater up over the outside deck, under the front door, and across the cabin floor.

Oh my word, Jill thought. Jim's out in this?

She hurried over to the CB radio, switched it on, and tried to reach her husband, but to no avail. She was clicking through the channels when she caught the sound of her husband's voice on Channel 16. He was talking to a Coast Guard helicopter pilot. The rescue of both her husband and son, she quickly surmised, was already under way.

"Are you guys going to get here pretty soon?" she head Jim ask the Coast Guard. "Cause my decks are awash."

Jill refused to panic. As the wife of a man who made his living on the sea, she was acutely aware of the inherent risks such a life involved. Besides, her husband was a strong, resourceful man who could fix or repair virtually anything. Turning to her son Curt, she said, "Daddy's in trouble, honey. Got to start praying."

With her head bowed, she began, "Oh, Father God, I just ask that you be with them out there tonight. Protect my little boy. Protect my husband. And bring them back safely to me."

Then Jill Blades struck on an idea. Switching channels, she used the radio to call Laura and Ben Hubbard, members of her church, and they began a prayer chain that quickly branched out into the community of Sitka.

"Mom," said little Curt, "when Dad and Clint get back, I'm never going to let 'em go out in a storm again."

Then Jill Blades caught the voice of the Coast Guard pilot on the radio. "Okay, we're coming up over the top of you," he said. Suddenly, all communications between the pilot and Jill's husband ceased. For the next twenty minutes, nothing more was heard from either of them.

Jill Blades had been all right up until that time. But now she felt fear beginning to well up. The helicopter has either crashed or the boat sank, and Jim and Clint are gone, she thought. And they're not going to tell me, because they're afraid that I'll freak out, being out here all by myself.

Then a friend, a commercial fisherman Ottie Florshutz, radioed Jill, offering to take his fishing boat out to their houseboat and get her and her son Curt to town.

"Fishing vessel *Adeline* to *Bluebird*," he began, "Jill, do you want me to come out and pick you up?"

"No, Ottie," she replied. "I don't want anybody else out in this stuff. It's really howling out here. The only thing is—I just wish they'd tell me. If they're dead, I just want them to tell me that they're dead, so I know. I just gotta know what happened."

It was then that the voice of a member of the Coast Guard came over Channel 16.

"Mrs. Blades," the man said.

"Yes?" she replied.

"We got them."

"Thank God!" she yelled, loudly enough for all to hear.

"I didn't know if God was going to make me a widow," she later told me when I visited their island home in Sitka Sound. "I didn't know what was going to happen, because I know that some people don't come back."

Rescuing the Rescuers

From *The Perfect Storm*

BY SEBASTIAN JUNGER

Junger's 1997 bestseller riveted thousands with its description of the last moments of a Gloucester fishing boat lost during the raging "storm of the century" in October 1991. But, caught in the same storm, a helicopter full of pararescue jumpers went down off the coast of New Jersey, and Junger here captures the hope and terror of their rescue.

★   ★   ★   ★   ★

Meanwhile, the worst crisis in the history of the Air National Guard has been unfolding offshore. At 2:45 that afternoon—in the midst of the *Satori* rescue—District One Command Center in Boston receives a distress call from a Japanese sailor named Mikado Tomizawa, who is in a sailboat 250 miles off the Jersey coast and starting to go down. The Coast Guard dispatches a C-130 and then alerts the Air National Guard, which operates a rescue group out of Suffolk Airbase in Westhampton Beach, Long Island. The Air Guard covers everything beyond maritime rescue, which is roughly defined by the fuel range of a Coast Guard H-3 helicopter. Beyond that—and Tomizawa was well beyond that—an Air Guard H-60 flies in tandem with a C-130 tanker plane, and every few hours the pilot comes up behind the tanker and nudges a probe into one of the hoses trailing off each wing. It's a preposterously difficult maneuver in bad weather, but it allows an H-60 to stay airborn almost indefinitely.

The Air Guard dispatcher is on the intercom minutes after the mayday comes in, calling for a rescue crew to gather at "ODC," the operations dispatch

Center. Dave Ruvola, the helicopter pilot, meets his copilot and the C-130 pilots in an adjacent room and spreads an aeronautical chart of the East Coast on the table. They study the weather forecasts and decide they will execute four midair refuelings—one immediately off the coast, one before the rescue attempt, and two on the way back. While the pilots are plotting their refueling points, a rescue swimmer named John Spillane and another swimmer named Rick Smith jog down the hallway to Life Support to pick up their survival gear. A crewcut supply clerk hands them Mustang immersion suits, wetsuits, inflatable life vests, and mesh combat vests. The combat vests are worn by American airmen all over the world and contain the minimum amount of gear—radio, flare kit, knife, strobe, matches, compass—needed to survive in any environment. They put their gear in duffle bags and leave the building by a side door, where they meet the two pilots in a waiting truck. They get in, slam the doors shut, and speed off across the base.

A maintenance crew has already towed a helicopter out of the hangar and fueled it up, and flight engineer Jim Mioli is busy checking the records and inspecting the engine and rotors. It is a warm, windy day, the scrub pine twisting and dancing along the edge of the tarmac and sea birds sawing their way back and forth against a heavy sky. The PJs load their gear in through the jump door and then take their seats in the rear of the aircraft, up against the fuel tanks. The pilots climb into their angled cockpit seats, go through the preflight checklist, and then fire the engines up. The rotors thud to life, losing the sag of their huge weight, and the helicopter shifts on its tires and is suddenly airborn, tilting nose-down across the scrub. Ruvola bears away to the southeast and within minutes has crossed over to open ocean. The crew, looking down out of their spotters' windows, can see the surf thundering against Long Island. Up and down the coast, as far as they can see, the shore is bordered in white.

In official terms the attempt to help Tomizawa was categorized as an "increased risk" mission, meaning the weather conditions were extreme and the survivor was in danger of perishing. The rescuers, therefore, were willing to accept a higher level of risk in order to save him. Among the actual crews these missions are referred to as "sporty," as in, "Boy, it sure was sporty out there last night." In general, sporty is good; it's what rescue is all about. An Air National Guard pararescue jumper—the military equivalent of Coast Guard rescue swimmers—might get half a dozen sporty rescues in a lifetime. These rescues are talked about, studied, and sometimes envied for years.

Wartime, of course, is about as sporty as it gets, but it's a rare and horrible circumstance that most pararescue jumpers don't experience. (The Air

National Guard is considered a state militia—meaning it's state funded—but it's also a branch of the Air Force. As such, Guard jumpers are interchangeable with Air Force jumpers.) Between wars the Air National Guard occupies itself rescuing civilians on the "high seas," which means anything beyond the fuel range of a Coast Guard H-3 helicopter. That, depending on the weather, is around two hundred miles offshore. The wartime mission of the Air National Guard is "to save the life of an American fighting man," which generally means jumping behind enemy lines to extract downed pilots. When the pilots go down at sea, the PJs, as they're known, jump with scuba gear. When they go down on glaciers, they jump with crampons and ice axes. When they go down in the jungle, they jump with two hundred feet of tree-rappelling line. There is, literally, nowhere on earth a PJ can't go. "I could climb Everest with the equipment in my locker," one of them said.

All of the armed forces have some version of the pararescue jumper, but the Air National Guard jumpers—and their Air Force equivalents—are the only ones with an ongoing peacetime mission. Every time the space shuttle launches, an Air Guard C-130 from Westhampton Beach flies down to Florida to oversee the procedure. An Air Force rescue also flies to Africa to cover the rest of the shuttle's trajectory. Whenever a ship—of any nationality—finds itself in distress off North America, the Air National Guard can be called out. A Greek crewman, say, on a Liberian-flagged freighter, who has just fallen into a cargo hold, could have Guard jumpers parachute in to help him seven hundred miles out at sea. An Air Guard base in Alaska that recovers a lot of Air Force trainees is permanently on alert—"fully cocked and ready to go"—and the two other bases, in California and on Long Island, are on standby. If a crisis develops offshore, a crew is put together from the men on-base and whomever can be rounded up by telephone; typically, a helicopter crew can be airborne in under an hour.

It takes eighteen months of full-time training to become a PJ, after which you owe the government four years of active service, which you're strongly encouraged to extend. (There are about 350 PJs around the country, but developing them is such a lengthy and expensive process that the government is hard put to replace the ones who are lost every year.) During the first three months of training, candidates are weeded out through sheer, raw abuse. The dropout rate is often over ninety percent. In one drill, the team swims their normal 4,000-yard workout, and then the instructor tosses his whistle into the pool. Ten guys fight for it, and whoever manages to blow it at the surface gets to leave the pool. His workout is over for the day. The instructor throws the whistle in again, and the nine remaining guys fight for it. This goes on until there's only one man left, and he's kicked out of PJ school. In a variation called "water harassment," two swimmers share a snorkel while instructors basically try to drown them. If either man breaks the surface and takes a breath, he's out of school. "There were times we cried," admits one PJ. But "they've got to thin the ranks somehow."

After pretraining, as it's called, the survivors enter a period known as "the pipeline"—scuba school, jump school, freefall school, dunker-training school, survival school. The PJs learn how to parachute, climb mountains, survive in deserts, resist enemy interrogation, evade pursuit, navigate underwater at night. The schools are ruthless in their quest to weed people out; in dunker training, for example, the candidates are strapped into a simulated helicopter and plunged underwater. If they manage to escape, they're plunged in upside-down and blindfolded. The guys who escape *that* get to be PJs; the rest are rescued by divers waiting by the sides of the pool.

These schools are for all branches of the military, and PJ candidates might find themselves training alongside Navy SEALS and Green Berets who are simply trying to add, say, water survival to their repertoire of skills. If the Navy SEAL fails one of the courses, he just goes back to being a Navy SEAL; if a PJ fails, he's out of the entire program. For a period of three or four months, a PJ runs the risk, daily, of failing out of school. And if he manages to make it through the pipeline, he still has almost another full year ahead of him: paramedic training, hospital rotations, mountain climbing, desert survival, tree landings, more scuba school, tactical maneuvers, air operations. And because they have a wartime mission, the PJs also practice military maneuvers. They parachute into the ocean at night with inflatable speedboats. They parachute into the ocean at night with scuba gear and go straight into a dive. They deploy from a submarine by air-lock and swim to a deserted coast. They train with shotguns, grenade launchers, M-16s, and six-barreled "mini-guns." (Mini-guns fire 6,000 rounds a minute and can cut down trees.) And finally—once they've mastered every conceivable battle scenario—they learn something called HALO jumping.

HALO stands for High Altitude Low Opening; it's used to drop PJs into hot areas where a more leisurely deployment would get them all killed. In terms of violating the constraints of the physical world, HALO jumping is one of the more outlandish things human beings have ever done. The PJs jump from so high up—as high as 40,000 feet—that they need bottled oxygen to breathe. They leave the aircraft with two oxygen bottles strapped to their sides, a parachute on their back, a reserve 'chute on their chest, a full medical pack on their thighs, and an M-16 on their harness. They're at the top of the troposphere—the layer where weather happens—and all they can hear is the scream of their own velocity. They're so high up that they freefall for two or three minutes and pull their 'chutes at a thousand feet or less. That way, they're almost impossible to kill.

The H-60 flies through relative calm for the first half-hour, and then Ruvola radios the tanker plane and says he's coming in for a refueling. A hundred and forty pounds of pressure are needed to trigger the coupling mechanism in the feeder hose—called the "drogue"—so the helicopter has to close on the tanker plane at a fairly good rate of speed. Ruvola hits the drogue on the first shot, takes on 700 pounds of fuel and continues on toward the southeast. Far below, the waves are getting smeared forward by the wind into an endless series of scalloped white crests. The crew is heading into the worst weather of their lives.

The rules governing H-60 deployments state that "intentional flight into known or forecast severe turbulence is prohibited." The weather report faxed by McGuire Air Force Base earlier that day called for *moderate* to severe turbulence, which was just enough semantic protection to allow Ruvola to launch. They were trained to save lives, and this is the kind of day that lives would need saving. An hour into the flight Dave Ruvola comes in for the second refueling and pegs the drogue after four attempts, taking on 900 pounds of fuel. The two aircraft break apart and continue hammering toward Tomizawa.

They are on-scene ten minutes later, in almost complete dark. Spillane has spent the flight slowly putting his wetsuit on, trying not to sweat too much, trying not to dehydrate himself. Now he sits by the spotter's window looking out at the storm. A Coast Guard C-130 circles at five hundred feet and the Air National Guard tanker circles several hundred feed above that. Their lights poke feebly into the swarming darkness. Ruvola establishes a low hover aft of the sailboat and flips on his floods, which throw down a cone of light from the belly of the aircraft. Spillane can't believe what he sees: massive foam-laced swells rising and falling in the circle of light, some barely missing the belly of the helicopter. Twice he has to shout for altitude to keep the helicopter from getting slapped out of the sky.

The wind is blowing so hard that the rotor wash, which normally falls directly below the helicopter, is forty feet behind it; it lags the way it normally does when the helicopter is flying ahead at eighty knots. Despite the conditions, Spillane still assumes he and Rick Smith are going to deploy by sliding down a three-inch-thick "fastrope" into the sea. The question is, what will they do then? The boat looks like it's moving too fast for a swimmer to catch, which means Tomizawa will have to be extracted from the water, like the *Satori* crew was. But that would put him at a whole other level of risk; there's a point at which sporty rescues become more dangerous than sinking boats. While Spillane considers Tomizawa's chances, flight engineer Jim Mioli gets on the intercom and says he has doubts about retrieving anyone from the water. The waves are rising too fast for the hoist controls to keep up, so there'll be too much slack around the basket at the crests of the waves. If a man were caught in a loop of cable and the wave dropped out from under him, he'd be cut in half.

For the next twenty minutes Ruvola keeps the helicopter in a hover over the sailboat while the crew peers out the jump door, discussing what to do. They finally agree that the boat looks pretty good in the water—she's riding high, relatively stable—and that any kind of rescue attempt will put Tomizawa in more danger than he is already in. He should stay with his boat. *We're out of our league, boys,* Ruvola finally says over the intercom. *We're not going to do this.* Ruvola gets the C-130 pilot on the radio and tells him their decision, and the C-130 pilot relays it to the sailboat. Tomizawa, desperate, radios back that they don't have to deploy their swimmers at all—just swing the basket over and he'll rescue himself. *No, that's not the problem,* Buschor answers. *We don't mind going in the water, we just don't think a rescue is possible.*

Ruvola backs away and the tanker plane drops two life rafts connected by eight hundred feet of line, in case Tomizawa's boat starts to founder, and then the two aircraft head back to base. (Tomizawa was eventually picked up by a Romanian freighter.) Ten minutes into the return flight Ruvola lines up on the tanker for the third time, hits the drogue immediately and takes on 1,560 pounds of fuel. They'll need one more refueling in order to make shore. Spillane settles into the portside spotter's seat and stares down at the ocean a thousand feet below. If Mioli hadn't spoken up, he and Rick Smith might be swimming around down there, trying to get back into the rescue basket. They'd have died. In conditions like these, so much water gets loaded into the air that swimmers drown simply trying to breathe.

Months later, after the Air National Guard has put the pieces together, it will determine that gaps had developed in the web of resources designed to support an increased-risk mission over water. At any given moment *someone* had the necessary information for keeping Ruvola's helicopter airborne, but that information wasn't disseminated correctly during that last hour of Ruvola's flight. Several times a day, mission or no mission, McGuire Air Force Base in New Jersey faxes weather bulletins to Suffolk Air Base for their use in route planning. If Suffolk is planning a difficult mission, they might also call McGuire for a verbal update on flight routes, satellite information, etc. Once the mission is underway, one person—usually the tanker pilot—is responsible for obtaining and relaying weather information to all the pilots involved in the rescue. If he needs more information, he calls Suffolk and tells them to get it; without the call, Suffolk doesn't actively pursue weather information. They are, in the words of the accident investigators, "reactive" rather than "proactive" in carrying out their duties.

In Ruvola's case, McGuire Air Force Base has real-time satellite information showing a massive rain band developing off Long Island between 7:30 and 8:00 P.M.—just as he is starting back for Suffolk. Suffolk never calls McGuire for an update, though, because the tanker pilot never asks for one; and McGuire never volunteers the information because they don't know there is an Air Guard helicopter out there in the first place. Were Suffolk to call McGuire for an update, they'd learn that Ruvola's route is blocked by severe weather, but that he can avoid it by flying fifteen minutes to westward. As it is, the tanker pilot calls Suffolk for a weather update and gets a report of an 8,000-foot ceiling, fifteen-mile visibility, and low-level wind shear. He passes that information on to Ruvola, who—having left the worst of the storm behind him—reasonably assumes that conditions will only improve as he flies westward. All he has to do is refuel before hitting the wind shear that is being recorded around the air field. Ruvola—they all—are wrong.

The rain band is a swath of clouds fifty miles wide, eighty miles long, and 10,000 feet thick. It is getting dragged into the low across the northwest quadrant of the storm; winds are 75 knots and the visibility is zero. Satellite imagery shows the rain band swinging across Ruvola's flight path like a door slamming shut. At 7:55, Ruvola radios the tanker pilot to confirm a fourth refueling, and the pilot rogers it. The refueling is scheduled for five minutes later, at precisely eight o'clock. At 7:56, turbulence picks up a little, and at 7:58 it reaches moderate levels. *Let's get this thing done,* Ruvola radios the tanker pilot. At 7:59 he pulls the probe release, extends it forward, and moves into position for contact. And then it hits.

Headwinds along the leading edge of the rain band are so strong that it feels as if the helicopter has been blown to a stop. Ruvola has no idea what he's run into; all he knows is that he can barely control the aircraft. Flying has become as much a question of physical strength as of finesse; he grips the collective with one hand, the joystick with the other, and leans forward to peer through the rain rattling off the windscreen. Flight manuals bounce around the cockpit and his copilot starts throwing up in the seat next to him. Ruvola lines up on the tanker and tries to hit the drogue, but the aircraft are moving around so wildly that it's like throwing darts down a gun barrel; hitting the target is pure dumb luck. In technical terms, Ruvola's aircraft is doing things "without inputs from the controls"; in human terms, it's getting batted around the sky.

Ruvola tries as low as three hundred feet—"along the ragged edges of the clouds," as he says—and as high as 4,500 feet, but he can't find clean air. The visibility is so bad that even with night-vision goggles on, he can barely make out the wing lights of the tanker plane in from of him. And they are right—*right*—on top of it; several times they overshoot the drogue and Spillane thinks they are going to take the plane's rudder off.

Ruvola has made twenty or thirty attempts on the drogue—a monstrous feat of concentration—when the tanker pilot radios that he has to shut down his number one engine. The oil pressure gauge is fluctuating wildly and they are risking a burn-out. The pilot starts in on the shut-down procedure, and suddenly the left-hand fuel hose retracts; shutting off the engine has disrupted the air flow around the wing, and the reel-in mechanism has mistaken that for too much slack. It performs what is known as an "uncommanded retraction." The pilot finishes shutting down the engine, brings Ruvola back in, and then reextends the hose. Ruvola lines up on it and immediately sees that something is wrong. The drogue is shaped like a small parachute, and ordinarily it fills with air and holds the hose steady; now it is just convulsing behind the tanker plane. It has been destroyed by forty-five minutes of desperate refueling attempts.

Ruvola tells the tanker pilot that the left-hand drogue is shot and that they have to switch over to the other side. In these conditions refueling from the right-hand drogue is a nightmarish, white-knuckle business because the helicopter probe also extends from the right-hand side of the cockpit, so the pilot has to come even tighter into the fuselage of the tanker to make contact. Ruvola makes a run at the right-hand drogue, misses, comes in again, and misses again. The usual technique is to watch the tanker's wing flaps and anticipate where the drogue's going to go, but the visibility is so low that Ruvola can't even see that far; he can barely see past the nose of his own helicopter. Ruvola makes a couple more runs at the drogue, and on his last attempt he comes in too fast, overshoots the wing, and by the time he's realigned himself the tanker has disappeared. They've lost an entire C-130 in the clouds. They are at 4,000 feet in zero visibility with roughly twenty minutes of fuel left; after that they will just fall out of the sky. Ruvola can either keep trying to hit the drogue, or he can try to make it down to sea level while they still have fuel.

We're going to set up for a planned ditching, he tells his crew. *We're going to ditch while we still can.* And then Dave Ruvola drops the nose of the helicopter and starts racing his fuel gauge down to the sea.

John Spillane, watching silently from the spotter's seat, is sure he's just heard his death sentence. "Throughout my career I've always managed—just barely—to keep things in control," says Spillane. "But now, suddenly, the risk is becoming totally uncontrollable. We can't get fuel, we're going to end up in that roaring ocean, and we're not gonna be in control anymore. And I know the chances of being rescued are practically zero. I've been on a lot of rescue missions, and I know they can hardly even *find* someone in these conditions, let alone recover them. We're some of the best in the business—best equipped, best trained. We couldn't do a rescue a little while earlier, and now we're in the same situation. It looks real bleak. It's not going to happen."

While Ruvola is flying blindly downward through the clouds, copilot Buschor issues a mayday on an Air National Guard emergency frequency and then contacts the *Tamaroa*, fifteen miles to the northeast. He tells them they are out of fuel and about to set up for a planned ditching. Captain Brudnicki orders the *Tam's* searchlights turned up into the sky so the helicopter can give them a bearing, but Buschor says he can't see a thing. *Okay, just start heading towards us,* the radio dispatcher on the *Tam* says. *We don't have time, we're going down right now,* Buschor replies. Jim McDougal, handling the radios at the ODC in Suffolk, receives—simultaneously—the ditching alert and a phone call from Spillane's wife, who wants to know where her husband is. She's had no idea there was a problem and just happened to call at the wrong moment; McDougal is so panicked by the timing that he hangs up on her. At 9:08, a dispatcher at Coast Guard headquarters in Boston takes a call that an Air National Guard helicopter is going down and scrawls frantically in the incident log: *"Helo [helicopter] & 130 enroute Suffolk. Can't refuel helo due visibility. May have to ditch. Stay airborn how long? 20–25 min. LAUNCH!"* He then notifies Cape Cod Air Base, where Karen Stimson is chatting with one of her rescue crews. The five airmen get up without a word, file into the bathroom, and then report for duty out on the tarmac.

Ruvola finally breaks out of the clouds at 9:28, only two hundred feet above the ocean. He goes into a hover and immediately calls for the ditching checklist, which prepares the crew to abandon the aircraft. They have practiced this dozens of times in training, but things are happening so fast that the routines start to fall apart. Jim Mioli has trouble seeing in the dim cabin lighting used with night-vision gear, so he can't locate the handle of the nine-man life raft. By the time he finds it, he doesn't have time to put on his Mustang survival suit. Ruvola calls three times for Mioli to read him the ditching checklist, but Mioli is too busy to answer him, so Ruvola has to go through it by memory. One of the most important things on the list is for the pilot to reach down and eject his door, but Ruvola is working too hard to remove his hands from the controls. In military terminology he has become "task-saturated," and the door stays on.

While Ruvola is trying to hold the aircraft in a hover, the PJs scramble to put together the survival gear. Spillane slings a canteen over his shoulder and clips a one-man life raft to the strap. Jim Mioli, who finally manages to extract the nine-man raft, pushes it to the edge of the jump door and waits for the order to deploy. Rick Smith, draped in survival gear, squats at the edge of the other jump door and looks over the side. Below is an ocean so ravaged by wind that they can't even tell the difference between the waves and the troughs; for all they know they are jumping three hundred feet. As horrible as that is, though, the idea of staying where they are is even worse. The helicopter is going to drop into the ocean at any moment, and no one on the crew wants to be anywhere nearby when it does.

Only Dave Ruvola will stay on board; as pilot, it is his job to make sure the aircraft doesn't fall on the rest of his crew. The chances of his escaping with his door still in place are negligible, but that is beside the point. The ditching checklist calls for a certain procedure, a procedure that insures the survival of the greatest number of crew. That Mioli neglects to put on his survival suit is also, in some ways, suicidal, but he has no choice. His duty is to oversee a safe bail-out, and if he stops to put his survival suit on, the nine-man raft won't be ready for deployment. He jumps without his suit.

At 9:30, the number one engine flames out; Spillane can hear the turbine wind down. They've been in a low hover for less than a minute. Ruvola calls out on the intercom: *The number one's out! Bail out! Bail out!* The number two is running on fumes; in theory, they should flame out at the same time. This is it. They are going down.

Mioli shoves the life raft out the right-hand door and watches it fall, in his words, "into the abyss." They are so high up that he doesn't even see it hit the water, and he can't bring himself to jump in after it. Without telling anyone, he decides to take his chances in the helicopter. Ditching protocol calls for copilot Buschor to remain on board as well, but Ruvola orders him out because he decides Buschor's chances of survival will be higher if he jumps. Buschor pulls his door-release lever but the door doesn't pop off the fuselage, so he just holds it open with one hand and steps out onto the footboard. He looks back at the radar altimeter, which is fluctuating between ten feet and eighty, and realized that the timing of his jump will mean the difference between life and death. Ruvola repeats his order to bail out, and Buschor unplugs the intercom wires from his flight helmet and flips his night-vision goggles down. Now he can watch the waves roll underneath him in the dim green light of enhanced vision. He spots a huge crest, takes a breath and jumps.

Spillane, meanwhile, is grabbing some last-minute gear. "I wasn't terrified, I was scared," he says. "Forty minutes before I'd been more scared, thinking about the possibilities, but at the end I was totally committed. The pilot had made the decision to ditch, and it was a great decision. How many pilots might have just used up the last twenty minutes of fuel trying to hit the drogue? Then you'd fall out of the sky and everyone would die."

The helicopter is strangely quiet without the number one engine. The ocean below them, in the words of another pilot, looks like a lunar landscape, cratered and gouged and deformed by wind. Spillane spots Rick Smith at the starboard door, poised to jump, and moves towards him. "I'm convinced he was sizing up the waves," Spillane says. "I wanted desperately to stick together with him. I just had time to sit down, put my arm around his shoulders, and he went. We didn't have time to say anything—you want to say goodbye, you want to do a lot of things, but there's no time for that. Rick went, and a split-second later, I did."

According to people who have survived long falls, the acceleration of gravity is so heart-stoppingly fast that it's more like getting shot downward out of a cannon. A body accelerates roughly twenty miles an hour for every second it's in the air; after one second it's falling twenty miles an hour; after two seconds, forty miles an hour, and so on, up to a hundred and thirty. At that point the wind resistance is equal to the force of gravity, and the body is said to have reached terminal velocity. Spillane falls probably sixty or seventy feet, two and half seconds of acceleration. He plunges through darkness without any idea where the water is or when he is going to hit. He has a dim memory of letting go of his one-man raft, and of his body losing position, and he thinks: My God, what a long way down. And then everything goes blank.

John Spillane has the sort of handsome, regular features that one might expect in a Hollywood actor playing a pararescueman—playing John Spillane, in fact. His eyes are stone-blue, without a trace of hardness or indifference, his hair is short and touched with grey. He comes across as friendly, unguarded, and completely sure of himself. He has a quick smile and an offhand way of talking that seems to progress from detail to detail, angle to angle, until there's nothing more to say on a topic. His humor is delivered casually, almost as an afterthought, and seems to surprise even himself. He's of average height, average build, and once ran forty miles for the hell of it. He seems to be a man who has long since lost the need to prove things to anyone.

Spillane grew up in New York City and joined the Air Force at seventeen. He trained as a combat diver—infiltrating positions, securing beaches, rescuing other combat divers—and then left at 21 to join the Air National Guard. He "guard-bummed" around the world for a year, returning to Rockaway Beach to lifeguard in the summer, and then signed up for PJ school. After several years of reserve duty he quit, went through the police academy, and became a scuba diver for the New York City Police Department. For three years he pulled bodies out of submerged cars and mucked guns out of the East River, and finally decided to go back to school before his G.I. Bill ran out. He started out majoring in geology—"I wanted to go stomping mountaintops for a while"—but he fell in love instead and ended up moving out to Suffolk to work full-time for the Guard. That was in 1989. He was 32, one of the most widely-experienced PJs in the country.

When John Spillane hits the Atlantic Ocean he is going about fifty miles an hour. Water is the only element that offers more resistance the harder you hit it, and at fifty miles an hour it might as well be concrete. Spillane fractures three bones in his right arm, one bone in his left leg, four ribs in his chest, ruptures a kidney, and bruises his pancreas. The flippers, the one-man raft, and the canteen all are torn off his body. Only the mask, which he wore backward with the strap in his mouth, stays on as it is supposed to. Spillane doesn't remember the moment of impact, and he doesn't remember the moment he first realized he was in the water. His memory goes from falling to swimming, with nothing in between. When he understands that he is swimming, that is *all* he understands—he doesn't know who he is, why he is there, or how he got there. He has no history and no future; he is just a consciousness at night in the middle of the sea.

When Spillane treats injured seamen offshore, one of the first things he evaluates is their degree of consciousness. The highest level, known as "alert and oriented times four," describes almost everyone in an everyday situation. They know who they are, where they are, what time it is, and what's just happened. If someone suffers a blow to the head, the first thing they lose is recent events—"alert and oriented times three"—and the last thing they lose is their identity. A person who has lost all four levels of consciousness, right down to their identity, is said to be "alert and oriented times zero." When John Spillane wakes up in the water, he is alert and oriented times zero. His understanding of the world is reduced to the fact that he exists, nothing more. Almost simultaneously, he understands that he is in excruciating pain. For a long time, that is all he knows. Until he sees the life raft.

Spillane may be alert and oriented times zero, but he knows to swim for a life raft when he sees one. It has been pushed out by Jim Mioli, the flight engineer, and has inflated automatically when it hits the water. Now it is scudding along on the wave crests, the sea anchors barely holding it down in the seventy-knot wind. "I lined up on it, intercepted it, and hung off the side," says Spillane. "I knew I was in the ocean, in a desperate situation, and I was hurt. I didn't know anything else. It was while I was hanging onto the raft that it all started coming back to me. We were on a mission. We ran out of fuel. I bailed out. I'm not alone."

While Spillane is hanging off the raft, a gust of wind catches it and flips it over. One moment Spillane is in the water trying to figure out who he is, the next moment he is high and dry. Instantly he feels better. He is lying on the wobbly nylon floor, evaluation the stabbing pain in his chest—he thinks he's punctured his lungs—when he hears people shouting in the distance. He kneels and points his diver's light in their direction, and just as he is wondering how to help them—whoever they are—the storm gods flip the raft over again. Spillane is dumped back into the sea. He clings to the safety line, gasping and throwing up sea water, and almost immediately the wind flips the raft over a third time. He has now gone one-and-a-half revolutions. Spillane is back inside, lying spread-eagle on the floor, when the raft is flipped a fourth and final time. Spillane is tossed back into the water, this time clinging to a rubberized nylon bag that later turns out to contain half a dozen wool blankets. It floats, and Spillane hangs off it and watches the raft go cartwheeling off across the wave crests. He is left alone and dying on the sea.

"After I lost contact with the raft I was by myself and I realized my only chance of survival was to make it until the storm subsided," he says. "There was no way they could pick us up. I'd just ditched a perfectly good helicopter and I knew our guys would be the ones to come out and get us if they could, but they couldn't. They couldn't refuel. So I'm contemplating this and I know I cannot make it through the storm. They might have somebody on-scene when light breaks, but I'm not going to make it that long. I'm dying inside."

For the first time since the ordeal began, Spillane has the time to contemplate his own death. He isn't panicked so much as saddened by the idea. His wife is five months pregnant with their first child, and he's been home very little recently—he was in paramedic school, and in training for the New York City marathon. He wishes that he'd spent more time at home. He wishes—incredibly—that he'd cut the grass one more time before winter. He wishes there was someone who could tell his wife and family what happened in the end. It bothers him that Dave Ruvola probably died taking the helicopter in. It bothers him they're all going to die for lack of five hundred pounds of jet fuel. The shame of it all, he thinks; we have this eight-million-dollar helicopter, nothing's wrong with it, nobody's shooting at us, we're just out of fuel.

Spillane has regained his full senses by this point, and the circumstances he finds himself in are nightmarish beyond words. It is so dark that he can't see his hand in front of his face, the waves just rumble down on him out of nowhere and bury him for a minute at a time. The wind is so strong it doesn't blow the water so much as fling it; there is no way to keep it out of his stomach. Every few minutes he has to retch it back up. Spillane has lost his one-man life raft, his ribs are broken, and every breath feels like he is being run through with a hot fire poker. He is crying out in pain and dawn isn't for another eight hours.

After an hour of making his farewells and trying to keep the water out of his stomach, Spillane spots two strobes in the distance. The Mustang suits all have strobe lights on them, and it is the first real evidence he has that someone else has survived the ditching. Spillane's immediate reaction is to swim toward them, but he stops himself. There is no way he is going to live out the night, he knows, so he might as well just die on his own. That way he won't inflict his suffering on anyone else. "I didn't want them to see me go," he says. "I didn't want them to see me in pain. It's the same with marathons—don't talk to me, let me just suffer through this by myself. What finally drove me to them was survival training. It emphasizes strength in numbers, and I know that if I'm with them, I'll try harder not to die. But I couldn't let them see me in pain, I told myself. I couldn't let them down."

Believing that their chances will be slightly less negligible in a group, Spillane slowly makes his way toward the lights. He is buoyed up by his life vest and wetsuit and swimming with his broken arm stretched out in front of him, gripping the blanket bag. It takes a long time and the effort exhausts him, but he can see the lights slowly getting closer. They disappear in the wave troughs, appear on the crests, and then disappear again. Finally, after a couple of hours of swimming, he gets close enough to shout and then to make out their faces. It is Dave Ruvola and Jim Mioli, roped together with parachute cord. Ruvola seems fine, but Mioli is nearly incoherent with hypothermia. He only has his Nomex flight suit on, and the chances of him lasting until dawn are even lower than Spillane's.

Ruvola had escaped the helicopter unscathed, but barely. He knew that the rotors would tear him and the helicopter apart if they hit the water at full speed, so he moved the aircraft away from his men, waited for the number two engine to flame out, and then performed what is known as a hovering auto-rotation. As the helicopter fell, its dead rotors started to spin, and Ruvola used that energy to slow the aircraft down, Like downshifting a car on a hill, a hovering auto-rotation is a way of dissipating the force of gravity by feeding it back through the engine. By the time the helicopter hit the water it had slowed to a manageable speed, and all the torque had been bled out of the rotors; they just smacked the face of an oncoming wave and stopped.

Ruvola found himself in a classic training situation, only it was real life: He had to escape from a flooded helicopter upside down in complete darkness. He was a former PJ, though, and a marathon swimmer, so being underwater was something he was used to. The first thing he did was reach for his HEEDS bottle, a three-minute air supply strapped to his left leg, but it had been ripped loose during the ditching; all he had was the air in his lungs. He reached up, pulled the quick-release on his safety belt, and it was then that he realized he'd never kicked the exit door out. He was supposed to do that so it wouldn't get jammed shut on impact, trapping him inside. He found the door handle, turned it, and pushed.

To his amazement, the door fell open; Ruvola kicked his way out from under the fuselage, tripped the CO_2 cartridge on his life vest, and shot ten or fifteen feet to the surface. He popped up into a world of shrieking darkness and landsliding seas. At one point, the crest of a wave drove him so far under the surface that the pressure change damaged his inner ear. Ruvola started yelling for the other crew members, and a few minutes later the flight engineer Mioli—who'd also managed to escape the sinking helicopter—answered him in the darkness. They started swimming toward each other, and after five or ten minutes Ruvola got close enough to grab Mioli by his survival vest. He took the hood off his survival suit, put it on Mioli's head, and then tied their two bodies together with parachute cord.

They've been in the water for a couple of hours when Spillane finally struggles up, face locked up with pain. The first thing Ruvola sees is a glint of light on a face mask, and he thinks that maybe it's a Navy SEAL who has air-locked out of a U.S. submarine and is coming to save them. It isn't. Spillane swims up, grabs a strap on Ruvola's flotation vest, and clamps his other arm around the blanket bag. What's that? Ruvola screams. I don't know, I'll open it tomorrow! Spillane yells back. Open it now! Ruvola answers. Spillane is in too much pain to argue about it, so he opens the bag and watches several dark shapes—the blankets—go snapping off downwind.

He tosses the bag aside and settles down to face the next few hours as best he can.

One can tell by the very handwriting in the District One incident log that the dispatcher—in this case a Coast Guardsman named Gill—can't quite believe what he's writing down. The words are large and sloppy and salted with excla-mation points. At one point he jots down, a propos of nothing: *"They're not alone out there,"* as if to reassure himself that things will turn out all right. That entry comes at 9:30, seconds after Buschor calls in the first engine loss. Five minutes later Gill writes down: *"39–51 North, 72–00 West, Ditching here, 5 POB [people on board]."* Seven minutes after that the tanker plane—which will circle the area until their fuel runs low—reports hearing an EPIRB signal for fifteen seconds, then nothing. From Gill's notes:

9:30—Tamaroa in area, launched H-65

9:48—Cape Cod 60!

9:53—CAA [Commander of Atlantic Area]/brfd—ANTHING YOU WANT—NAVY SHIP WOULD BE GREAT—WILL LOOK.

Within minutes of the ditching, rescue assets from Florida to Massachusetts are being readied for deployment. The response is massive and nearly instantaneous. At 9:48, thirteen minutes into it, Air Station Cape Cod launches a Falcon jet and an H-3 helicopter. Half an hour later a Navy P-3 jet at Brunswick Naval Air Station is requested and readied. The P-3 is infrared-equipped to detect heat emitting objects, like people. The *Tamaroa* has diverted before the helicopter has even gone down. At 10:23, Boston requests a second Coast Guard cutter, the *Spencer*. They even consider diverting an aircraft carrier.

The survivors are drifting fast in mountainous seas and the chances of spotting them are terrible. Helicopters will have minimal time on-scene because they can't refuel, it's unlikely conditions would permit a hoist rescue anyway, and there's no way to determine if the guardsmen's radios are even working. That leaves the *Tamaroa* to do the job, but she wasn't even able to save the *Satori* crew, during less severe conditions. The storm is barreling westward, straight toward the ditch point, and wave heights are climbing past anything ever recorded in the area.

If things look bad for Ruvola's crew, they don't look much better for the people trying to rescue them. It's not inconceivable that another helicopter will to have to ditch during the rescue effort, or that a Coast Guardsman will get washed off the *Tamaroa*. (For that matter the *Tamaroa* herself, at 205 feet, is not necessarily immune to disaster. One freak wave could roll her over and put eighty men in the water.) Half a dozen aircraft, two ships, and two hundred rescuers are heading for 39 north, 72 west; the more men out there, the higher the chances are of someone else getting into trouble. A succession of disasters could draw the rescue assets of the entire East Coast of the United States out to sea.

A Falcon jet out of Air Station Cape Cod is the first aircraft on-scene. It arrives ninety minutes after the ditching, and the pilot sets up what is known as an expanding-square search. He moves slightly downsea of the last known position—the "splash point" —and starts flying ever-increasing squares until he has covered an area ten miles across. He flies at two hundred feet, just below cloud cover, and estimates the probability of spotting the survivors to be one-in-three. He turns up nothing. Around 11:30 he expands his search to a twenty-mile square and starts all over again, slowly working his way southwest with the direction of drift. The infrared-equipped P-3 is getting ready to launch from Brunswick, and a Coast Guard helicopter is pounding its way southward from Cape Cod.

And then, ten minutes into the second square, he picks up something: a weak signal on 243 megahertz. That's a frequency coded into Air National Guard radios. It means at least one of the airmen is still alive.

The Falcon pilot homes in on the signal and tracks it to a position about twenty miles downsea of the splash point. Whoever it is, they're drifting fast. The pilot comes in low, scanning the sea with night-vision goggles, and finally spots a lone strobe flashing below them in the darkness. It's appearing and disappearing behind the huge swell. Moments later he spots three more strobes half a mile away. All but one of the crew are accounted for. The pilot circles, flashing his lights, and then radios his position in to District One. An H-3 helicopter, equipped with a hoist and rescue swimmer, is only twenty minutes away. The whole ordeal could be over in less than an hour.

The Falcon circles the strobes until the H-3 arrives, and then heads back to base with a rapidly-falling fuel gauge. The H-3 is a huge machine, similar to the combat helicopters used in Vietnam, and has spare fuel tanks installed inside the cabin. It can't refuel in mid-flight, but it can stay airborn for four or five hours. The pilot, Ed DeWitt, tries to establish a forty-foot hover, but wind shear keeps spiking him downward. The ocean is a ragged white expanse in his searchlights and there are no visual reference points to work off of. At one point he turns downwind and almost gets driven into the sea.

DeWitt edges his helicopter to within a hundred yards of the three men and tells his flight engineer to drop the rescue basket. There's no way he's putting his swimmer in the water, but these are experienced rescuemen, and they may be able to extract themselves. It's either that or wait for the storm to calm down. The flight engineer pays out the cable and watches in alarm as the basket is blown straight back toward the tail rotors. It finally reaches the water, swept backward at an angle of 45 degrees, and DeWitt tries to hold a steady hover long enough for the swimmers to reach the basket. He tries for almost an hour, but the waves are so huge that the basket doesn't spend more than a few seconds on each crest before dropping to the end of its cable. Even if the men could get themselves into the basket, a shear pin in the hoist mechanism is designed to fail with loads over 600 pounds, and three men in waterlogged clothing would definitely push that limit. The entire assembly—cable, basket, everything—would let go into the sea.

DeWitt finally gives up trying to save the airmen and goes back up to a hover at two hundred feet. In the distance he can see the *Tamaroa*, searchlights pointed straight up, plunging through the storm. He vectors her in toward the position of the lone strobe in the distance—Graham Buschor—and then drops a flare by the others and starts back for Suffolk. He's only minutes away from "bingo," the point at which an aircraft doesn't have enough fuel to make it back to shore.

Two hundred feet below, John Spillane watches his last hope clatter away toward the north. He hadn't expected to get rescued, but still, it's hard to watch. The only benefit he can see is that his family will know for sure that he died. That might spare them weeks of false hope. In the distance, Spillane can see lights rising and falling in the darkness. He assumes it's a Falcon jet looking for the other airmen, but its light are moving strangely; it's not moving like an aircraft. It's moving like a ship.

The *Tamaroa* has taken four hours to cover the fifteen miles to the splash point; her screws are turning for twelve knots and making three. Commander Brudnicki doesn't know how strong the wind is because it rips the anemometer off the mast, but pilot Ed DeWitt reports that his airspeed indicator hit 87 knots— a hundred miles an hour—while he was in a stationary hover. The *Tamaroa's* course to the downed airmen puts them in a beam sea, which starts to roll the ship through an arc of 110 degrees; at that angle, bulkheads are easier to walk on than floors. In the wheelhouse, Commander Brudnicki is surprised to find himself looking up at the crest of the waves, and when he orders full rudder and full bell, it takes thirty or forty seconds to see any effect at all. Later, after stepping off the ship, he says, "I certainly hope that was the high point of my career."

The first airman they spot is Graham Buschor, swimming alone and relatively unencumbered a half mile from the other three. He's in a Mustang survival suit and has a pen-gun flare and the only functional radio beacon of the entire crew. Brudnicki orders the operations officer, Lieutenant Kristopher Furtney, to maneuver the *Tamaroa* upsea of Buschor and then drift down on him. Large objects drift faster than small ones, and if the ship is upwind of Buschor, the waves won't smash him against the hull. The gunner's mate starts firing flares off from cannons on the flying bridge, and a detail of seamen crouch in the bow with throwing ropes, waiting for their chance. They can hardly keep their feet in the wind.

The engines come to a full stop and the *Tamaroa* wallows beam-to in the huge seas. It's a dangerous position to be in; the *Tamaroa* loses her righting arm at 72 degrees, and she's already heeling to fifty-five. Drifting down on swimmers is standard rescue procedure, but the seas are so violent that Buschor keeps getting flung out of reach. There are times when he's thirty feet higher than the men trying to rescue him. The crew in the bow can't get a throwing rope anywhere near him, and Brudnicki won't order his rescue swimmer overboard because he's afraid he won't get him back. The men on deck finally realize that if the boat's not going to Buschor, Buschor's going to have to go to it. *SWIM!* They scream over the rail. *SWIM!* Buschor rips off his gloves and hood and starts swimming for his life.

He swims as hard as he can; he swims until his arms give out. He claws his way up to the ship, gets swept around the bow, struggles back within reach of it again, and finally catches hold of a cargo net that the crew have dropped over the side. The net looks like a high rope ladder and is held by six or seven men at the rail. Buschor twists his hands into the mesh and slowly gets hauled up the hull. One good wave at the wrong moment could take them all out. The deck crewmen land Buschor like a big fish and carry him into the deckhouse. He's dry-heaving seawater and can barely stand; his core temperature has dropped to 94 degrees. He's been in the water four hours and twenty-five minutes. Another few hours and he may not have been able to cling to the net.

It's taken half an hour to get one man on board, and they have four more to go, one of whom hasn't even been sighted yet. It's not looking good. Brudnicki is also starting to have misgivings about putting his men on deck. The larger waves are sweeping the bow and completely burying the crew; they keep having to do head counts to make sure no one has been swept overboard. "It was the hardest decision I've ever had to make, to put my people out there and rescue that crew," Brudnicki says. "Because I knew there was a chance I could lose some of my men. If I'd decided not to do the rescue, no one back home would've said a thing—they knew it was almost impossible. But can you really make a conscious decision to say, 'I'm just going to watch those people in the water die?' "

Brudnicki decides to continue the rescue; twenty minutes later he has the *Tamaroa* in a beam sea a hundred yards upwind of the three Guardsmen. Crew members are lighting off flares and aiming searchlights, and the chief quartermaster is on the flying bridge radioing Furtney when to fire the ship's engine. Not only do they have to maneuver the drift, but they have to time the roll of the ship so the gunwale rides down toward the waterline while the men in the water grab for the net. As it is, the gunwales are riding from water-level to twenty feet in the air virtually every wave. Spillane is injured, Mioli is incoherent, and Ruvola is helping to support them both. There's no way they'll be able to swim like Buschor.

Spillane watches the ship heaving through the breaking seas and for the life of him can't imagine how they're going to do this. As far as he's concerned, a perfectly likely outcome is for all three of them to drown within sight of the ship because a pickup is impossible. "My muscles were getting rigid, I was in great pain," he says. "The *Tam* pulled up in front of us and turned broadsides to the waves and I couldn't believe they did that—they were putting themselves in terrible risk. We could hear them all screaming on the deck and we could see the chemical lights coming at us, tied to the ends of the ropes."

The ropes are difficult to catch, so the deck crew throw the cargo net over the side. Lieutenant Furtney again tries to ease his ship over to the swimmers, but the vessel is 1,600 tons and almost impossible to control. Finally, on the third attempt, they snag the net. Their muscles are cramping with cold and Jim Mioli is about the start a final slide into hypothermia. The men on deck give a terrific heave—they're pulling up 600 pounds deadweight—and at the same time a large wave drops out from underneath the swimmers. They're exhausted and desperate and the net is wrenched out of their hands.

The next thing Spillane knows, he's underwater. He fights his way to the surface just as the boat rolls inward toward them and he grabs the net again. This is it; if he can't do it now, he dies. The deck crew heaves again, and Spillane feels himself getting pulled up the steel hull. He climbs up a little higher, feels hands grabbing him, and the next thing he knows he's being pulled over the gunwale onto the deck. He's in such pain he cannot stand. The men pin him against the bulkhead, cut off his survival suit, and then carry him inside, staggering with the roll of the ship. Spillane can't see Ruvola and Mioli. They haven't managed to get back onto the net.

The waves wash the two men down the hull towards the ship's stern, where the twelve-foot screw is digging out a cauldron of boiling water. Furtney shuts the engines down and the two men get carried around the stern and then up the port side of the ship. Ruvola catches the net for the second time and gets one hand into the mesh. He clamps the other one around Mioli and screams into his face, You got to do this Jim! There aren't too many second chances in life! This is gonna take everything you got!

Mioli nods and wraps his hands into the mesh. Ruvola gets a foothold as well as a handhold and grips with all the strength in his cramping muscles. The two men get dragged upward, penduluming in and out with the roll of the ship, until the deck crew at the rail can reach them. They grab Ruvola and Mioli by the hair, the Mustang suit, the combat vest, anything they can get their hands on, and pull them over the steel rail. Like Spillane they're retching seawater and can barely stand. Jim Mioli has been in sixty-degree water for over five hours and is severely hypothermic. His core temperature is 90.4, eight degrees below normal; another couple of hours and he'd be dead.

They two airmen are carried inside, their clothing is cut off, and they're laid in bunks. Spillane is taken to the executive officer's quarters and given an IV and catheter and examined by the ship's paramedic. His blood pressure is 140/90, his pulse is a hundred, and he's running a slight fever. *Eyes pearled, abdomen and chest tenderness, pain to quadricep,* the paramedic radios SAR OPS [Search-and-Rescue Operations] Boston. *Fractured wrist, possibly ribs, suspect internal injury. Taking Tylenol-3 and seasick patch.* Boston relays the information to an Air National Guard flight surgeon, who says he's worried about internal bleeding and tells them to watch the abdomen carefully. It it gets more and more tender to the touch, he's bleeding inside and has to be evacuated by helicopter. Spillane thinks about dangling in a rescue litter over the ocean and says he'd rather not. At daybreak the executive officer comes in to shave and change his clothes, and Spillane apologizes for bleeding and vomiting all over his bed. Hey, whatever it takes, the officer says. He opens the porthole hatch, and Spillane looks out at the howling grey sky and the ravaged ocean. Ah, could you close that? He says. I can't take it.

The crew, unshaven and exhausted after thirty-six hours on deck, are staggering around the ship like drunks. And the mission's far from over. Rick Smith is still out there. He's one of the most highly trained pararescue jumpers in the country, and there's no question in anyone's mind that he's alive. They just have to find him. *PJ wearing black ¼" wetsuit, went out door with one-man liferaft and spray sheet, two 12 oz. cans of water, mirror, flare kit, granola bar, and whistle,* the Coast Guard dispatcher in Boston records. *Man is in great shape—can last quite a while, five to seven days.*

A total of nine aircraft are slated for the search, including an E2 surveillance plane to coordinate the air traffic on-scene. Jim Dougherty, a PJ who went through training with Smith and Spillane, throws a tin of Skoal chewing tobacco in his gear to give Smith when they find him. This guy's so good, Guardsmen are saying, he's just gonna come through the front door at Suffolk Air Base wondering where the hell we all were.

Part Four

Men at War: Saving Lives in Terrible Peril

An American Combat Doctor in Dachau

From *Our War for the World*

BY BRENDAN PHIBBS

During the winter and spring of 1945, Brendan Phibbs was a young combat surgeon with a lead point unit of the Seventh U.S. Army as it invaded Germany. His memoir, *Our War for the World*, is probably one of the finest ever written about practicing medicine in the heat of battle. But the selection below is all about a rescue, or an attempted one—how Phibbs entered Dachau at war's end only to discover its typhus-ridden inhabitants starving while surrounded by food and plenty.

★   ★   ★   ★   ★

Captain Levy, a medical officer traveling back to Dachau, stopped at our mess for lunch; he and I naturally sat together and he told me where he worked—in a typhus hospital in the concentration camp. There had been a number of British and American hospitals organized in the camp, he told me, chiefly to deal with the typhus then raging among the human wreckage with appalling results.

I asked him how they were treating them (this was in the days before antibiotics; there was no definitive treatment for typhus).

Well, he hesitated, they had started out just feeding everybody. They had dumped all the army rations they could find into a big stew and ladled out as much as everybody could eat. The patients did fine, he commented; even with their TB and their beriberi and their typhus they started gaining weight and healing infections—and then some flaming ass in the quartermaster corps discovered a regulation forbidding the feeding of GE rations to foreign civilians and cut off their supply. The medics were told to get food from a German warehouse in Munich, but the general of the X Infantry Division for some arcane reason had the key and wouldn't give it up and there was, for practical purposes, no food in the American field hospital.

The whole table stared. "What the hell are you doing?" I asked.

"Scrimping out leavings of rations," he mumbled, acutely embarrassed. "Sometimes we have to use our plasma for food. I mean it," he assured my disbelief. "We make up the damned plasma units and feed the stuff to them with a spoon."

The mess was silent, genuinely shocked. I dropped the subject until we were standing near his jeep as he left, when I pressed him further with incredulous questions. Could we help? Wasn't somebody doing something? Couldn't they just go out and scrounge food for these people? Finally I asked if he thought I could help if I came down. I had nothing special to do where I was. He assured me they'd be glad of any help, and the next day, with permission from the division surgeon and my commanding officer, I drove my ambulance down the autobahn past Augsburg to Dachau and the seventy-seventh field hospital. My motives weren't entirely altruistic; not a dozen physicians in the United States had ever seen typhus, and the chance to work with a rare and almost legendary disease was irresistible, particularly after four years of mindless army surgery. More practically, I had some vague idea of showing the helpless rear-echelon medics how to forage for food as we'd done all across Germany. As I drove along I mused that in May of 1945 Germany still bugled with the looted food of all Europe and it was hard to imagine in that cornucopia why concentration camp inmates should go hungry. I made sure my carbine with the usual sixty rounds was in the rack in the ambulance, and I noted the cows and pigs thronging the fields all around Dachau. There didn't seem to be any real shortage of animal protein.

After I'd been thoroughly dusted with DDT powder, I introduced myself to the commanding officer, a squatty major named Karff: from what Levy had told me I gathered he was trembling toward promotion.

"Always glad of extra hands, Major," he assured me and sent me off to dump my gear in a barracks.

I began daily rounds and patient care in the typhus ward in one of the giant green barracks with the mocking *"Arbeit macht Frei"* still lettered in white across its front.

The room seemed bigger than a gymnasium; it was filled with long rows of cots a few inches apart, each holding a shriveled remnant of a human fighting with pathetic resources against diseases that could tear the life out of vigorous, well-nourished people in their prime.

Starvation was the diagnosis that met the eye; the faces and the voices were those of the cold, muddy nightmare near Landsberg with the same naked, painful eyeballs, the same fleshless lips, the same bird-rasping voices, and, under the blankets, remnants of bodies of unbelievable fragility, every tissue wasted right down tautly around the skeleton, deep concavities between ribs, plunging hollows where the skin fell from the rib cage down to the almost empty abdomens, arms and legs where there was no muscle one could feel. I marveled at their ability to move.

After an initial tour of the ward, I sat down with the physicians of the unit to look at X rays. I hadn't actually looked at an X ray since we left the States; from the vantage point of a battalion aid station, the ability to look at something as medical as an X ray was a luxury. In addition to the four American physicians, there were two foreigners. One was a young Yugoslavian who had been surgeon of a "Divisie" in the partisan army and, until recently, a prisoner in Dachau. The other was an elderly Dutch physician who had been in Dachau for a long time; he had been, he informed me proudly, a member of the Dutch Communist party. The Yugoslavian hadn't been in long and was almost back to normal health; dressed in an American army uniform, he functioned as a ward officer. The Dutchman was a collection of bones barely mobile; he had been starved almost to death. He was still in his blue-striped pajamas, which fluttered loosely around his feeble frame as he walked, but he sat among us with great professional pride, squinting at the X rays, manifesting a dignity that could come only from a man so near death asserting the achievement of his life.

We began by looking at X rays of chests. Most of the lungs showed evidence of tuberculosis, many in stages so advanced it was obvious there could be no cure. A great number of the hearts were enlarged, some grotesquely, suggesting severe heart failure. The physicians of the ward explained that I was looking at the terminal stages of beriberi, when the heart, having been pathologically overactive, declines to a swollen, feebly pulsing organ. (Studies of American survivors of Japanese prison camps five and ten years after the war showed that at this stage the disease is irreversible and that even though feeding and vitamins appeared to restore health for a time, the heart muscle was so scarred that the victims died slowly of progressive heart failure over a period of years.)

Typhus is a savage disease; added to starvation, tuberculosis, and beriberi, it ravaged the wards like a machine gun. The steady flow of new cases into the unit, I was told, was balanced—sometimes more than balanced—by the dead who left. The louse, the transmitter of the disease, was being attacked throughout the main camp, but the infestation was so profound, the population so large, and the preexisting infection was so widespread that new cases kept turning up every day.

I didn't realize it at the time, but I was in the middle of what was probably the last major typhus epidemic in the history of the human race. In 1945 there was no treatment for the disease once it had started, but it could be largely prevented by DDT delousing and by a typhus vaccine that was at least fairly effective. When the first broad-spectrum antibiotic appeared in the late forties, the rickettsial diseases, including typhus, suddenly became minor nuisances instead of lethal, large-scale scourges.

Typhus is caused by an organism of a peculiar class named the *Rikettsiae*, smaller than ordinary bacteria, larger than viruses. The *Rikettsiae*, named for their discoverer, Ricketts, are remarkably widespread, since they have penetrated almost every part of the globe, surviving in insect reservoirs until they attack the definitive human victim. Each region has its characteristic and slightly different disease; all have some features in common. Rocky Mountain spotted fever is transmitted by ticks, tsugsugamuchi fever by the Japanese river mite, rickettsialpox by the mouse flea. All the rickettsial infections are acute, febrile illnesses characterized by a rash and a varying degree of mortality. The mortality of typhus tends to be very high.

"Classic" louse-borne typhus was endemic to, and often epidemic in, Eastern Europe, the Near East, and Russia. The disease figured in European literature as a daemon ex machine; typhus often destroyed besieging armies, saving cities, or conversely, left cities full of dead ready to contaminate conquerors. Napoleon's armies were ravaged by it as they dragged their lice from the English Channel to Moscow; the protagonist in Turgenev's *Fathers and Sons* died of typhus acquired while performing a post-mortem examination, thereby figuring forth the helplessness of the enlightened "nihilistic" generation in the face of an antique horror. Pathologically, typhus is characterized by an acute inflammatory and necrotizing process in the cells of the capillaries through the body, a kind of swift inflammatory degeneration of the lung cells in the smallest blood vessels, often with catastrophic results for the area or organ where this takes place. The disease begins with fever, followed soon by a rash. After a time the characteristic degeneration of blood vessels in the skin transforms the rash into a dark, red-purply process that mottles most of the body, hence the term "Fleck Typhus" or spotted typhus.

Since there was no definitive treatment for typhus in 1945, all that could be done was to treat the specific manifestations of the disease and hope for survival. The basic problem of recognizing typhus in the first place before coming to grips with its complications and permutations was very difficult for American physicians, who had never seen a case. Our chief resource was the young Yugoslavian, who, in his army career, had lived with typhus in the primitive, lousy encampments of the partisans. Like everyone else close to the disease, he had learned to dread it and to look minutely for its presence and its manifestations. He was a recent graduate of the University of Belgrade just before the war and had had no sophisticated postgraduate training, but he knew typhus, I suppose, better than anyone else in the world. As we walked down the wards, he demonstrated the characteristic rash, the early stage with a deep pink eruption that blanched under light pressure, the second, a mass of dark red hemorrhagic eruptions, dark massy speckles all over the body.

Even in the short time the hospital had been functioning, the American physicians had started to learn the danger signs. Invasion of the central nervous system produced a peculiar agitation, followed within hours by delirium. On the first day I began to see patients who would suddenly begin babbling wildly, trying to lift themselves from the cot, so weak they needed only a hand or a finger to restrain them. Most of the time, I learned, death followed within twenty-four hours, with convulsions and agonal screaming. After a couple of days of going around with Tito Minor, as our young Yugoslavian was delighted to be called, I had also learned to look for a rapid heartbeat and a falling blood pressure indicating invasion of the circulatory system. Tito Minor would take a pulse, note a blood pressure reading, and put a blanket back with a headshake. "*Bald todt,*" he would mutter, and he was almost always right. Within a day or two a shocklike state would produce deadly cold, a weak, rapid, thready pulse, a blue color to lips and earlobes, and gasping, wheezing death.

We treated the central nervous system complications with sedatives and anticonvulsants; circulatory collapse was treated with digitalis and adrenaline—the latter to sustain blood pressure (It was the only pressor agent then available). Nobody was sure the treatment helped very much, and the death rate was appalling once the more virulent stages of the disease took over. I remember standing with Tito Minor one evening watching a man die of terminal inflammation of the brain and spinal cord. He suddenly drew up in the terrifying position called opisthotonus, commonly seen in the last stages of tetanus, when the body is arched like a drawn bow, only the heels and the back of the head touching the bed, muscles drawn to an unbelievable rigidity. The man's groans turned to screams; the screams seemed to cycle with the convulsive arching of his body, growing louder and higher in pitch while his body pulled into more intense contortions until one feared the spinal cord would shatter. In midscream he collapsed, the sounds cut off, the muscles loosed in a series of jerking releases, and the man was dead, a pathetic, shriveled testament to the virulence of the *Rickettsiae* and the savage degeneracy of humans.

To which add the final mocking element: The only real treatment we could offer was food, and my friend had been right. The medical bureaucrats had pulled off the final, staggering stupidity of the Second World War. It was the absolute top of an impressive list, starting with the clods in Italy who threw combat men from Cassino in jail for coming on leave without neckties, proceeding through the record of the criminal incompetents in army ordnance who sent our men into battle with obsolescent death-trap tanks, reaching flood tide with the rear-echelon satraps who kept regiments of able-bodied men busy with janitor work far behind the lines while we sent sick and wounded infantrymen back out to fight, and finally, small but dazzling, incomparable, this paradigm, this illumination of a kind of mindlessness that percolates through our corporations, our governments, our institutions, our armed forces, corrupting, castrating, infuriating, wasting, and finally destroying—here it was, focused to a brilliant point of light. We couldn't feed the patients. Army regulations said we couldn't feed them army rations at a time when those rations were the specie of Western Europe, traded for sexual favors, for war souvenirs, for black-market profit, moldering in mountains in every depot, generating towering profits for manufacturers and traders and pilferers, wasted and dumped in garbage cans by the ton, but denied to our poor patients whose only hope for life they were.

As I walked along the rows, patients called to me, beckoned me. By now the word was out that I spoke German, the lingua franca of prisoners and victims, and they tried with varying degrees of desperation to convey to me that surely some monstrous mistake was being made, something that I or any rational man could correct with a word.

"Hunger, hunger," this often with the clutching of my sleeve to hold my attention. "Herr Major, we are starving. I don't believe this. We were finally rescued, we never thought we could be rescued, we never thought it was possible, but we were rescued by the Americans; after everything we were rescued, and now we're starving."

A meal might consist of a cup of milk and two crackers from a K ration. One inmate looked at this repast and commented bitterly to another, "*Guten Appetit!*"

"Please," one mumbled, "I'm dreaming. This is a nightmare."

Translations were incredibly involved; a Hungarian might speak to a Czech who knew enough German to speak to me. An enormous effort went on to convey to me as a sympathetic ear the mass conviction among the prisoners that nobody understood that they weren't getting enough to eat. They were sure that if somebody simply understood . . .

I kept asking the administrative officers. They were trying, they answered, with memos and phone calls to Third Army, largely ignored. Military government officials were manifesting their true colors early in the game. Nothing was their fault or their responsibility. See the people at the captured food warehouse in Munich. See the general who had the key to the warehouse; he wasn't around! Then see his aide. Not around either! Well, what could you do?

The medical officers themselves had gone around to the local Germans for food, meeting, of course, a blank wall. Didn't the Americans have all the food in the world? How could the poor, starving Germans possibly part with anything, pressed as they were by four years of war? The rear-echelon medics lived with the pretense of law, and it hadn't occurred to any of them simply to take food from the well-stocked larders around.

After a week, desperate myself, I went to see Major Karff, the commanding officer. I explained that there was a critical shortage of food.

Yes. His nod was solemn. Agreement. "Some administrative problems. Administrative."

I waited. Silence. Apparently the word *administrative* had been hauled in from the wings to explain and excuse everything.

"They're starving." I blurted it. "These people are really starving to death. Right in this United States hospital."

"Starving is a strong word, Major." (Calming, conciliatory, minimizing, smiling, tolerant.) "Supply problems. . . . "

I described that day's menu on the wards. I asked the major if he thought he or anybody else could live on it.

"A couple of cups of milk a day," I finished. "The only treatment we have for these people is food. It could save a lot of their lives, but we aren't feeding them."

The major spread his hands. I thought of a French general in 1940, bathing in happy, relieved hopelessness, in cleansing disavowal.

"We can do something," I put the point strongly. "I can do something, but I'll need help." Raised eyebrows, genuine surprise, unspoken question. I went on. "I have a carbine and sixty rounds of ammunition in my ambulance. Give me some men from the mess crew and I'll bring in all the fresh meat we can use."

"Fresh meat?" The major started to beam. Apparently he thought the fresh meat was going to be for him.

"There," I pointed out the window. The major's gaze followed my finger, focusing on some cows and pigs in nearby fields. Then he swung back to me. The dawn of comprehension was followed swiftly by a high noon of genuine alarm.

"You mean those cows, that livestock?"

"Just shoot the goddamned things. Make stew. Feed these people. The military government can pay them or something later, and what if they don't?"

"Just take them? Take people's property?" The idea was still battering at the outworks of the major's mind. Tough sledding.

"Major, the Germans did this to these people. They can damn well feed them."

"*Take* people's private property?"

"Hell, the Germans took their lives, if you want to think of it that way. Food, medicine, it's life-saving. It's an emergency." The words were tumbling out. I had to penetrate that glassy incomprehension. Inhalation, retreat to back of desk, official pose, steely gaze.

"Major, the United States Army doesn't steal. We are not criminals."

I forbore to point out that the army killed and burned as a matter of duty, because a category was knocking.

"Foraging," I said, "it's just foraging. Foraging is okay, it's official. Armies forage; they have foraging parties. Officers are in charge of foraging parties. If an army didn't forage when it ought to, people would get court-martialed."

The major hung firm. I had him by the throat. The official resonance of the word *forage* was something he couldn't get around. It was standard military jargon, and he knew it. It suggested something he ought to do that he wasn't doing.

I pressed on. "Sherman, Stuart, Grant—all the great American generals did it. Had to. Armies are supposed to forage when they don't have food. Rules of war."

The major looked trapped; I began to relax, thinking I had snared him in officialese and that the mess truck would soon be forthcoming, but I reckoned without the major. He was, after all, a career survivor; he had survived too many half-witted encounters, too many *imbecilia bureacratica* to be hoisted by any engine of mine. In a way it was wonderful to watch him recover. With the deepest, most studious, kindly explanatory air he began a lecture, not really much sillier, now that I think of it, than many I have since heard from learned podia or corporate board-tables.

"Armies forage, of course; they always have, but armies forage *to feed their own soldiers*. That's their duty, that's legal. Rules of war. On the other hand, if armies took people's private property and gave it to other civilians ... " (long pause, tapping of fingers on desk with each word) "that, Major, would [pause] be [pause] stealing!"

Silence. I waited for a silly giggle or some other more obvious sign of lunacy, but the studious lecture continued. The major looked steely-eyed. He pointed at me.

"You'd get in ... " (again a pause) "trouble."

Apparently I continued to look untroubled, or at least unimpressed, for the major fused and fired his ultimate weapon.

"You'd get ... " (very long pause) "a REPRIMAND!!!"

Studied silence. Hand that had pounded on desk now pointed a finger to the floor, indicating nethermost hell served for damned souls who have gotten themselves reprimanded.

I tried to talk, but nothing came out. Discuss mercy and reason with Caligula? Shout a message to Antares? My head was spinning with a feature of pure unreason. I left.

Across the muddy yard I slammed into the mess and began talking agitatedly, angrily, with some of the other medical officers. They all knew about the problem; they were all distressed; why not ignore the major and order the mess crew out on our own? Nobody could argue with success, and anyway, none of us was going to stay in the army after the war. We were all going home to residencies or to practices, and what the hell did we care what our army 201 files looked like? Certainly no one was going to get into very serious trouble for feeding concentration camp prisoners—not in May of 1945. I didn't convince anyone and, in fact, the more I talked the more I sensed embarrassment, a growing hostility, a concentration of a lot of frustration and guilt on me as an outsider daring to make them more uncomfortable than they were already. After all, they had tried within their own lights.

Two officers came in and sat down while we were talking; fragments of the conversation reached them.

"Oh shit." The speaker was a red-faced, food-stuffed officer punctuating his words with forkfuls of food. "Hunger, hunger"—he gave the words the German pronunciation as the inmates did—"that's all I hear. I'm sick of it. We're doing our best; I'm in the fuckin' ward all day on my feet for hours and do you think they appreciate it? Hunger—all I hear is this goddamn complaining."

His neighbor gave a relieved giggle and began to chant, "Hunger, hunger," in the singsong whining tones of the prisoners, shaking his head to convey wonder at their affrontery.

The two made a jeering chant of the phrase, repeating it to each other. I felt Levy's hand on my shoulder, restraining me, and I realized I had been about ready to plant a plateful of food on the fat officer's mocking mouth. I walked out.

Across the yard in the ward I made rounds with the Dutch physician, stopping while he rested, sitting down every third or fourth bed. We had offered him rations like ours, because after all he was a working physician and insisted on staying on his feet as long as he could, but he refused. To have accepted extra food, he explained, would have been a betrayal of his friends, his patients, as he thought of them. I kept thinking that I should ignore him and simply carry him off someplace and feed him, but he probably would have refused even then. I thought then, and I have thought many times in the years since, that nobody who hasn't been desperately hungry or close to real starvation could begin to grasp the sacrifice of that splendid old Hollander. It was a triumph of idealism and dedication over the atavistic lifesaving reflexes of the human organism beyond anything in my experience. We wanted to bring him food and put it in front of him to try to make him eat, but that would have tormented the old man beyond endurance, so we let him sit there on the cot with his friends and patients, munching a couple of K ration crackers, quietly accepting with them the agonies of slow starvation.

Next day Tito Minor asked me to drive him to a bookstore in the village of Dachau to find a German-English dictionary. I was delighted; a few hours out of the camp was welcome, and somehow, even in Nazi Germany, the idea of a bookstore conveyed an aura of learning and decency. I half-expected to find some scholarly old gentleman who had been hiding volumes of Heine and Brecht from the Nazis, but when I confided all this to Levy, he snorted.

"We looked that place over when we moved in. It's wall to ceiling Nazi propaganda, race books, stuff about *Übermenschen* and *Lebensraum*. Scholarly old bookseller my Jewish ass!"

When Tito and I walked in the door, any shred of illusion vanished; the proprietor was a rodent-faced version of Joseph Goebbels, deep in hunched conversation with two Germans. Since I took pains to look uncomprehending and talked loudly in English to Tito Minor, I was soon hearing phrases about the god-damned Jews in the camp, and all this ridiculous fuss the Amis were making, and why didn't people get them all killed in time?

I waited until the conversation, subdued on our entrance, had hits its stride before introducing myself in my most fluent German, explaining what I wanted. The effect was marvelous: the two customers backed against a shelf, staring at me as if I'd pointed a gun, while the proprietor pasted the sickliest smile I've ever seen across his receding chin and froze. At that stage of the war most Germans supposed we had some equivalent of the Gestapo, since they couldn't imagine running a war or a country without one. Obviously they felt they had been blabbering unguardedly in the presence of an *Obersturmbann-führer*.

A dictionary, I reminded the bookseller forcefully. He ran to get one.

"We work at the camp there." I pointed out the window. "In the typhus hospital."

Rodent-face began to talk. Wasn't it awful; my God, they were appalled; they never suspected.

The words *nie gemütet*—never suspected—uncorked all the bad temper I'd been holding back for days. Ever since we'd crossed the German border all we had heard was how nobody suspected, nobody was a *Naziparteigenosse*, nobody ever dreamed, if they had only known, and besides, what could they do? We really didn't give a damn, and reactions had varied from uh-huh to bullshit, but to hear this same whine right in the village of Dachau, in the lee of the horror of horrors, blew all restraint to the winds.

"Didn't suspect, you goddamn pimp." I found myself dragging Rodent-face to the window, holding his head out, pointing him toward the camp a mile away. "What the hell was there not to suspect when you saw all those furnaces and barbed wire and railroad sidings and trucks loaded with human beings coming in to get burned? Christ, the stink must have knocked you over. Couldn't you see? Couldn't you smell?"

I picked up the dictionary. Rodent-face started to say something, but before he did I seized a piece of paper from the counter, wrote "requisitioned for the inhabitants of Dachau" across it and started for the door. Before I went out I turned back, trying to say something more impressive, more chilling. The Germans hadn't moved; their expressions had hardly changed.

"*Leb' 'wohl, Naziparteigenosse*," I told them, "Live well, Nazi party members, soon comes the American Gestapo," and with that completely empty but satisfying threat I slammed out to the jeep.

At the end of three weeks, the food shortage improved; somebody got the word somewhere, and I had the pleasure of hearing a prisoner tell me he had "*mehr als genug*" to eat one day. It was time to go back to my unit, and I packed up and left.

How many had died of the stupidity? Hard to say—there was so much else to die of. On the way through the village of Dachau I stopped at military government headquarters with some idea of tracking down the responsible dunce, or at least finding out if the machinery could possibly admit to having broken down. Military government headquarters was very well bestowed in a mansion, and the officer in charge, typically, was a quartermaster corps captain who stood behind a large desk wearing riding breeches and highly polished boots, twiddling a riding crop.

I tried in reasoned tones to explain what had happened, but the captain kept shaking his head all the time I talked and ended up by telling me that it really hadn't. I next told him what I'd actually seen the prisoners eat, and he implied strongly that I was making it all up. We both started shouting; the captain retreated behind his desk and struck what he obviously thought was a military pose, hand on hip, riding crop tapping the desk. In the first place, he explained, I was all wrong; there had been lots of food in the camp all the time, and anyway, it wasn't his responsibility.

Whose was it?

Not clear, certainly not his.

Well, how would he have known there was enough food if it wasn't his responsibility? It must have been in his department?

Lines of administrative responsibility, problems I wouldn't understand.

I exploded. I told him he was either a fool or a liar; I pointed out the incongruity of his Georgie Patton get-up in the light of his real role in the army, i.e., that of a glorified grocery clerk. I commented further that he was an incompetent grocery clerk. (Military joke: Only two members of the quartermaster corps died in the whole war: a case of toilet paper fell on one and the other died laughing.)

Again I slammed out of doors and realized I was being bad tempered, emotionally exhausted, floundering, and ineffectual. I should have gone to the inspector general of the Third Army and nailed the culprits; someone should have burned, but by now I was sick of the camp, sick of my own footling efforts, sick of the mindless bureaucracy I saw closing around us, and I simply turned my ambulance north and headed toward the mansion on the Danube.

Even as I drove along the autobahn, somewhere in the large centers of Germany businessmen in uniform were finding it easier to deal with former Nazis than with the heroes of the concentration camps. One Demaree Bess, a writer for the *Saturday Evening Post*, was to comment with stupid loftiness that one couldn't turn the government of postwar Germany over to men who were still capable of hiding fish sandwiches under their beds, thereby betraying his bottomless ignorance of the real greatness of mind and soul that had been penned in the concentration camps and of the grinding compulsions of starva tion. In offices in New York and Boston men whose moral imperatives began and ended with greed were limning the corporate structures of the next incar- nation of Krupp and I.G. Farben; all through Germany the military govern- ment units, staffed by the incompetent rejects of the combat army, the men with no war to forget, the compromisers trapped in immediacy and the need for personal advancement, were creeping through everything we had con- quered, leaving trails of expediency and comprise across the footsteps of heroes while back in our mansion in the willows, we, the innocent warriors, still in the glow of victory, propped our boots on the marble tables, drank our cap- tured beer, and talked of battles won and the battles still ahead of us in Asia. What a relative pleasure it would be to match our long-barreled seventy-six- millimeter guns against the cracker-barrel tanks of the Japanese!

Precious Cargo

From *The Rescue*

BY STEVEN TRENT SMITH

Another incredible World War II rescue mission takes place in the Philippines, and is described in white-knuckled detail in Steven Trent Smith's *The Rescue*. The time is 1944, the place is the island of Negros. A rag-tag band of 40 American missionaries and their children, plus a few escaped POW, are under death warrant by the Japanese. They trek to a secluded beach to await evacuation by submarine to Australia. They are picked up by the USS *Crevalle*—but their adventures are only beginning.

★   ★   ★   ★   ★

Unbeknownst to the refugees and the Salvador Abcede, *Crevalle* was even then patrolling a few thousand yards offshore, looking for any signs of life on the beach. At 8:55 A.M., just a few minutes after John Maille began his periscope watch, he suddenly pulled away from the eyepiece. With urgency in his voice he called out, "Mr. Ruhe? Is this what you're looking for?" Ruhe took a quick look. Smiling at the motormac, he said, "Well done, Maille. Captain to the conning tower!" Walker rushed up the ladder and grabbed the scope from Ruhe. He carefully scanned the shoreline. Two white squares hanging from coconut palms caught his eye. "Looks right." Still, there were no people, no boats, just the panels. "Let's move in for a closer look. All ahead slow, course one-two-zero." When the submarine was a mile off the beach, Walker reexamined the area, turning over in his mind the chances of this whole thing being a ruse to destroy or capture his ship. The sailboat he had seen earlier had tacked to the south and was now headed in his direction. He felt a vague uneasiness. "Take some pictures," he ordered. A call went out for the ship's photographer. While the sailor rigged the 35mm Kodak to the main periscope, Walker asked him to shoot the signals on the beach. "And grab a shot of the little boat while you're at it."

For the rest of the day, submerged and undetected, *Crevalle* cruised warily off Negros. That afternoon Walker returned to his stateroom, there to devise plans for the rendezvous.

The captain had to work out how he was going to get the passengers aboard without putting his ship in danger. While he wanted to have as few of his people on deck as possible, he also wanted to be able to defend *Crevalle* from Japanese attack. He resolved to use his gunners to assist the refugees as they came aboard. If trouble developed, they could immediately jump on the four-inch gun, ready to fire on the beach or to seaward at his command. Their ammunition would come from the ready lockers below the bridge. The 20mm crews were to load their weapons, then join Lieutenant (jg) Walt Mazzone's special security detail patrolling the deck. *Crevalle* would have to depend upon them to repel any attempt to take the ship. Walker would post a continuous watch on radar and both scopes, a duty that would fall to the junior officers, Lieutenant (jg) Jim Blind and Ensign Howard Geer. Ensign Richard Bowe would man the TDC if a threat from the sea developed. The assistant diving officer, Lieutenant (jg) T.W.E. "Luke" Bowdler, would stay below in the control room, ready to take the boat down in a hurry if there was any trouble. Bill Ruhe would assist the deck operations on the bridge.

The captain also had to consider how his submarine, already crowded with eighty men, was going to sleep and feed another twenty-five. He could put the majority of passengers up in the forward torpedo room, the rest aft. Because *Crevalle* had expended most of her torpedoes, there was extra space in each room. The torpedo support racks—the *skids*—normally crowded with deadly missiles, could be turned into beds; hard, uncomfortable, cold steel beds. The passengers would have to make do with a blanket or two. The object was to get the boarders out of the way of the crew as much as possible. As for meals, the cooks would have to be in the galley around the clock, the number of mess seatings doubled.

Walker had concerns about provisions, too. During the depth charging five days earlier, the freezers below the crew's mess had been shut down so enemy listeners would not pick up the sound of their compressors. Hundreds of pounds of spoiled meat had been tossed overboard afterward. He checked with his commissary officer, who reassured him there would still be plenty of food to make it down to Darwin. Confident that all was ready for the rendezvous, that all the bases were covered, Walker relaxed in his cabin.

★   ★   ★   ★   ★

By midafternoon the boatmen had hidden their craft upriver under the cover of overhanging trees. Upon Ramon Monsale's signal they were ready to slip their moorings, drift downstream to the pickup point, load, and head out to sea. Toward late afternoon Colonel Ausejo and others fanned out across the groves to tell the evacuees it was nearing time to depart. They made it clear to all that only one small suitcase and nothing more would be permitted aboard. Many people had no belongings at all. But the news upset Kenneth Ossorio—he had two bags stuffed with classified papers. When he realized that Ausejo was deadly serious, he crammed as many papers as he could into one valise, leaving the other in the care of his father.

At four-thirty precisely, Colonel Abcede called for the boats. One by one they emerged from hiding, sliding into the river's current. As they approached the mouth of the Tyabanan, their crews skillfully steered them to the shallows. Shouting through a megaphone from a sandbar across the river, Abcede told the group that there were now many more passengers for the submarine than the twenty-five he had radioed MacArthur about. He assured them he would do his best to get them all aboard. When he called their names, he said, each person must hurry to the big banca, the *Susing*. When that one was full, he told them to move on to the next boat. One by one, Abcede began to read the names in a booming voice: "Viola Schuldt Winn . . . Rodger Lewis Winn . . . Norman . . ." and shortly, "Sergeant Howard Tom Chrisco." Chrisco was surprised to be called so quickly, perhaps surprised to be called at all. There were officers and ladies ahead of him. "Howard Chrisco," came an impatient second call. The weary sergeant climbed into the boat and moved up to the bow. No sooner had he settled than Jamie Lindholm jumped into his arms. The boy looked up, a great big smile on his face. The battle-hardened former prisoner of war was charmed, and moved, by this simple familial act. Chrisco was soon joined by Snell, Dyer, and Young. After a long wait Kenneth Ossorio heard his name called. He and his parents boarded a small banca next to another boat filling up with the seven Reals.

For Bill Real, the dreaded moment had come. It was time to say good-bye to Thunderbolt. The two had shared great adventures. More than once the dog had alerted the boy to danger, had probably saved his life. He knelt beside the rangy mongrel, knowing in his heart he would never see the dog again. He gently rubbed its belly and scratched behind its ears—just the way Bill knew Thunderbolt liked. He told the dog he would never forget him. The creature was very subdued, almost as if he understood what was about to happen. To

Bill, this was the most difficult thing he had ever had to do. After a final hug and with a tear in his eye, the boy joined his family in the outrigger. "Hurry now!" the colonel implored. "We haven't much time."

When the four boats were loaded Abcede, with Viloria and a radioman, climbed into a small banca carrying an American flag atop its mast. With a wave of his arm, all the boats slipped into the stream. Prows pointed seaward, the little convoy sailed toward the rendezvous a mile off Balatong Point.

Aboard *Crevalle* a routine periscope sweep finally showed activity on the beach. "Captain to the conning tower," blared the speaker. Walker hurried out of his cabin. Through the scope he could see there were now boats on the beach, and a large number of people were gathered around them. Thereafter Walker took more frequent looks. At 5:00 P.M. he saw two large boats and other, smaller outriggers stand out from the beach. "This is it."

For the next half hour the commander watched the progress of the little banca convoy as it slowly made its way out to the meeting point, looking like a bunch of ants coming out of an anthill. *Crevalle* circled, submerged, at two knots, staying close to the rendezvous coordinates. Wanting to remain concealed as long as possible, Walker kept his looks through the scope brief— just a few seconds each. Aboard ship the tension was palpable. Orders were orders, but these orders did not sit well with some old hands. To veteran submariners, surfacing the ship a mile off enemy territory to pick up passengers seemed totally unnatural, if not downright suicidal. On the other hand, because they did not know any better, newcomers such as Ensign Bowe thought that being pinned to the bottom by raining depth charges and picking up refugees under the nose of the Japanese were standard submarine operating procedures. By 5:30 P.M. the bancas and boats were just a few hundred yards off the submarine's starboard beam.

"Security and gun details, stand by. Lookouts to the conning tower. Prepare for surfacing." Men scurried through the narrow passageway. Rifles and submachine guns were issued from the small-arms locker. Drums of 20mm ammunition were broken out from the belowdecks magazine. Pharmacist's Mate Fred Loos stood by with his medical kit. Over the intercom the captain announced, "If something comes over, you close the topside hatch and jump over the side. We'll come back to pick you up." No one relished such a circumstance. But from bow to stern, the crew was at action stations. Walker returned to the scope.

When Abcede's armada reached the rendezvous point, the boats dropped sail. And they waited. Bobbing in the water, in the stillness of early evening, they waited. Forty-one pairs of eyes strained to see any sign of a submarine. More than once someone shouted, "Look, the periscope!" All eyes would shift to the spot, but there was nothing to be seen. Kenneth quickly grew discouraged, convinced there was no submarine out there, that it was all a great hoax.

At 5:46 P.M. the wait ended. Two hundred yards ahead of the lead boat, *Crevalle's* great black nose suddenly broke the surface. Everyone gasped as the ship slowly revealed herself—first the foredeck, then the conning tower, then the afterdeck, finally the stern. Men appeared on the bridge while the decks were still awash. When they hoisted the American flag above the cigarette deck, a huge cheer went up from everyone in every boat. Some of *Susing's* passengers began to sing "The Star Spangled Banner." Loretta Ossorio began to cry. By the time the song was finished there was not a dry eye on any boat. To Howard Chrisco it all felt like being a kid at Christmas. It *was* Christmas—Christmas in May.

Suddenly the deck was swarming with men. The armed ones were the security detail. The others were the gun crews. Still dripping, the deck gun was quickly unlimbered. The 20mm cannons were loaded and cocked and ready to fire. Walker ordered all four engines started—two for propulsion, two for battery charge. The big diesels coughed to life, white smoke pouring from exhausts along both sides of the submarine's afterdeck. "Come about to course two-nine-zero, all ahead standard."

As his ship turned toward the boats, Walker turned his attention to the task of getting the refugees aboard. "Open the after battery hatch." He looked aft to see a horizontal black wheel spinning amidships. A round door swung upward. Out crawled Chief Petty Officer Fred "Hook" Sutter, who would assist the passengers down the tricky ladder into the crew's mess. Everyone was alert as *Crevalle* approached the bancas. "All back full. All stop."

One of the boats, flying a small American Flag, came alongside the submarine as she churned to a halt. "Dayon! Welcome to Negros!" hailed a man standing in the prow of the banca. After exchanging passwords, he introduced himself as Lieutenant Colonel Salvador Abcede, commander of the 7th Military District of U.S. Armed Forces in the Far East. He asked permission to come aboard.

"Come ahead!" shouted Walker.

Colonel Abcede leaped onto the hull, then scampered up the superstructure toward the bridge fairwater. He was followed by Ben Viloria and a young soldier with a spanking-new U.S. Army radio strapped to his back. The Filipino commander climbed up the ladder to the cigarette deck, met there by the American captain. As they shook hands, Walker thought him a striking figure. Abcede looked nothing like the tatty, dirty guerilla warrior he had imagined. The young colonel—he was only thirty-one—was dressed in crisp, clean khakis and carried himself with a decidedly military swagger. Pointing to the big boat seaward, Abcede informed Walker that he had not twenty-five passengers for *Crevalle*, but forty-one. The soldier motioned to a second banca as he continued what had become a plea. "Can you take that many? Twenty-one are children, eight are women." They were all American citizens.

Walker thought for a moment. He knew that life aboard his ship was going to be uncomfortable no matter now many boarded. But he also knew that there were no insurmountable problems in feeding and bedding all of the refugees. He turned back to Abcede. "Sure. We'll take them all. Just hurry them aboard."

The evacuees watched as the guerrilla negotiated with the captain. The boats bobbed in the water for an interminable time. People began to wonder why it was taking so long. No sooner had distress overcome them than a signal was flashed, telling the boats to approach the submarine. Another loud cheer came when word was passed that *Crevalle* would take not twenty-five, but all forty-one. Everybody was going to go home. The tiny flotilla converged on the submarine. It was three minutes to six.

When *Susing* was made fast, sailors, dressed mostly in shorts and sandals and reeking of diesel fumes, began pulling passengers out of the boat, passing them to other men on the deck, who pushed them down the open hatch. When the big banca was empty the second took its place and the operation was repeated.

From Abcede's boat a small wooden box was carried up to the deck by another guerrilla officer. The soldier told Walker that the box contained extremely important documents, captured from the Japanese on Cebu by Jim Cushing's patriots. He added that MacArthur was most anxious to see them. A sailor picked up the box, lugged it to the bridge, passing it down through the conning tower. From there it was handed to diving officer Luke Bowdler in the control room with orders to stow it in the captain's cabin.

As the sun began to drop across the Sulu Sea, *Crevalle* bustled with activity. While Walt Mazzone stood by the after hatch, the guerrilla commander approached and introduced himself. "I am Colonel Abcede," he said, then added with a mirthful grin, "That's spelled A-B-C, E-D-E." Abcede walked on, toward the stern, where he had posted his own guard. He had another man on the bow. Abcede seemed very much in control of the situation. Using radios just arrived from America, he communicated with his boats, with his command post on the beach, even with his lookouts in the hills. If they saw an enemy airplane approaching they would transmit a warning in time for the submarine to submerge.

Salvador Abcede had a lot at stake ensuring that *Crevalle's* brief call was trouble-free. The aftermath of *Narwhal's* previous visit had caused concern at GHQ in Brisbane about sending another submarine to Basay. Off Balatong Point on 7 February *Narwhal* had successfully unloaded a shipment of supplies badly needed by the guerrillas. She then evacuated two dozen refugees, most of them civilians. But within hours the Japanese had learned, in detail, of her exploit. Five days later the enemy launched a punitive expedition against Abcede's district. They swept through villages, burning and looting as they went. They destroyed crops and livestock. They killed men and women, and children, too—eighty-nine people in all. And then they left. Brisbane was dismayed by the breach of security. To overcome their apprehensions, Abcede had personally guaranteed the safety of this operation to General MacArthur.

The stillness of the evening was broken by the clamor of children, a strange and disturbing sound to men at war. It caught Walker off guard. He turned from Abcede to look for the source of the noise. In the fading twilight he watched as ragtag kids clambered up the side of the submarine, looking not unlike pirates boarding a prize vessel. The children ranged from small to large, and there seemed to be many of them. Indeed half his passengers were under seventeen years of age—the youngest, Janet Lindholm, born the day the war began two and a half years before. A couple of children were in tears, fearful of boarding the black sea monster. Mothers and sailors did their best to reassure them.

One by one the children went down the ladder to the crew's mess. Some climbed down. Others, the small ones, were dropped down the hatch by "Gooberhead" Johnson, a seventeen-year-old gunner's mate. Seven mothers followed. But only four fathers boarded *Crevalle* that Thursday evening. Three—Ricardo Macasa, Paul Lindholm, and George Ossorio—did not intend to leave Negros. Macasa was not an American citizen. Even though he had lived in the States for seventeen years, he had never applied for citizenship. Lindholm and his family had talked about his staying behind for weeks, but only at this moment, on the deck of the submarine, had he finally made up his mind. He helped his children below, giving each a quick peck on tear-streaked cheeks. Then he bade his wife farewell. Their parting was brief, hardly tender. In her heart Clara had known he would stay, but to hear his words just now, to realize she alone would have to care for her family for the duration of the war, still came as a shock. In disbelief, Clara Lindholm descended into the boat, hearing her husband say to Bill Ruhe, "I think I'll stay up here for a little while."

Paul Lindholm had come to believe that staying behind to continue his ministry was the right and proper and Christian thing for him to do. For days he had wrestled with that weighty issue; it troubled him greatly. His decision came slowly, painfully, then firmly and resolutely. He could endure the hardships of living in the mountains of Negros, a hunted man, so the men and women and children who had come to depend upon his caring and wisdom these past thirty months would not be disappointed. But he would do so only if he truly believed his family would be safe aboard the submarine. Earlier in the week Lindholm had gone to Abcede with his quandary. The guerrilla leader tried to persuade the missionary to leave; he may even have believed he had succeeded.

"Aren't you going down, Mr. Lindholm?" Abcede asked sternly, now knowing full well he would have one more passenger on the banca back to Basay. The minister replied simply that his job on Negros was unfinished. Walt Mazzone, standing nearby, was deeply moved by the words of the missionary. "Here's a guy," he thought, "who has freedom in the palm of his hand and he walks away from it to carry on his work." It was a very meaningful moment in Mazzone's life. But Abcede was not pleased that his earlier arguments to persuade the missionary to leave had failed. "I have orders from MacArthur to send you to Australia." The Reverend Lindholm quietly replied, "Sir, I have orders from headquarters higher than MacArthur's to remain here with your people." Abcede shook his head and smiled. Turning to his adjutant he said, "Ben, these are the kind of people worth fighting for."

On *Crevalle's* deck Kenneth and Loretta said their brief good-byes to George. There was no big scene in the short time the family had together. It was all rather matter-of-fact. Mother and son felt secure that father would be safe. Father felt the same about wife and son. Fleeting hugs, fleeting kisses, down the hatch they went, leaving George very alone on the deck.

When he climbed from *Susing*, Howard Chrisco looked up into the faces of the palest men he'd ever seen. Even in the dead of winter nobody could be that colorless. Deeply tanned himself, he was puzzled until someone explained, "No sun. Most of us have been cooped up inside the hull for five weeks." A seaman stretched out a hand and pulled the sergeant up to the deck. "Where you from soldier?" asked Gooberhead the gunner. "Missouri," drawled Chrisco. "Me, too! Welcome home!" the young sailor replied as he helped the sergeant, whose still painful arm hung loosely in its sling, negotiate the steep ladder down. At the bottom another sailor greeted him cheerfully, then pointed him in the direction of the forward torpedo room.

For Russ Snell, leaving the Philippines was bittersweet. Before the war, before 8 December 1941, he had resolved to reenlist, to stay in the islands he had grown so fond of. But after what he had gone through since, he was now very glad to be getting out. He took one last look at Negros, one last gulp of warm Philippine air, then disappeared down the hatch.

As the evacuees went down into the brightly lit crew's mess they were assaulted by a noxious combination of smells: rancid frying grease, cigarette smoke, diesel fumes, and the unmistakable odor of unwashed bodies. To their left, through a narrow doorway, they could see the crew's quarters, a darkened Quonset-shaped room crowded with triple bunks. Men not on duty peered out from under their bedding, astonished to see women and children. Looking around the mess, the passengers could see it was rather basic. Four metal tables affixed to the deck provided seating for meals and for recreation. The top of each table was covered in linoleum and inset with red and black checkers and acey-deucey boards. Beyond the tables was the tiny galley, where the ship's three cooks slaved over their hot griddle. In one corner a fancy radio sat on a recessed shelf, blaring forth music from some far distant station. Across from the galley a huge stainless steel coffee urn, percolating away, was bolted to the wall. A jungle-weary mother asked if the coffee was "real." "You bet. Help yourself," a sailor replied.

From the crew's mess the evacuees were marched forward through the busy control room into officers' country and on to the forward torpedo room. The control room was bathed in eerie red light, which greatly impressed the children. On their way through, some slowed to "ooh" and "ahh" at all the gauges and wheels and multicolored lights. "Don't touch," cautioned Luke Bowdler.

When they got to the torpedo room, the refugees were asked to find a place to sit. Though there was only one torpedo in the racks, it still quite awed the children. Little hands pawed cautiously at the giant missile. Small eyes turned curiously toward the bow and the six gleaming bronze torpedo tubes festooned with numerous pipes and dials and valves. This looked like a grand jungle gym. As they approached the tubes they were summarily shooed away by torpedoman Francis Thomas MacGowan, although with a smile he told the children to call him "Mac." Unhappy at not being permitted to climb about, they settled on the empty skids.

Up on deck, the evacuees' baggage was being brought down the hatch. While supervising the guerrilla stevedores, a thirsty Major Ben Viloria was handed a jug of water from the galley—his first cold drink after nearly three years in the jungle. He was delighted by the refreshing treat. From the bridge Colonel Abcede viewed the quieting scene with satisfaction. He was pleased with the speedy progress his men had made getting the passengers out to the submarine and safely on board. Walker, too, was pleased with the short turnaround. The young colonel descended to his banca, there joining Paul Lindholm for the trip back to the beach. As the boat pushed off, a voice shrieked out of the darkness.

"Hey! Wait for us!"

Startled, Abcede spun around to see one last banca pull alongside. "The Reals!" Hands reached out to pull five children and two parents aboard, then hustled them belowdecks—Rose shaking and sobbing as she climbed down the narrow ladder. "My God, I thought we were going to be left behind."

The Reals' banca had been loitering two hundred yards off the submarine's bow, waiting its turn to approach the big ship. As the empty *Susing* pulled past the outrigger, a man shouted to Sam, "The sub is full! There's no more room. You better turn back now."

That news practically sank the little boat. Rose burst into tears. Bill and John were ashen. Sam grew sullen. Disappointed, restrained, he told the boatman to head for shore. The bow swung around and began to gain speed when all of a sudden a voice called out, "Ahoy, small boat—return to disembark your passengers!" The relief was immense and immediate. In Visayan, Sam urged the boatman to turn the boat. The banca spun a quick half circle and tacked back to *Crevalle*, where sailors were waiting to haul the family aboard. Nancy, Berna, and Fritz were passed up in the arms of submariners. John and Bill climbed up the steep sides themselves. Rose enjoyed flirting with the men who helped her to the deck. Sam, scowling, followed behind. The family was the last to board. When the family was safely below, Abcede finally took his leave.

When the colonel's banca had cleared *Crevalle*, Walker issued orders to get his ship under way. "Secure the deck. Steer course two-one-six. Standard speed." He then went below to sort things out. The time was 6:37 P.M., just thirty-eight minutes after the first passenger came over the side.

Lieutenant George Morin led Viola Winn and her children to the officer's wardroom in the forward battery compartment. There, in the center of the table, was a pile of candy. Viola pulled a chocolate bar from the stack. She slowly unwrapped it, snapped off a corner, laid it on her tongue. Tears rolled down her cheeks as she savored the sweetness. Memories of chocolate bars past flashed through her mind. It was the best she had ever tasted. The Lindholm children joined their friends in the wardroom. Eleven-year-old Beverly's eyes lit up when she saw the treasures on the table. She eagerly grabbed a candy bar, practically devouring it in one bite. Then she grabbed another, and another, until she began to feel quite queasy. She would not touch chocolate again for years to come.

On her way through the galley Loretta Ossario stopped to ask the cook if she could have a piece of "real bread." He gave her a quizzical look. In the jungle, she told him, "we didn't have real bread—wheat bread." Wheat flour had run out years before. Cassava bread made a poor substitute. "I don't ever remember having any in the hills," she said wistfully as she took her first, happy bite of American white bread.

Twelve-year-old Bill Real stopped dead in his tracks when his family passed through the control room. He had never seen such an array of lights and dials, knobs and wheels, switches and gauges. The machinery at sugar central had nothing on this submarine. He approached a small metal table near the center of the room and peered down at a large circular dial. "What's this?" he asked. "How's it work?" All he got for his curiosity was a stern look. He turned to rejoin his family, but his considerable curiosity about how this great vessel functioned had been thoroughly piqued.

Major Edward Franklin McClenahan was quite happy to be aboard *Crevalle*. He had spent, by his own account, two and half miserable years in the jungles of northern Negros. Passing Walt Mazzone in the passageway, McClenahan said, "Do you know what I had for breakfast the other day?" Mazzone gave the army man a quizzical look. "I had Japanese liver!" The diving officer decided then and there to steel clear of the major. McClenahan was not happy with his bunking arrangements in the after torpedo room, so he sought out Frank Walker. "You know, you're a lieutenant commander and I'm a major. Where do I really sleep?" Annoyed, Walker replied, "In the bunk you've been assigned." "Well," said the major, "what do I call you?" More annoyed, Walker curtly replied, "Captain!"

As things began to settle, Chief Yeoman Al Dempster moved through each compartment recording the names of his passengers.

In the forward torpedo room Dempster encountered the apparition that was Howard Tom Chrisco. "I was a prisoner of war on Bataan." The Yeo, startled to hear the word "Bataan," stopped writing. Before him stood a thin, dirty, barefoot man in tattered fatigues, his right arm in a sling. The soldier was deeply tanned. His eyes, deeply set in a hollow face beneath a horizontal wave of brown hair, darted constantly, warily, full of suspicion. His voice was tired as he spoke slowly in an Ozark drawl. "We was prisoners for fifteen months. Drove trucks for the Japanese. We escaped last Fourth of July—seven of us. Spent ten months in the jungle with the guerrillas. I got wounded on an ambush, bullet tore right through my elbow. My arm's pretty bad. You got a doctor?"

Dempster knew the story of the terrible Death March on Bataan, knew that Chrisco had been lucky to survive. "You must've been through hell," he said, shaking his head slowly. "There's no doc, but we got a pharmacist's mate. Loos. We call him 'Pinky.' I'll send him up."

In the forward torpedo room Dempster found the sixteen-year-old Ossorio boy, looking for a place to put his suitcase. Kenneth did not tell the sailor it was stuffed with secret guerrilla maps and papers he had collected while working for the resistance on Negros. "Where do I put it?" the boy asked. The chief looked down at the battered bag. "Well, kid, we'll stow it below the torpedo tubes. It should be safe there." The teenager seemed relieved. He climbed into his bunk, the first real bed he had seen since leaving the house on the tree-lined street. He was disappointed to find it hard and uncomfortable. Nevertheless, he was thrilled to be aboard.

In his travels around the boat the Yeo came across two civilians turned soldier, one soldier turned recluse, an ailing Filipino guerrilla who had been on a secret mission for General MacArthur, and three more ex-POWs. A trio of comely young women gave Dempster cause for concern—sailors were already eyeing them. In all, the chief recorded the names of forty people.

As he returned to the control room he passed a shaken Clara Lindholm moving toward the comfort of her children.

Their mother found them on a skid near the torpedo tubes, playing with a tiny chick one of the other children had brought on board. Clara gathered them around. The children asked about their father's decision. "We have to learn to take whatever comes and try not to question it," their mother whispered above the steady drone of the motors and the pumps and the sea rushing by outside. The five Lindholms then bowed their heads in silent prayer.

At dinner that night sixteen children and mothers squeezed around the wardroom table to give thanks for their deliverance. Stewards Willie Gregory and Waymon Davis then delivered a feast the likes of which no diner had ever seen. Out came heaping plates of meat, potatoes, vegetables, pitchers full to the brim with milk, bowls of canned peaches, fresh bread, real butter, and more. It was a dazzling array of food. The adults filled their plates, ate ravenously, relished every bite. The children, many of whom had no memory of food such as this, were certain it was no good. One of the boys held up a slice of bread and asked, "What's this?" The meat was not to their liking, and the milk was not right either—it did not taste at all like carabao milk. Howard Chrisco was amazed at the quantity of food given him in the crew's mess. But after the second bite he knew he could not finish it. "Pardon me," he said as he rose, "I've got to go feed the fish." It would be months before he could eat normally again.

That first night aboard was a restless one for many of the passengers. For their benefit George Morin played Brahms' "Lullaby" (sung by Bing Crosby) on the wardroom phonograph. The soothing tones were carried over the intercom throughout the ship, gently encouraging the smaller children to sleep. Older ones, such as Kenneth Ossorio, found that sleep did not come so easily. He went back to the crew's mess to grab a cup of cocoa and swap stories with the sailors. Chrisco made friends with some of the motormacs in the engine room. He spent most of the night amid the deafening roar of the diesels, losing his voice telling his own tales of war. One submariner gave him a pair of black dress shoes to cover his bare feet. The shoes barely fit, and were certainly uncomfortable to a soldier who had spent most of the past two years unshod. But he appreciated the gift nevertheless.

In the captain's cabin, hidden beneath his bunk, sat the sealed wooden box that Abcede had sent aboard. It would sit undisturbed—indeed, mostly forgotten—during the long voyage south.

By dawn the next day *Crevalle* was nearly two hundred miles from Balatong point, cruising south-southeast at fourteen knots. Walker intended to stay on the surface as long as possible, to increase the distance between his ship and Negros. At 2:35 P.M. lookouts spotted two bancas at a range of eight thousand yards. The captain worried that these boats were coast watchers, that they might spot *Crevalle* and report her position to the Japanese. He decided to annihilate them.

Frank Walker felt he had good cause to sink the little boats. On the evening of 9 May, while transiting the dangerous Balabac Strait, en route to his special mission, the big ship spotted a small sailing banca with three men aboard apparently heading for Comiran Island. The captain concluded that the banca was harmless, that it did not harbor watchers. *Crevalle* steamed right past the little boats. When it was well astern of the sub its crew fired two green flares high into the sky. Walker was furious—at himself for being duped by the innocent-looking boat. Next time, he had decided, he would just shoot up little boats like that. And now he had his chance.

The submarine closed the bancas at high speed. As they dropped their sails and paddled furiously for Pearl Bank Island, Walker ordered the gun crew to fire ahead of the boats with the forward 20mm machine gun. The shells only incited the outriggers' crews to paddle harder. "Empty the pan," the captain told Morin, his gunnery officer. As the shells pumped into the wooden boats, the four Filipinos jumped into the sea. The ship circled the hulks, then closed for a closer inspection. The larger of the two bancas contained nothing but a straw hat, a few dried fish, and a basket. There was no evidence of a radio or of flares. Walker called the guerrilla officer, Captain Emilio Quinto, to the bridge to interrogate the men. Quinto questions the bobbing sailors. They told him they were Moro fishermen. Walker decided to believe them. He would not take them prisoner (where would he find room for them?), nor would he kill them. He let them go, knowing they could still sail the small boat to Pearl Bank. *Crevalle* returned to her original course, heading for Sibutu Passage.

The second night out, while the boat was entering Sibutu, *Crevalle* celebrated Dean Lindholm's birthday. One of the cooks, Ship's Cook 3rd Class Frank "Mother" Stokes, had baked him a cake, topped with mounds of icing and nine flickering candles. After a hearty round of "Happy Birthday," passengers and crew hungrily devoured the fancy confection.

By the third day, life aboard the submarine had grown routine. The five bunks in chiefs' quarters, a small compartment abutting the wardroom, had been turned over to the ladies, including—especially including—the comely Modesta Hughes. Mothers with small children slept alongside their kids on the decks of the forward torpedo room. Most of the men were quartered in the after torpedo room, though Howard Chrisco and Kenneth Ossorio got bunks forward. *Crevalle's* crew resorted to hot bunking: one bunk served two or three men sleeping in shifts, an unpopular but at the time quite necessary practice. The use of the toilet—the "head"—was a problem that plagued the ship. More was involved than simply flipping the flush lever. Indeed, the instructions on the use of the head listed eighteen separate steps: "See that bowl flapper valve A is closed, gate valve C in discharge line is open, valve D in water supply line is open. Then open valve E to admit necessary water. Close valves D and E." A missed step or a step in the wrong order would have (and did have) grave consequences. The problems (and mess) grew so numerous that Captain Walker had to order his passengers not to attempt to flush the head on their own, but to let the crew do it for them.

The young children spent most of their day in the wardroom, where their mothers read to them or helped them play games such as Monopoly, Parcheesi, and dominoes. The rest of the refugees, basically confined to the torpedo rooms, stayed in their bunks, read, wrote letters, or chatted with the crew. A favorite pastime was catching up with current events in the many recent copies of *Life* magazine carried by *Crevalle*. A reader might learn that *A Tree Grows in Brooklyn* was a national best-seller; that German prisoners of war in the United States were well treated, well fed, and generally happy; that young Red Skelton was one of the country's favorite comedians; or that ten Americans escaped from a Japanese prison camp in Mindanao and lived to tell their story. While the picture magazines entranced Bill Real, he really preferred to wander about the boat, trying to figure out how things worked. He was not above cranking a knob, yanking a lever, or throwing a switch. One of the chiefs, wise to Billy's ways, put up a sign: "Any children found in the control room without their parents will be shot." The message was ineffective. Having spent the past two years being pursued by the Japanese, Bill was not about to be intimidated by a bunch of sailors.

Radioman Jerry Stutzman let the kids come into the radio shack for a few minutes every day. They delighted in pecking at the telegraph key and spinning the dials on the radios. In the evening he let them put on the headset to listen to the dits and dahs of Morse as they danced through the air. Walt Mazzone quickly made friends with four-year-old Nancy Real. He had grown a particularly spectacular beard accented by a fine handlebar mustache. Nancy was greatly amused by tugging on Mazzone's face. When he was on watch, she would take him a cup of coffee. The situation with the passengers was so chaotic that Mazzone thought Nancy was an orphan. He had two godchildren her age back in the States; it grieved him to think she might be alone in the world.

The crew enjoyed ribbing Chrisco, Snell, and the other soldiers despite the horrible experiences they had lived through. The sailors learned, for example, that if they dropped a metal platter on the mess deck their guests would jump out of their seats. Navy thought it very funny. Army was unamused. But the crew members were genuinely interested in the amazing stories the soldiers had to tell: about the Bataan Death march, about the atrocities they had witnessed, about their escape from the Japanese, about fighting with the guerrillas.

Each evening, when the submarine was running on the surface, Captain Walker would order the hatches opened to ventilate the ship. Fetid air, built up during the day-long submergence, was quickly purged by fresh sea air, which cleansed the ship, the lungs, and the soul. Loretta Ossorio stood beneath the circular opening in the forward torpedo room, watching intently the small patch of star-speckled sky above. It was her favorite time of the day, for it hinted at the freedoms soon to come.

The submarine steamed across a vacant Celebes Sea. Soon she would have to transit Bangka Strait, then weave her way around the island-dotted, enemy-patrolled inner seas of the Dutch Indies. Australia was still twelve hundred miles to the south.

Three days after receiving orders for the special mission, Captain Frank Walker had effected the rescue of forty passengers, not twenty-five. To everyone's amazement—crew, guerrillas, and passengers—the rescue had been perfectly executed. The entire operation, from surfacing to departure, had taken only fifty-one minutes—a far cry from the five days it took *Searaven* to rescue the thirty-three Australians in 1942. Walker was pleased. As *Crevalle* cruised easily toward Darwin, spirits were high. Everyone aboard felt safe and secure.

Just past midnight on Sunday, 14 May, *Crevalle* was nearing Bangka Passage at the northernmost finger of Celebes Island. While most aboard slept, Chief Yeoman Al Dempster was busy in his tiny office typing up *domain Neptunus Rex* cards. It was the crew's idea to pass these out to their passengers as mementos of crossing the equator, scheduled for the next day. In the galley, Mother Stokes was busy with prebreakfast chores, baking a batch of bread and rehydrating the powdered eggs. Up on the bridge, Captain Walker took over the con as his ship began the tricky transit through Bangka. Two and a half hours later he went below to catch some sleep after *Crevalle* had crossed into the Molucca Sea. As dawn overtook the boat Luke Bowdler relieved Jim Blind on the bridge, assuming the duties of Officer of the Deck (OOD). For the next four hours the boat would be his. As he looped his binoculars around his neck, Bowdler noted the low-hanging cumulus clouds. These, he thought, would give the submarine some protection from being spotted from the air. At 5:55 A.M. he was proved dead wrong.

A twin-engine Betty bomber dropped out of the clouds just a few hundred yards off the port beam, intent on sinking *Crevalle*. Bowdler instantly hit the diving alarm. As the Klaxons rang throughout the boat he yelled, "Clear the bridge! Dive! Dive!" The lookouts were dropping from the periscope shears before he finished shouting. Within seconds the bow was covered by the sea. Luke, the last down the hatch, saw the plane drop a bomb, noting with some relief that it would fall astern of his plunging ship.

The crash dive and the bomb explosion woke the entire boat. Captain Walker raced from his stateroom on hearing the alarm. Billy Real, sound asleep on a skid in the forward torpedo room, was jolted awake. Howard Chrisco rose with such a start he banged his head on an overhead pipe. But the crew seemed barely excited by the incident, which many of the passengers found reassuring. *Crevalle* remained submerged for more than an hour. Before giving the order to surface, Frank Walker called Bowdler into his cabin for a dressing down. What happened? the skipper wanted to know. As his OOD explained the situation in detail, Walker's ire dissipated. With a word of caution, he sent the young jg back to his post. "Surface. Surface," Bowdler called from the conning tower, and at two minutes after seven that gray morning *Crevalle* emerged from the depths. Within half an hour another Betty was sighted, eight miles distant. Again Bowdler dived the boat. Again the plane swooped in and dropped a bomb. And again it was not close. But just two minutes later, a third bomb suddenly exploded directly above the ship, jarring her from bow to stern. Walker decided to stay down to give things time to cool off.

Later that morning, at nine-forty, the high periscope watch sighted the smoke of six ships passing west of Tifore Island, a small atoll midway between Celebes and Halmahera, the vigilant Betty circling above the convoy. *Crevalle* still had four torpedoes in her stern tubes and one forward, and Frank Walker wanted to use them up. Despite the special mission, the secret papers, and the forty passengers aboard, Comsubs had never rescinded the ship's original orders to "wage unrestricted submarine warfare against the enemy." Walker, ever aggressive, decided to attack the enemy ships. At 10:05 A.M. he sent his crew to battle stations.

The tracking party began its work. By ten-eighteen they had identified six marus, two destroyers of the Shinonome class, two destroyer escorts of the Chidori class, and a fifth escort, a converted minesweeper. It took twenty minutes more to determine the enemy ship's precise course and range. Then came discouraging news. The TDC operator, Dick Bowe, said his calculations showed *Crevalle* could not get into position to launch her torpedoes. "The closest we could get would be seven thousand yards from the sternmost ship." Walker scowled. Seven thousand yards—three and a half nautical miles—put the convoy out of range. The captain asked Ruhe to release the men from battle stations. Disappointment showed on his face as Walker dropped down the control room ladder, heading to the wardroom for a fresh cup of coffee. But five minutes later the scenario unexpectedly changed. "Captain to the conning tower!" He was told that the convoy had just changed course, zigging right toward the submarine. Walker had not expected this favorable turn of events but was glad of it. The gongs rang out as the ship returned to battle stations. The flurry of alarms wrought confusion and concern among the passengers in the forward torpedo room. The crew told them only the basics: "The captain's going after an enemy convoy." Those words were not comforting, especially after having already been thrice bombed. In the wardroom Viola Winn, oblivious to the commotion, had gathered the small children, as she did every morning, for reading and playing games. Dean and Jamie Lindholm took a pile of dominoes from a box and began another elaborate construction, while the Real boys serenely played cards.

Things were anything but serene in the tense conning tower as the pursuit continued. Crowded into the tight chamber, seven sweaty men concentrated upon waging war. By ten fifty-five the distance to the convoy had closed to twenty-eight hundred yards. Captain Walker picked his target, the third ship in the line. He would shoot when the range dropped below two thousand yards—a nautical mile. Peering at the fat freighter through the attack scope with just moments to go, Walker heard Bill Ruhe ask, "Frank, did you do a sweep? Do you know where the escorts are?" The captain grumbled at his exec's criticism but followed the suggestion. As he spun the periscope, Walker suddenly pulled his eye from the finder, shouting, "Get me down! Get me down! Flood negative!"

For all his submarine experience, the captain had made a textbook error: he failed to search a three-hundred-sixty-degree arc. The skipper never spotted the smoke bomb the Japanese aircraft had dropped above him, signaling his presence to the convoy. Nor had he seen one of the deadly Chidoris break rank and turn toward him, belching thick black smoke behind a fearsome bow wake. One hundred twenty men, women, and children were about to pay for Frank Walker's mistake. As *Crevalle* plunged toward the safety of the deep, everybody aboard heard the loud, whining screws of the high-speed sub killer bearing down on them, passing directly overhead, steaming away. Only sonarman Grandma Biehl heard the telltale splashes.

As the submarine passed through one hundred ninety feet, the first depth charge exploded just forward of the conning tower. The boat shook violently. And then hell broke loose. There were no clicks. Only whams. Seven more gigantic whams in rapid order. *Crevalle* was tossed about in the incompressible deep like a mere toy. She pitched, she rocked, she rolled, she swayed, groaning all the while. Crew and passengers were thrown to the deck, against bulkheads, out of bunks, under tables. The concussion caused many to see a bright flash of red and to set off loud ringing in their ears. Throughout the ship light bulbs shattered, fittings snapped, cork insulation showered down like tiny snowflakes. The thick bronze locking rings on the torpedo tube doors started to rotate open. Amid the bedlam the crew managed to close and dog all the intercompartment watertight doors.

In the first seconds of the attack all manner of things took to the air. Loose wrenches flew through the engine rooms. A two-hundred-pound tool locker levitated and spun completely around in the forward torpedo room. The steel bowl in the officers' head blew off its stanchions. The blinker gun in the conning tower sailed out of its holder, smashing into Captain Walker's head. The ship's library cascaded down upon the children playing in the wardroom. Dean Lindholm's domino edifice careened deckward.

The sea streamed in through the steering wheel, soaking the helmsman and the talker. "Clear the conning tower!" Al Dempster, who had been sitting in the hatchway recording the attack approach, jumped to the control room deck, followed rapidly by others. Things were bad there, too. Water poured down from the conning tower, drenching the electronic bays full of delicate radar and sonar equipment. The emergency alarm from the master gyro compass blared. The mercury from the auxiliary compass had been blown out. Their failure meant shifting to an army tank compass bolted to the forward bulkhead. Two ominous green lights glowed on the otherwise all-red Christmas tree, the panel that showed any open hatches. Diving officer Walt Mazzone struggled to keep *Crevalle* under control as the flooding shifted the balance of the submarine in devilish ways.

The walls in the officers' quarters broke loose when their fasteners sheared. A light bulb had exploded directly above Rodger Winn's head. The shards showered down around him, but none hit him. From beneath the table scared eyes peered out. Eight-year-old Berna Real, claustrophobic and trembling with fear, watched sailors stuff mattresses around leaking pipes. "Gulp air!" Mrs. Winn told the children. "Otherwise your ears will hurt from the pressure." Two young ones grabbed the legs of electrician's mate Jack William Singer as he came to check on them. Looking down into their frightened faces, he gave them a paternal pat on their heads, struck by the fact that though obviously terrified, the children did not panic. "Be as quiet as you can. If you talk or make any sound at all they can get our exact position," he told them. "You don't want the Japanese to hear us, do you?" Little heads shook no.

The situation in the forward torpedo room, where most of the passengers were quartered, was alarming. Water poured in through myriad fractured vents, flanges, and gaskets. The sonar head connection leaked. The pitometer connection leaked. The starboard vent riser leaked. All the sea valves leaked. The space below the deck plates filled with water, submerging the two lower torpedo tubes. And if that was not enough, the torpedo room's heater burst into flames.

The sledgehammer blows against the hull quickly became too much for one woman. When she became hysterical, torpedoman "Rocky" Langfeldt seized her hard by the arms, shook the panic out of her, and told her to keep quiet. Howard Chrisco was awed when the two cast steel dogs sealing the lower escape trunk hatch suddenly sheared off during the explosions. The oblong door flopped open, swinging crazily on a single hinge, as water tricked in.

Chief Torpedoman Jim Howard calmly peered into the passage. He shouted to his men that the gasket on the upper hatch had blown, ordering them to rig a chain fall to close it up. Men raced for the block and tackle. They hooked one end to the hull, the other to the lower hatch, then quickly hauled the fall tight. They knew that if the outer hatch failed, the chain would not hold the lower door, nor stop the sea from pouring in. In the middle of it all, Loretta Ossorio wrapped her arms around torpedoman Mac MacGowan. "I'm scared," she told him. "So am I, ma'am." Kenneth jumped down from his bunk to join them. The pair felt safer clinging to the veteran submariner as the blasts continued to rock the ship.

On the torpedo room deck Clara Lindholm worked at keeping her daughters calm. They had been through many scary times in the mountains, but this was downright terrifying. Here they had no control over anything. They were now truly in God's hands. Beverly asked gravely if the ship was sinking, asked if they would all die. "I don't know," Clara told her honestly. Silently she prayed her husband would not lose his family aboard *Crevalle*. When toddler Janet began to cry, a sailor gave the girl a piece of a candy bar to quiet her.

The barrage was over in less then a minute, leaving behind a cyclonelike trail of destruction. In the stillness of the deep, all eyes instinctively strained upward, hoping to see through the thick steel hull, hoping to see that their enemy had broken off his attack, moved on, and would not return. A spooky silence spread throughout the boat, punctuated only by the sound of leaking water. After some moments all eyes leveled on their neighbors as if to check them out, as if to make sure everyone was all right. Clara Lindholm could clearly see terror in the eyes of her fellow refugees, perhaps, too, in the eyes of the crew. Kenneth Ossorio watched in horror as his suitcase full of secret guerrilla documents floated in the flooded bilges. Russ Snell, lying in his bunk, looked around at the mess in the torpedo room. He thought about the danger he was now in, comparing it to past perils. Fighting as a guerrilla was certainly dangerous, too, but in the jungles he could always get up and run away. "In this damn submarine there ain't no place to run!"

People moved slowly and quietly around the crippled submarine. "Is it over?" they whispered among themselves. "Is it done?" Through the hull they could still hear the faint sounds of propellers and the distinct and dreaded sound of sonar actively pinging for the ship. *Crevalle* was deeper now, and depth meant safety. At four hundred feet, the sub crawled along at two-thirds speed. With his own sonar knocked out, Captain Walker had no way of determining the position of the enemy above. Suddenly the screws of the Chidori grew louder. "He's shifting to short scale. He's making a run!" "Steady as she goes," replied the skipper. All eyes again soared toward the surface. No splashes. No clicks. Only whams. Without warning a string of eight more charges exploded close aboard. The shock waves slammed against the hull with the roar of a freight train. Then the sea went silent again.

The second attack unnerved some of those who had weathered the first. Now fear gnawed at their insides, churned their stomachs, and constricted their throats. There was nothing to do but sit it out. Billy Real, dangling his feet over the edge of a top bunk, thought the whole thing was fun until he saw a sailor crying. Then he got worried. Some crewmen, such as motormac William John Curran, were more circumspect about their condition. He truly did believe this was the end, that he was about to die. But he would not give himself over to his fears. A mate asked, "How can you be so calm?" Curran looked at the man closely. "What the hell good is it to get excited?" Loretta Ossorio had felt strangely composed after the first attack. A devout Catholic, she prayed silently to herself as the explosions rocked the boat. When the second attack came she felt strong enough to tell her son, "Don't ask me how I know, but everything will be all right."

Crevalle crept silently away from her pursuers—undetected, or so Captain Walker hoped. Though he never gave the order for "silent running," his crew had spontaneously shut down all noise-generating systems that might give away her location, in particular the ventilation. Within minutes the temperature inside had reached one hundred twenty degrees, with the humidity in rivulets, saturating the decks while beads of condensation covered the hull walls. Dean Lindholm, sitting in the dimness of the wardroom, grew concerned that water from burst pipes was drenching him. He looked around the room to find the source until he realized he was being soaked by his own perspiration. Doc Loos cruised the passageway, passing out salt tablets. When he reached the wardroom, he fetched some cool water for the children. He cautioned them to stay put while the captain evaded the enemy. Walker himself stopped by, too, telling Viola Winn and her wards they were doing just fine. When he left, Rodger Winn asked his mother to say a prayer. "Dear Heavenly Father, we thank you that you took care of us in the mountains and on the trip to this submarine. Watch over us now and keep us safe." Twelve hushed voices finished the prayer, "Amen."

As minutes became hours the air inside *Crevalle* grew foul; the finite amount of oxygen within the pressure hull was slowly being replaced by carbon dioxide. To preserve precious air, Walker ordered the crew not to smoke.

By then the oxygen was so depleted a match would not have stayed lit. He also ordered CO_2 absorbent to be spread around the compartments. The white powder soaked up carbon dioxide, prolonging the atmosphere a little longer. In the wardroom the kids began to fall asleep. "Blessed is the sleep of little children," thought Viola Winn, not perceiving the danger. Breathing became difficult, and with the suffocating heat came enervation. Those who could, lay in their bunks. Few men were on their feet. Walt Mazzone was one of them. He fought to keep the boat level and neutrally buoyant. Knowing how critical his job was to the survival of the submarine, he steadied himself with one arm wrapped around the control room ladder, his eyes constantly scanning the depth gauges, woozily alert for even minute variations in pitch or depth.

Forty minutes after the second attack Grandma Biehl managed to get the passive sonar working. He huddled in the damp conning tower, straining to hear the noises of the sea. The first pattern had knocked out the sound training motors; it was necessary for radioman Albert Bower to move the sonar heads manually up in the forward torpedo room. Biehl and Bower communicated via talkers. "Give me another two degrees right," Biehl would ask. "Two degrees right," would come back the response. It was slow going, but eventually Biehl provided his captain with an accurate tactical picture of the enemy's activities. As the noon hour approached, the captain knew there were three ships circling and pinging. Biehl whispered some good news to Walker: the enemy could not find the submarine. At 12:02 P.M., Walker ordered the boat's speed cut from two-thirds to one-third to conserve the battery. He then concentrated upon lightening the ship—there were twenty-two tons of water in the forward bilges, making control precarious. Any slight change in the sub's angle sloshed thousands of gallons of water, shifting the boat's balance. At her last refit in Fremantle, *Crevalle* had been given a powerful new centrifugal trim pump for an occasion such as this. In short order tons of water were forced back into the sea. Walker was very pleased with the new pump. It was, he wrote in his report, "wonderful and pumped quickly and quietly." For the next hour and a half, while the pump ticked silently away, the Japanese continued their sweep for the submarine. Many times they passed directly overhead *Crevalle* without picking her up. At 1:29 P.M. Biehl could no longer hear screws, only pinging. At 3:00 P.M. he could hear nothing but the Molucca Sea. The talker in the forward torpedo room passed on the news. Everyone was thrilled that their five-hour ordeal was over.

People finally began to relax. Compartments filled with the sound of chatter as crew and passengers compared their experiences. "They're all severe," said Jack Singer to one of the civilians. "Most of the crew take it matter-of-factly. But you gotta have confidence that everything's gonna be okay. When you've made a few runs you get used to in—to a degree. Well, you're never totally used to it, but after you settle down, it's mind over matter. You say a silent prayer and you go through it."

At five-thirty that afternoon Walker ordered Mazzone to take the ship up to sixty-six feet—periscope depth. Hoping against hopes, he ordered the main scope raised. When he peered through the eyepiece he could see nothing. "Down scope." Walker moved to the attack scope and tried again. "Down scope." They were both smashed and *Crevalle* was blind. Walker ordered the boat down to one hundred fifty feet, the course held at three-one-zero.

An hour later Walker ordered the ship up to radar depth, forty-five feet. Radar operator Biehl had already warmed up the SJ search set when the captain gave the signal to start the motor that would rotate the parabolic dish. He flipped the switch and waited. He flipped it again. And waited. A frustrated Biehl told him the set was dead. Frank Walker now faced a dilemma. He believed that if he surfaced there would not be any ships in sight. But he was not sure. Japanese escort captains had more than once caught an unwary submarine in just such a predicament. The sub killers would shut down their engines and drift, while their sonarmen listened very, very carefully. He mulled the risks over in his mind. "Lookouts to the conning tower. Surface! Surface!" The Klaxons rang out three times as *Crevalle* rose from the depths.

All hands were alert to the dangers as *Crevalle* slowly rose to the surface. Decks awash, lookouts and captain raced up the ladder to the bridge. A quick scan across the horizon revealed nothing. A relief. A more leisurely survey also revealed nothing. Greater relief. Once Walker was satisfied there was no enemy threat, he ordered the hatch in the forward torpedo room opened to ventilate the submarine. The room immediately became a maelstrom as fresh air was sucked the length of the boat, feeding the four hungry diesels near the stern and rapidly replacing the dank, lifeless atmosphere within the hull. Dean Lindholm was drawn like a magnet to the opening, there gulping down great lungfuls of ocean air. Up on the main deck, repair parties surveyed the damage in the waning light. The first depth charging had smashed the breech cover off the four-inch gun. The forward bridge fairwater was dimpled and the ammunition ready locker blown open. All running lights and the searchlight were smashed. The 20mm gun mounts had been torn loose. Most serious of all, the bow planes would not rig in, which would make running on the surface difficult. After reviewing the list, Captain Walker counted his blessings, for he knew the damage might have been much worse, even fatal. His ship was less crippled than she was hobbled. But she was out of commission as an offensive weapon. She had lost two of her eyes—the radar and periscopes. And her hearing—the sonar—was impaired. But she was still afloat, she could still dive, and though it would take a little longer, she could still get safely down to Australia.

Throughout the night of 14 May *Crevalle* cruised southward on the surface at sixteen knots. Belowdecks the mood was subdued. Sailors worked through the night trying to fix the long list of damaged equipment. Radarman Biehl sat on the deck of the conning tower, patiently disassembling the electronics bay. Albert Bower carefully dried each component as Biehl pried it out of the rack, fragile tubes and condensers spread at his feet. With the radar out, Captain Walker cautioned his lookouts to be extra alert. He did not want the enemy springing out of the pitch-black night. The passengers slept fitfully, fearing another attack might come. But many took comfort in the fact that familiar routines had not changed. Mother Stokes still baked his bread. Al Dempster still typed his reports in his tiny office. Captain Walker still strolled through the boat, making sure everybody was okay.

On Monday morning Clara Lindholm woke up feeling paralyzed. The intensity of events the day before had drained away all her strength. Doc Loos came to check on her. He took her pulse. He listened to her lungs. He looked at her throat. Then he asked her a few questions. After mulling over the symptoms he announced that she was suffering from "battle fatigue." Clara was amused by the diagnosis. Loos gave her some tranquilizers and within a few hours she was her normal, cheerful self again.

Midmorning, sonar picked up distant pinging. A sense of fear instantly permeated the boat. *Crevalle* was in no shape to go through another encounter with a determined enemy. For two hours Biehl, Bower, and Dempster tracked the active sonar. By noon they lost contact. Word was quickly passed through the boat. People relaxed again. At 4:30 P.M. the master gyro compass was restarted, and by eight-twenty that evening it was back in commission. That night, navigator Bill Ruhe went up on deck to shoot the stars with his sextant. With a good reading he was able to calculate the submarine's true position. At 9:00 P.M. on Monday Walker was able to send a radio message to Comsubs, outlining his failed attack and the resultant damage to his ship.

Shortly after midnight on Tuesday, 16 May, the submarine finally crossed the equator. Al Dempster brought cheer to his passengers by passing out the *domain Neptunus Rex* cards he had prepared before the attack, each signed by Frank Walker and Bill Ruhe. Many of the refugees had looked forward to the "crossing-the-line" party planned for the occasion, but events intruded; the cards would have to suffice. The quality and quantity of food began to change. This was not unusual at the end of a long war patrol, but was now exacerbated by the further loss of fresh meat, spoiled when the freezers were shut down during the depth charge attack in the Molucca Sea. Mother Stokes and the other cooks were forced to use more rice, a shift in the diet that pleased no one but the children, who had survived on the grain in the jungles. Having toiled nearly nonstop since the attack on Sunday, early Tuesday evening Henry Biehl and Albert Blowers got the SJ search radar working. Partially. The pair had stripped every component from the radar rack, cleaned it, checked it, replaced it if they could, then reassembled the conglomeration. Next they tackled the radar projector unit. That involved removing a large flange in the conning tower, held fast by twenty long bolts. The work was slow and tedious. When they took off the cover, a circuit board fell out. Grandma said he had found the problem. "The standing wave resistance card was blocking the circular wave antenna." Luke Bowdler, the OOD, looked puzzled. Biehl, waving the card in his hand, explained he was now sure he could fix the SJ. Topside, a repair crew had been working on the jammed radar mast. "Try it now!" somebody yelled down the hatch. When Biehl flipped the rotator motor switch, the dish failed to spin. He thought for a few moments, then turned to Walker. The radar could be turned by hand, he suggested. The captain agreed to try, and soon the SJ hummed back to life. At first the radar could see but a mile around the boat, but it was better than being totally blind, especially at night.

At eleven minutes past midnight on Wednesday, Captain Walker sent a second message to Comsubs, giving *Crevalle's* estimated time of arrival at Port Darwin. He then knuckled down to write his patrol report.

Every submarine captain was expected to submit a detailed report of all aspects of his patrol when he returned to port. Comsubs had established an outline that skippers were expected to follow closely. Walker, with the help of Bill Ruhe, began writing a time line of all noteworthy events on the patrol. Based upon the ship's log, and ending each day's entry with *Crevalle's* position, miles steamed, and fuel used. There were sections on the weather encountered and all ship and aircraft contacts that had been made. Each attack was covered in detail, including the serial numbers and maintenance history of the torpedoes expended. Because of the depth chargings, the section "Major Defects and Damage" ran six pages. When he got to "Personnel," Walker cited the top-secret nature of the special mission, Walker elected to submit a separate report for 9–11 May. Chief Yeoman Al Dempster typed up the completed report on Multilith stencils, ready for immediate duplication and distribution upon arriving back in Fremantle.

Leaks continued to plague the crew and passengers throughout the voyage. Walker's new trim pump worked overtime keeping the bilges relatively dry. And the bow planes continued to cause trouble, too. When *Crevalle* surfaced on Wednesday evening the planes, critical to depth control submerged but a hindrance to the helm on the surface, would not rig in. They had to be laboriously cranked back into position by hand. The captain urged his repair crew to concentrate on fixing the plane motors and linkage. They succeeded in restoring the bow planes to full operation by Thursday morning. And Biehl continued to work on the SJ radar—managing to increase its effective range. Late on the seventeenth it saw land at thirty-seven miles.

Just before sunrise on Friday, 19 May 1944, *Crevalle's* radar picked up the outline of northern Australia. And at 6:29 A.M. her lookouts spotted two boats to the south. As the vessels got closer they could make out the lines of a sleek Fairmile-class Australian Navy motor launch and a dumpy motor ketch. They were heading for the American submarine. When Captain Walker rang up All Stop, his ship rapidly lost way in the slight chop. The launch approached *Crevalle*, the launch's skipper hailing through a megaphone that he was there to pick up the passengers. This was a surprise to Walker. He had always assumed he would drop them off at the boom jetty inside Darwin Harbor. Another man, in U.S. Navy khakis, called out that he was there for the "mail" Walker had brought out from Negros. The one-hundred-twelve-foot HMAS *ML815* came alongside and was tied up to the submarine. Commander S.M. Smith, who headed the American base at Darwin, clambered up the side. Walker ordered the sealed wooden box brought from his stateroom. He had wondered what was in the container, what was so important that a base CO came to pick it up personally, but Walker was never to find out. Smith gave the submariner a signed receipt for the box. Sailors cautiously lifted it into the launch.

Her duty done, the Fairmile pulled away to let the sixty-ton trawler *Chinampa* nuzzle alongside.

Belowdecks in the submarine word spread quickly among the forty that they were disembarking now, not later, in Port Darwin. There was a sudden frenzy of activity. Sailors descended into the torpedo room bilges to retrieve still-soggy suitcases. Howard Chrisco pulled on the navy-issue black dress shoes a seaman had given him. Clara Lindholm and Viola Winn donned their best dresses. Nancy Real grabbed a last kiss and hug from Walt Mazzone. In short order, everybody was ready.

Chief Hook Sutter opened the after battery hatch. One by one the evacuees climbed the steep ladder into the bright Australian sunshine. They had not seen the sun since they left Negros eight days before. It seemed brighter than they ever remembered. Captain Walker called the group together on the deck—they assembled next to the battered four-inch gun. He addressed them in his deep, rich Down East voice: "You have been our precious cargo," he began. "Your conduct aboard this ship was magnificent." He continued by apologizing for hauling his passengers into a dangerous situation; he was sorry for the inconvenience caused. He explained that *Crevalle* was a warship on a war patrol, she still had five live torpedoes. He said he had felt duty-bound to fire them if a target presented itself. He thanked his passengers for bearing with the hardships his decision entailed. And he ended by warning them "not to mention at any time the name of this ship, the locality of your embarkation, or the means by which you have been evacuated." To Walker's surprise the gathering then applauded him.

There was just time to pose for a picture. The captain took his place next to Loretta Ossorio and Virginia Macasa in the front row. "Squeeze together a little more," cried the photographer. They squeezed. "You, in the back, with the wavy hair, stand taller!" He did. "Everybody smile!" Click. "One more, please." Click. And then it was time to leave. "Hey, 'depth-charge buddy'!" Mac MacGowan called out to Loretta. "Here's my mom's address in Los Angeles. Call her if you can, tell her I'm fine. If you get down to L.A., be sure to stop by, she'd love to see you." MacGowan gave her a big hug and a peck on the cheek. Then there was a flurry of final good-byes, hugs, kisses, shaking hands, don't-forget-to-writes. And, of course, tears. Many eyes, many cheeks, were moist that morning.

Over the side they went—women first, then the small children, carefully passed from hand to hand. The caretaker of the group, Colonel George H. Yeager of the AIB, signed a receipt for his wards. By 8:45 A.M. everyone was aboard, the lines cast off. Then *Chiampa* turned from the submarine and pulled away. It was headed to a remote intelligence base on the eastern side of the harbor. Waving continued on both boats for many minutes. When Walker returned to the bridge, he snapped a series or orders to get under way. *Crevalle*, under the protection of the Fairmile, still had a two-hour cruise before she would dock in Darwin.

Behind Enemy Lines

From *MIA Rescue: LRRPs in Cambodia*

BY KREGG P.J. JORGENSON

The story of America's LRRPs (Long Range Reconnaissance Patrolers) during the Vietnam War is one of triumph and tragedy. These men risked their lives slipping far behind enemy lines to bring back important information, but the cost was high. Here, a strike force races against time to bring out wounded LRRP's trapped by the NVA in Cambodia.

★   ★   ★   ★   ★

On the flight to the remote fire support base, Warrant Officers John Bartlett and Tyrone Graham led the mission in the Cobra gunship, but when the three Huey lift ships took off in search of the missing LRRPs, Bartlett and Graham took up their standard covering position.

Taking the lead in the first leg of the journey had maybe more to do with restoring confidence; the second leg of the journey was tactical.

The rockets, machine guns, and grenade launchers made the gunship attack helicopter a formidable weapon. For this mission, it would be the lift ships' responsibility to scour the countryside, searching for the missing LRRP team, while the attack helicopters would lay back, watching over the flight formation and, when needed, scream down from above to cover them with a deadly array of automatic weapons. The NVA were often leery of any helicopter because of this tactic. They could never be certain whether the helicopter was alone or simply being used to draw them out. From time to time, they'd set traps for the gunships, but they had to do it very carefully because if the gunships encountered more than they could handle, then they could easily call in fixed artillery on the enemy heavy machine-gun site. Once out of range of the NVA's weapons, they could easily pinpoint the 105mm howitzer rounds called in from a forward fire support base.

More often than not, though, pilots like John Bartlett and Jerry Boyle preferred rolling in on the enemy locations. Some said it was because they were hot dogs or showboats; others knew it was because they were the closest support to any unit who desperately needed their help on the ground. Sure, they thought they had brass balls, and a few even swaggered from time to time. But maybe it was the job that made them that way.

John Bartlett was better known by his nickname Bloody Bart. He had more than 1,200 combat assault hours in Cobras. The 22-year-old Apache Troop pilot was a gunship hotshot, an attack helicopter ace. Many of the scouts breathed a little easier when they had him shadowing as their high bird. When the smaller OH-6 scout helicopters flew at treetop level to draw enemy fire, Apache Troop gunship pilots like Bartlett flew in lazy circles thousands of feet above, waiting for the chance to assist the action. These hunter-killer or Pink Teams, as they were called, formed the backbone of the aerial reconnaissance arm of the troop, not to mention accounting for the majority of the kills credited to the 1st Cav Division. That effectiveness lay in the hands of the young pilots like Bartlett, who made it seem easy. But nothing is every easy in combat. Locating a target on the ground and then sighting in on it at a hundred miles an hour or more isn't easy, and when the enemy soldiers on the ground in fortified fighting positions are doing their best to shoot you out of the sky, it helps to have more than just a little bit of flying talent; you had to have nerve.

Bartlett had that, and multiple awards for heroism said as much officially, using phrases like "with total disregard for his own safety" and "gallantry in action." Bartlett had earned the acclaim and awards along with the Bloody Bart nickname for always staying in the middle of the fight, which came to be a trademark he shared with a handful of other pilots in Apache Troop. Most had been shot down more than once or had watched their best friends die in fiery explosions, so their commitment was always personal. Their collective attitude formed a collective bravery.

Ranger Hancock, who just the night before had barely escaped and evaded the enemy in a harrowing ordeal, was aboard the lead helicopter, ready to go back into the ambush site. His face was tense, something not lost on the rescue force accompanying him.

The lead helicopter would focus on the team's insertion point and last known position, and Hancock would fine-tune the search, retracing the team's steps from memory. The fate of the wounded Rangers lay in his ebony hands.

The weather was still dictating the mission. The fog was diminishing, but slowly. The ceiling was still ridiculously low, so the helicopters made do with what visibility they had. They flew low-level up a narrow valley with large, thick-branched trees lining each side. Wet open grassland, less than 20 feet below, blew back beneath the helicopters' passage as they thundered through the morning. Rounded hilltops peeked out of the fog as others disappeared menacingly in the loose gray backdrop.

Whenever they flew into the pockets of fog that refused to give, and those were frequent, the pilots switched to instrument readings, frantically calling out their headings. By luck, they avoided colliding into each other, hidden trees, and hilltops.

As they climbed to 4,000 feet, the fog gave way to blue sky and sunshine. Reassembling, the four helicopters took their bearings and once again looked for an opening in the fog. When they found one, they tried a different tack.

"Hang back in a loose formation," McIntosh suggested to the others. "That'll give us room to maneuver."

"Roger One One," the pilots replied while Bartlett and Graham said they'd take the lead and see how it was below.

Harris' order broke from the SOP but then this wasn't a standard mission. There wouldn't be a second chance. Fuel consumption dictated as much as the weather, and the unusual mission called for unusual tactics. Even so, a few of the rescue pilots were disturbed by the departure from the safe routine. On the ground, the helicopters would be sitting ducks, their only protection being the 21-man infantry platoon and the helicopters' door gunners. Neither could stop enemy mortar rounds from disabling or destroying the flight in just one volley.

Bartlett said as much but was overruled. Shaking his head at the idea, he remained in his gunship, watching the Huey. Helmet on and monitoring the radio, he wondered when the battle would begin.

He knew it was just a matter of time.

The two Rangers stared at each other for what seemed like eternity, and what went unsaid was transmitted in volumes. Andrus was in mild shock, teetering on going deeper, but elation and glee won out over his pain. Hancock seemed to find new energy as well. However, their adrenaline could only carry them so far, and they were both well beyond the limit for anyone, even Rangers.

"I told you I'd come back!" he said while Andrus nodded, staring back over his shoulder; back toward the hiding place. "I told you."

Andrus nodded and then turned back toward the Blues. "Clark . . . he's down there," Andrus said, motioning with a pained gesture to a small patch of underbrush. His wounds could easily be seen. The area around the collarbone was swollen and disfigured, dried blood crusted on his uniform. He pointed toward a line of dense vegetation. A purple-yellow cut ran the length of his wrist. "There are gooks all around here. We've got to get him," he said, moving toward the site as the rescue force hurried after him. His gait was stiff and slow, like that of a tired old man.

"Hold on," Sergeant Beal said to Andrus, stepping in front of the wounded Ranger and holding him back. "We'll take over from here. You just take it easy."

Several soldiers moved off in two separate directions to search for Clark. The Wise Guy was surprised to see that Major Harris, the Apache Troop commander, was following Hancock's lead.

"I'll be a son of a bitch!" he said as the pilot followed the uninjured Ranger while Sergeant First Class Kenneth Yeisley—the acting platoon sergeant for the Blues on the mission—the Wise Guy, and Sergeant Beal went in the direction Andrus had indicated.

Yeisley was a career soldier who had carried a Browning automatic rifle until the weight of the weapon under the sweltering heat, and maybe the difficulty of tracking down magazines for it, made him go back to a more accommodating M16. He also had the annoying habit of playing his bagpipes every day in the rear area, which the Wise Guy said probably scared the enemy more than the damn BAR. But Yeisley knew his way in the field, and the Wise Guy and Beal followed his lead with confidence.

"Did you see that?" the Wise Guy asked while Beal shook his head.

"What?" asked Beal.

"Look who's going around the other end?"

Beal turned to see the major and one other member of the Blues disappear into the underbrush.

"Who's watching his helicopter?"

"McIntosh," the Wise Guy said. "He and Bartlett are staying with the aircraft."

"Good. This ain't exactly a secured landing zone. Looks like Blue is setting up a perimeter, so fuck it."

Beal followed Yeisley's lead while the Wise Guy covered him.

The point squad would find and secure a knoll overlooking the LZ while the rest of the rescue force took a tactical stance. Other helicopters were ferrying in more of the multiunit rescue force.

The Ranger Company commander, Captain William Carrier, who was also ferried in with the rescue force, was studying the last known map coordinates the team had called in.

A combat tracker team arrived a short time later, but the area wasn't secure enough to let them work. The dog and handler might be able to get a fix on the missing Rangers if they could get into the ambush site.

Setting up protective cover, using the rolling hills to maneuver, Lieutenant Hugele had the Blues seal the area. The platoon's medic, Specialist Four Richard DeValle, waited with the main body of the rescue force.

The point squad, minus Beal and the Wise Guy, included Specialists Cortez and Bloor, who set up a machine-gun position to cover the immediate area. Their additional firepower and wealth of combat experience gave them more than the high ground—something that made the rest of the squad feel more at ease, considering the situation. Bloor and Cortez were veteran machine-gunners, although on this particular mission, Cortez carried an M16 since he had been unable to procure a light M60 from one of the platoon's assigned gunners. In combat, few people wanted to give up their weapons, especially on a rescue mission where contact with the enemy could be expected.

Almost on top of the LRRP's hideout, the troop commander was surprised to find Clark well concealed in a waist-high clump of elephant grass, hardly the place you'd expect someone to hide, but then maybe the perfect location just for that reason.

"Over here!" Cortez called to DeValle, the medic, and pointed toward the Old Man's position. DeValle quickly moved in to assist the wounded LRRP medic.

Clark's leg wound was menacing behind the makeshift bandage. He had lost a lot of blood, and his face was pallid and drawn. Helping Clark back to the main body of soldiers, DeValle had his hands full.

"Doc, you might want to take a look at him when you're done," the Wise Guy said, gesturing to Andrus. The medic was rummaging through his aid bag for morphine and bandages. He looked up and saw that something was seriously wrong with Andrus.

"You okay?" Beal asked Andrus, who tried to shrug his response and failed miserably. "The team leader's down there," he said, pointing to the ambush site. "We got to get him, too. We can't leave him. Them," he added correcting himself, recalling the dead assistant team leader's face when he turned him over in the ambush site.

Talking it over with Staff Sergeant Burrows and Blue, the two point men quickly decided on a course of action. Beal took the lead as the rest of the point squad started to move toward the ambush site, a hundred yards to their front.

Meanwhile, Doc DeValle's assessment confirmed the Wise Guy's suspicions about Andrus' condition. He was seriously wounded. A bullet had ripped into his collarbone and bored deep into his chest without exiting. A preliminary inspection showed shrapnel wounds to his back and wrist, but it was the thought of the lodged bullet and the internal damage it must have produced that bothered the medic most. The medic suggested that Andrus be medevacked as soon as possible.

Andrus, by then, was going into shock, his attention span was slipping. He had been up for almost 24 hours, and it was a wonder he was hanging in at all. How he managed to walk was something even the medic couldn't figure out. If there was a mystery about Andrus' hold on reality, Sergeant Beal and the Wise Guy knew what it was—it was searching for the two remaining LRRPs that kept him going. Beal and the Wise Guy had both been LRRPs with Hotel Company and had served well. LRRPs were like family—the team was everything—and until the remainder of the missing patrol was located, Andrus wouldn't surrender to his wounds. Period.

His concern for his teammates carried him over his pain. He wouldn't give in to the shock. He couldn't. There wasn't time.

"We have two Whisky India Alphas," the lieutenant said, using the radio phonetic code to tell the brigade's temporary facility at David that several of the missing LRRPs had been found and that the two MIAs were wounded.

"We're going to check out the ambush site for any others," Beal radioed the platoon leader a few minutes later. The platoon leader told him to take it slow and stay close to the radio.

"You stay with the medic," Lieutenant Hugele said to Andrus, who still wanted to help.

"I'm okay, sir," Andrus said. "I can help."

The lieutenant looked to the medic, who shrugged, and then back to Andrus. "You can stay a little longer," he said. "But after we check the area, you're going out on a medevac. You got that?" Andrus reluctantly agreed.

Through the background noise on the radio, Specialist Jim Braun was calling in a medical evacuation helicopter (medevac) while Lieutenant Hugele maneuvered several squads around to cover the point squad's bounding advance.

As Clark was being helped back to the rescue helicopters by the medic, Staff Sergeants Burrows, Beal, Tony Cortez, Duane Bloor, and the Wise Guy cautiously moved forward, splitting their lead and approaching the ambush zone from different entry points.

Awaiting the next discovery, Major Harris, Captain Carrier, and the others would remain in place. The two commanders divided the responsibilities for a more complete and methodical search.

Meanwhile, the point squad did what it did best. The men moved toward their objective slowly and carefully. Up a slight lime-green hill, a golf course-like knoll, the squad paralleled a "runner" —a small, orange dirt path leading into a patch of jungle—and a fresh clearing generated by the NVA's ambush against the LRRPs.

Unlike the unsuspecting Ranger team that had walked into the ambush site, the Apache Blues point squad knew what to expect, but knowing the very real and probable danger didn't lessen the advancing point squad's apprehension.

Staying off the jungle path, they bounded into the kill zone from different directions, flanking directions overlapping their fields of fire in case the fighting positions were still occupied. What they discovered left little to the imagination.

The horseshoe-shaped kill zone of the ambush site was nearly cleared from the previous evening's small battle; the gunfire and explosions ripped underbrush and branches, exposing a battle site that smelled like a newly mowed lawn with just a tinge of cordite.

There were no bodies to be seen, and no one was visible. But that didn't mean shit to the Wise Guy or Beal, who had the task of being the first into the kill zone. Dark pools of blood lay clotted on the leaves as insects moved through them, tasting it before making off with the small shreds of flesh. The two point men had seen it many times before. Deep, arterial blood, more purple than red. If the team leader and assistant team leader had survived the brief but intense battle, then it would have been a miracle.

Pieces of equipment were haphazardly left around the ambush site: a Chinese canteen, one of the Rangers' M16 magazines, a hunting knife that had fallen off the Rangers' web gear.

The fighting positions surrounding the kill zone were empty, hastily abandoned. The rope ladder was nearly severed, hanging like a kite caught in a tree. The lean-to was collapsed and bullet scarred. Beal and the wise-guy squad leader crawled in and out of as many of the fighting positions and bunkers as they could without losing sight of each other or the rest of the squad. Their actions were naturally synchronized, a practice developed over the time spent together on point covering each other, watching out for anything unexpected, and knowing that the other would always be there.

With a keen eye and an M60 barrel surveying the wall of jungle to their front, Specialist Bloor oversaw their inspection, while Andrus, losing strength rapidly, was led back to safety by the medic. Cortez provided cover support for them as they made their way back to the platoon, then turned his attention back to the point squad.

Beal's rough-hewn face held a stern expression while that of the usually gregarious Wise Guy told Cortex and Bloor both that the search was useless. The two missing LRRPs were gone.

And, too, there was something more; something Beal saw that made him give up any hope as he studied the kill zone for any positive signs. A piece of an arm lay near an exposed fighting position. Beal shuddered in dismay. Quickly crossing to it, he saw the severed limb was unusually thin and yellow-brown. Vietnamese!

"Andrus and Clark were lucky they even got out," he said to Cortez, who quietly agreed.

"There's no way the others could have survived this," he added. The ambush had been costly on both sides.

"We better call it in," the Wise Guy said just as the first explosions rocked the quiet countryside, and enemy mortar fire rained down on the Blues and the point squad still in the ambush site. The sniper fire immediately followed.

The NVA were springing their next trap.

Singular Courage

From *The Rescue of Bat 21*

BY DARREL D. WHITCOMB

The saga of the SAR mission which plucked Air Force Colonel Iceal "Gene" Hambleton (call sign Bat 21 Bravo) from the clutches of four NVA divisions has been celebrated in a Hollywood movie. But the true story was not known publicly until recently. Now, using declassified documents and interviews with survivors, Darrel Whitcomb tells the dramatic tale of how it all came down to one courageous American SEAL, Lieutenant Tom Norris, who moved, on foot, at night, to reach Hambleton and another downed airman.

★   ★   ★   ★   ★

On 9 April, activity picked up on the ground. The NVA force that had been building up in the Cam Lo area attacked to the east along Route QL-9. They were met by the 20th Armor and 5th Ranger Group, both under the operational control of the 1st Armor Brigade, about six kilometers west of Dong Ha. In a battle that lasted several hours, the friendly units used naval gunfire, airstrikes, and the direct fire of their main tank guns to stop the attack before it could gain any ground.

The ground commanders in the area declared a tactical emergency, meaning that they needed immediate help. Captain Icke, Bilk 11, was scrambled from Da Nang in his intrepid O-2 to support the ARVN. But before he could arrive overhead, the ground situation stabilized and he was diverted to work in support of the SAR operations. As he orbited and talked to the survivors, he watched and dodged more SAM launches. One of the missiles hit a B-52; the aircraft was seriously damaged but landed at Da Nang.

At almost the same time, the NVA also launched an attack against Fire Base Pedro, to the south. The day before, the 6th Vietnamese Marine Battalion had taken over defense of the position from a Ranger battalion. Upon arriving, they were advised that an attack was imminent. They were ready: the battalion commander, Major Tung, had learned from watching the NVA. He moved the majority of his battalion off of the fixed fire support base and dispersed it along a battle line. Then he devised a combined-arms plan, including the use of land mines, artillery, tanks, and airstrikes, to stop the enemy force.

The battle for Pedro started at about sunrise. NVA tanks charged right into the bunkers of the base and methodically began destroying them. The Marines counterattacked, but the enemy seemed to be gaining the momentum. Then the low clouds partly broke, and two VNAF A-1s were able to get in and destroy four enemy tanks. The NVA had moved in antiaircraft guns with the attacking units, and they shot down one of the VNAF planes. The pilot was killed.

Some NVA tanks attempted to bypass Pedro and became entangled in the minefield. Simultaneously, a counterattack force of mounted infantry and tanks from Ai Tu struck them. Using well-coordinated artillery, airstrikes, and direct fire, they routed the NVA force and blunted the enemy's effort to drive deep into the ARVN rear.

These two ARVN actions were significant. For the first time since the beginning of the offensive, ARVN units had stopped and defeated major NVA units. And both had been almost exclusively Vietnamese actions. In the Route 9 action, 653 enemy soldiers were reported killed and twenty-four tanks destroyed or captured. At Pedro, twenty-two more tanks were destroyed or captured, eighty-five crew-served weapons were seized, and 424 enemy soldiers were killed. In both battles, friendly losses were minimal.

Significant actions were also taking place in the air. Rockly Smith and Rick Atchison were back flying yet another mission in the continuing effort for the three survivors. While orbiting over them, they observed a large column of tanks coming down QL-1 toward Dong Ha. They immediately reported this through secure voice radio, and a few minutes later, six B-52s were diverted to catch the NVA in the open. Long strings of bombs devastated the enemy column. Later, the province chief for that area reported that three artillery pieces and twenty-seven tanks had been destroyed. He had also seen large explosions for thirty minutes. Thus, on this one day the enemy lost seventy-three tanks. The defense was stiffening.

While these battles were raging, Anderson and his team were helilifted to 3d ARVN Division headquarters. There he briefed the commander,

Brigadier General Giai, on the operation. The general was very pessimistic about the operation and made it clear that he could not guarantee their safety. Norris also noted, that, given the size of the battle in which he was engaged, he was not too concerned about three downed airmen. But the general did agree to provide them transportation to his forwardmost unit. This was a platoon of Rangers supported by three M-48 tanks from the 20th Armor, positioned along QL-9 to keep an eye on the Cam Lo bridge.

From there they traveled to the headquarters of the 1st Armor Brigade near Dong Ha. They met with the commander and his senior U.S. adviser, Lt. Col. Louis Wagner, who gave them a comprehensive briefing on their situation. They exchanged a set of frequencies and codes and decided how best to proceed with the "ball game." The next morning they moved by armored personnel carrier (APC) to the forward location. Anderson did not like what he found: the platoon consisted of about twenty soldiers under the command of a young and obviously scared second lieutenant. The position itself was strong. It consisted of an old French bunker on top of a small hill overlooking Cam Lo and the river. The tanks were dug in, covering QL-9, but each only had three rounds of main-gun ammunition. Out from the position about 150 yards were the hulks of three burned-out T-54 tanks, remnants of the previous day's battles.

The Vietnamese troops were tired and hungry. Wisely, Anderson had brought extra rations for just this contingency: he needed to establish a quick rapport with these troops. But when he explained his mission to the Vietnamese lieutenant, the latter wanted no part of it. Anderson, who could speak Vietnamese, stated that he had immediate access to airstrikes if any sizable threat developed. He then threatened to shoot anyone who deserted the position. As the Vietnamese troops were digesting all of that, Anderson got on the radio to his covering FAC and had him tell Bat 21 Bravo and Nail 38 Bravo to plan on a pickup that night.

By nightfall they were ready to begin the operation. Anderson contacted the survivors to make sure that they were moving. Hambleton was getting weak; Nail 38 Bravo was the closest to the team and would be first. He was instructed to be ready to get in the water and let the current carry him down. Lieutenant Norris took his team and began moving to the river. But the area was heavily patrolled by NVA troops, so the going was very slow. Anderson and his team of Rangers positioned themselves farther downstream to catch Clark if he got by Norris.

Movement had to be very precise, because Anderson had pre-planned both airstrikes and artillery to disrupt enemy forces in the area. Both teams had to pause several times during their movement because of enemy patrols. Norris initially moved his team to the river to test the water for temperature and current. He decided that it was too strong for the Vietnamese to swim against and that they would have to move overland. He also decided that they would go beyond the one-kilometer restriction that Anderson had given them. But as he began to move through the fields, he became concerned when he saw a column of NVA tanks, trucks, and support vehicles move down across the Cam Lo bridge and turn east along QL-9. As the column approached, he debated calling in an airstrike on it. But approximately five hundred meters west of his position, the vehicles turned off on a side road and proceeded south.

Norris and his team had to skirt numerous NVA patrols and positions as they moved generally parallel to the river. The enemy security was uncharacteristically lax, and the soldiers were easy to see even in the dark. But the team still had to move slowly and carefully, because they could not afford to give up the element of surprise. They traveled about two kilometers before they finally set up an observation point on the river and began to wait for Nail 38 Bravo. The position gave the team good cover while also allowing them excellent visibility of the river. Norris had two of his Vietnamese go down to test the water and wait for the first survivor. He had one of the ships on the gun line occasionally fire an illumination flare into the area for light. Now they had to just sit and wait.

As directed by the FAC overhead, Clark had gotten into the water and begun his journey. He had not gone too far when one side of his life preserver snagged on a branch and inflated. The sudden sound horrified him, but it did not draw any enemy response. Fortuitously, it was just enough to keep his head above water while the rest of his body was hidden. He also wore his mosquito net over his head as camouflage. But while passing through the rapids, he got caught in some debris along the shore. The current forced him underwater and he lost his footing. To keep from drowning, he quickly inflated the other side of the preserver, which brought him back to the surface. It also helped him to decide to get out and walk for about one hundred yards. Then he got back in the water. He figured that the distant flares were for the benefit of the pickup team and that he did not have much farther to go.

Sometime between 2:00 and 3:00 A.M., Norris heard and then saw Clark floating down with the current. The water was cold and the survivor was breathing hard. At the same time, an NVA patrol passed between him and the cold and tired Mark Clark. Norris could not move; he had to let Clark pass by. The patrol consisted of six soldiers. Norris immediately considered killing them, but again, he did not want to make his presence known. So he let them pass off to the west. But after the patrol had cleared, he could no longer see Clark. So he slipped into the water and attempted to swim after him. After a few hundred yards, he could not find his target. He got out of the water and proceeded to patrol along the south bank, back as far as his team. Still he made no contact. He quickly reported the situation to Anderson.

Anderson promptly called Clark and ordered him to the south shore. He then directed Norris to begin patrolling to the east. Additionally, he requested a situation update from Norris. Norris did not feel like explaining the situation, so he acknowledged Anderson's directive, turned off his radio, and moved out with his team. He got back in the water while the commandos searched the shore. This was a meticulous, drawn-out process, since the river had areas of twisting rapids and heavy undergrowth. But as dawn approached, Norris rounded a bend and noticed movement near a sunken sampan. He knew that it was Clark and called him by name.

Clark did not realize who Norris was. Instinctively he moved for cover. Norris tells the story: "He had no idea who I was. I don't even think that he got a good sight of me, he just heard something and went for cover. So I started talking to him. I took off my hat, put my gun behind me, and started telling him who I was. I gave him . . . you know, when a pilot goes down he has a series of codes that he leaves, something only he or his family would know. That's how you identify who you are when you come up on the radio, to show him you are not a bad guy. I used that to talk to him and slowly his head came up from behind the sampan and he realized that I was an American. He stood up and there was relief in his eyes."

Norris rendezvoused with the rest of his team and notified Anderson that Clark had been recovered. He then gave the Air Force navigator a quick course in being an infantryman, since they had to thread their way back through enemy territory to the platoon location. Upon arriving back at the bunker, Clark was given some first aid and food. An APC arrived from the brigade to medevac him to Dong Ha. From there, he was flown by helicopter to Da Nang.

At 10:15 A.M., the 3d ARVN Division Tactical Operations Center (TOC) received the following message: "1LT MARK N CLARK, USAF . . . 23d TAC air SPT SQK, arrived Tm 155 location accompanied by LTC WAGNER, SA, 1st ARMD Bde. Lt. CLARK, downed Pilot, was recovered by team on night of 10 Apr."

One survivor down, two to go. Anderson thought that the mission had gone fairly smoothly. Norris did not tell him how far west they had gone or the number of enemy patrols or tanks they had observed. He also did not mention that for most of the time he had had his radio turned off. Norris, when given a mission, liked to do things his way, with minimal supervisory interference. When queried about some missed radio calls, he said that he was having some problems with his radio.

Anderson next turned his attention to planning the pickup of Bat 21 Bravo that night. He gave the FACs targets that he wanted struck in preparation. He spotted another tank column crossing at Cam Lo and had it attacked. Three tanks were destroyed, and several trucks were left burning. Meanwhile, Bilk 11 came back on station for yet another sortie in support of the SAR. Anderson had him inform Hambleton that Anderson was now on the radio, and his call sign was Leatherneck. Bilk 11 also told Hambleton to stay by the river with his eyes open and not be surprised at anything he saw coming down the *klong* (river).

As Bilk 11 was overhead, the NVA struck back: NVA artillery began to fall around the position. The first round was well over their heads; several of the ARVN laughed at the inaccuracy. But Norris and the Vietnamese lieutenant began shouting for the troops to take cover. Then the rounds began to impact squarely on the position. These were accompanied by B-40 rockets and mortars. Several soldiers went down with serious wounds. Norris and the lieutenant jumped up and began directing the soldiers into protective positions and ordering them to begin firing back at the enemy infantry, but the ARVN began to panic. Anderson had to threaten again to shoot deserters to keep them in their positions.

Bilk 11 was still orbiting overhead. Anderson called him and told him that he needed an immediate airstrike. Prior to the arrival of the strikers, Captain Icke had directed artillery on the enemy. Then his fighters arrived, and Icke led them in. The airstrike stopped the infantry attack, silenced the mortars, and restored ARVN confidence. But the attack did take a toll on the friendly force. Lieutenant Colonel Anderson, while out trying to rally and calm the AVN, was himself hit. Additionally, Lieutenant Tho was seriously wounded in the arm, and many of the Rangers and one other sea commando were killed or injured. Lieutenant Norris called for APCs to come and medevac the wounded. All of them were evacuated; a helicopter picked up Anderson and Tho and flew them to Da Nang.

Lt. Col. Andy Anderson was transferred back down to a hospital in Saigon. But he could not keep his mind off of the mission. He knew that Norris was in a tough position. The next day he climbed out of the window of his room and talked General Marshall into using his T-39 to fly him back to Da Nang. From there he intended to return to the site of the operation.

His concern was well placed, for Norris was in dire straits. He only had three commandos, none of whom spoke much English. His covering force was badly beaten up and low on ammunition. His survivor had been out nine days now and was very weak. Norris checked with him: he was making progress to the river, but slowly. He was not going to last much longer.

Throughout the rest of the day, Norris and his team planned and prepared to move out that night and snatch Hambleton. Just before sunset, they watched a column of tanks and trucks move west from near Hambleton's original position across the Cam Lo bridge and proceed east along QL-9 toward their position. Norris was surprised by all of this activity, but the Vietnamese Rangers said that it had been going on every night for a week.

After dark, Norris set out with his team of three. But two of his troops began to balk: they did not want to go through such a concentration of enemy regulars for an American. In fact, one stated that he was no longer going to follow an American just to rescue another American. It was a tense moment. In a firm tone, Norris explained to them that he was going to proceed and that they were safer staying together as a group. They reluctantly stayed with him. Norris led them to a position about three and half kilometers northwest and set up an outpost to watch for the survivor to move to him.

But Bat 21 Bravo had notified the orbiting FAC that he had reached the river and just could not go any farther. Norris could occasionally hear Hambleton, but his descriptions of his location were confusing. So Norris began a search along the shore back toward the platoon position. But he could not make contact, and as dawn approached, he returned his team to the bunker. There he dropped off the two reluctant commandos and returned with PO Nguyen Van Kiet to the river. They grabbed a sampan and searched for two more hours, until it was too light to continue. Disappointed, they headed back to the bunker.

Later that morning, the members of the 37th ARRS gathered outside the south hangar at Da Nang to hold a memorial service for their six lost comrades. Squadron mates eulogized each of the fallen and sang several hymns in their memory. It was hard not to notice the tears as the brave crewmen and pararescuemen sang, "Lord guard and guide the men who fly."

During the day, Norris and his team rested. He had some extra supplies brought for his troops and some paddles for a sampan. Bilk 11 was back overhead; he plotted Hambleton's new position. The tired and weak survivor had only moved fifty meters the night before. Two Sandy A-1s were also on station over him. While a B-52 strike was going on nearby, Sandy 01 came in and dropped a Madden survival kit to Hambleton, filled with food and other supplies. But it landed fifty meters past him and slightly uphill, and he was too weak to climb up and get it. Instead, he came out on a sandbar in the river and began waving a white handkerchief. Captain Icke could not believe what he was seeing: he told Hambleton to get back under cover. The Sandy pilots also saw him and dropped another kit. But he could not reach that one either. Concerned for his obviously failing condition, Icke and the Sandys considered trying another helicopter pickup with whatever they could get into the area. But once again they all agreed that it was too dangers. They had to stay with the plan—but they did not have much time left.

Hambleton had to come out soon or he was not going to make it. He simply could not move any farther. Norris sensed this, having monitored the conversations between Hambleton and the aircraft. He knew that he would have to go to Hambleton. His original orders had been to proceed no more than one kilometer beyond the bunker position and wait for the survivor to come to him. He had already gone well beyond that. Norris thought it all over, weighing the risks against the possibility of success. The stubborn, tenacious wrestler from Maryland decided to go for it. There really was no other choice. He talked it over with Petty Officer Kiet, the ranking South Vietnamese sea commando. Kiet would accompany him; the other two would remain behind.

After dark the two of them set out, dressed as Vietnamese fishermen. They threaded their way to a bombed-out village on the river. There they found a sampan that was not damaged, and they jumped in and paddled up-stream. Fortunately, it was a dark night. But they had to advance very cautiously, because they could hear enemy troops on both banks of the river. At one point Norris stopped along the bank for a map check. Not ten meters away, he spotted two enemy soldiers sitting in a bunker—sound asleep.

Overhead, the FACs monitored their progress. As they moved upriver, Norris constantly passed targets along both banks; some of these were very significant. Coming around one bend, they were startled by the sound of many tanks starting up their engines. Apparently they had stumbled into an armor battalion assembly area.

Just beyond the tanks, they encountered a fog bank, which gave them added cover. They cautiously continued west until they began to emerge from the fog. To their horror, they discovered that they were directly under the Cam Lo bridge and could see troops crossing. They quickly did a U-turn and proceeded back downstream.

They slowly paddled back down the river and started a sweep of the shore. And then they found him, sitting in a clump of bushes. Hambleton, awake but partly delirious, recognized Norris as an American. Norris quickly checked him over for injuries. He had some minor cuts but was otherwise okay. He could walk but was very weak. Norris considered spending the day there and traveling the next night, but there was just too much enemy activity. So he and Kiet laid Hambleton in the sampan, covered him with some bamboo, and notified the FAC that they were coming out. They had to get him out quickly, because dawn was approaching. Norris also told the FAC to have lots of airstrikes available, just in case. Once again the FAC overhead was Bilk 11, Capt. Harold Icke. He had been on station since before dawn and had launched while the air base at Da Nang was under rocket attack.

The team slipped back into the water and headed downstream. A few hundred yards down, they encountered a patrol that began to shout and run after them. Kiet noted that they spoke with a North Vietnamese accent; he also noticed the white stars on their belt buckles. Norris was becoming concerned: Hambleton was beginning to babble. An American voice would definitely give them away. Additionally, he could not use his radio, because this would also give away their identity. Fortunately, a bend in the river and heavy foliage along the bank allowed them to separate from the threat. But Norris was worried about the tank park and reported it to Icke. As he approached, though, he could see that the tanks were gone.

A little farther on, a soldier on the north bank opened up on them with a heavy machine gun. There was no way around him, so Norris and Kiet paddled to the south bank, hid the boat in some vegetation, and called Bilk 11 for an airstrike. But the FAC did not have any fighters on station. American airstrikes had been reduced because the main air effort was not against North Vietnam. So Bilk 11 came up on the emergency frequency and called for any fighters available in the immediate area.

The response was instantaneous. Garfish, a flight of five A-4s from the USS *Hancock* and led by Lt. Denny Sapp, answered the call. Bilk 11 directed them to his discrete strike frequency and talked them in to the target area. Once they were overhead, he explained the situation. The target was the guns hidden in houses on the north shore of the river. First he visually talked them on to the target. Then to confirm it, he marked the position with a smoke rocket. The Navy fliers had a solid fix on the guns, so Icke cleared them in hot. Antiaircraft fire was surprisingly minimal, so the fighters set up a low bombing pattern and dropped their bombs from three thousand feet. Having lots of gas, they dropped one bomb per pass and worked over the village with tremendous accuracy until the positions were obliterated. Norris was impressed and very thankful. He then gave the FAC all of the enemy positions that he had noticed along the river and told him to unload on them, too.

The orbiting King rescue aircraft was also monitoring the action. They diverted two U.S. A-1s to Bilk 11, and he also had them strike the north shore. First Lt. Tim Brady was the wingman in this flight. Just new in the squadron, he was not yet checked out as a Sandy. He and his lead had been launched as a normal strike flight. But instead of carrying the normal load of Mk-82 500-pound bombs, they were carrying the "soft" load of ordnance, including napalm, rockets, and M47 smoke bombs. This ordnance was designed for pinpoint accuracy and could be dropped near unprotected friendlies without danger to those being supported. It was the ideal load to give Norris the last bit of support he needed. Under the direction of Bilk 11, they devastated what enemy positions remained on the north shore. The last thing they dropped was their M47 smoke bombs. This created a curtain that Norris could then use for cover. Above, Captain Icke pulled out his camera and snapped a picture of the airstrike.

As the A-1s were finishing, Norris and his crew got back in the boat and made the last dash back to the friendly outpost. But as they beached their boat, they began taking small-arms fire from the north shore. ARVN soldiers returned fire. Hambleton could not walk, so several of the Vietnamese helped him up the hill to the bunker.

Upon reaching the bunker, Norris gave Hambleton some quick first aid and then called for an armored personnel carrier to carry him back to the brigade. While waiting for the AOC, Hambleton had a cigarette given to him by one of the Vietnamese soldiers. The arrival of the APC was delayed by another mortar and rocket attack on the position; Bilk 11 used more A-4s and A-1s to beat off the heavy ordnance and the enemy troops on the north shore.

After the enemy fire ended, the personnel carrier arrived and carried Hambleton and Norris and the remnants of his team back to Dong Ha. A waiting helicopter then lifted Hambleton back to Da Nang. There he was accosted by a news team. The weak and dazed survivor was asked by the reporter about all that had been done to rescue him. His answer was terse: "It was a hell of a price to pay for one life," he said. "I'm very sorry." Concurrently, another reporter at Dong Ha found Norris and asked, "It must have been tough out there. I bet you wouldn't do that again!" The SEAL bristled. Then coldly he replied, "An American was down in enemy territory. Of course I'd do it again."

Tom Norris and his team were then driven to Quang Tri. There they met with officers from the 3d ARVN Division and briefed them on all of the enemy positions that they had observed. In the meantime, the third survivor, Covey 282 Alpha, had not been able to move through the enemy units to rendezvous with the team along the river. Consequently, Norris and the remnants of his team returned to Da Nang and began to work up an alternative plan to get 1ˢᵗ Lt. Bruce Walker.

So it was done. After eleven and a half days trapped behind enemy lines, Bat 21 Bravo, Lt. Col. Iceal Hambleton, was returned to friendly control. But the cost was high. Among the soldiers and airmen, ten men were killed working or supporting the SAR; one other, like Hambleton, was rescued; two were captured but later released; and one, First Lieutenant Walker, was still evading. On the ground, several members of the recovery team, including Anderson, were injured. Six more aircraft were shot down, and numerous others were damaged, some so badly they would never fly again. More than eight hundred strike sorties, including B-52s, were flown in direct support of this rescue.

For his part in the operation, Petty Office Kiet was awarded the U.S. Navy Cross, the only Vietnamese of the war to be so honored. For the rescue of the two fliers, Lt. Tom Norris, the stubborn wrestler from Maryland, would be awarded the Medal of Honor by President Gerald Ford on 3 April 1976.

Out of the Jaws of Hell

From *Black Hawk Down*

BY MARK BOWDEN

Bauden's celebrated bestseller (and basis for the Ridley Scott movie of the same name) tells a story pivotal in recent American history: how 100 Special Forces troops were dropped on a steaming marketplace in Mogadishu, Somalia, on October 3, 1993. And how, for 72 hours, their compatriots attempted to rescue them from the jaws of hell.

★　★　★　★　★

Captain Drew Meyerowich was with the Delta operators who were leading his portion of the rescue convoy toward Steele and Miller's position. It had been a pitched battle much of the way in. Two of the Malaysian drivers had taken a wrong turn and driven about thirty of Meyerowich's men off in the wrong direction. They'd been ambushed and caught up in a severe firefight, and one of their men, Sergeant Cornell Houston, had been mortally wounded.

For all his careful planning, Specialist Squeglia ended up in a Humvee. The banging of gunfire was constant, most of it coming from the convoy, which stretched so far in both directions Squeglia could not see the front or rear. No one had lights on, but muzzle flashes and explosions lit up the whole line. In the reflected light he saw two dead donkeys by the side of the road, still strapped to cars. The air was filled with diesel fumes, and through the open side window of the Humvee Squeglia smelled the gunpowder from his weapon mingled with the burning tires and trash and the general pungent, rotten smell of Somalia itself. He was out in it now.

In a sudden volley of gunfire an RPG bounced off the hood. The explosion a few feet away sounded like somebody had dropped an empty Dumpster off a roof. Squeglia felt the concussion like a blow to the inside of his chest, and then smelled smoke. Everybody had ducked at the blast.

"Holy shit, what was that?" shouted Specialist David Eastabrooks, who was driving.

"Jesus," said Sergeant Richard Lamb, who was in the front passenger seat. "I think I've been hit."

"Where you hit?" Squeglia asked.

"In the head."

"Oh, Jesus."

One of the men in the Humvee fished out a red light flashlight and they shined it on Lamb. He had a trickle of blood running down his face and a neat hole, a small one, right in the middle of his forehead.

"I think I'm okay," Lamb said. "I'm still talking to you."

He wrapped a bandage around his head. Doctors would later determine that a piece of shrapnel had lodged between the frontal lobes of his brain, missing vital tissues by fractions of an inch in either direction. He was all right. It felt like he had just banged his head. It hurt a lot worse minutes later when he took a bullet to his right pinkie, which left the tip of it hanging by a piece of skin. Squeglia could see the bone of his finger jutting from the mangled flesh. Lamb just swore and stuck the fingertip back on, wrapped it with a piece of duct tape, and continued working his radio.

All the way out from the base, Specialist Dale Sizemore was shooting. He'd cut the cast off his arm to join the fight, and at last he was in it. Night vision gave him and the other men on this massive column a tremendous advantage over the Somalis. Sizemore spread out on his stomach in the back of the Humvee just looking for people to shoot. When there weren't people he shot windows and doorways. Most of the time he couldn't see whether he'd hit anybody or not. The NODs severely restricted peripheral vision. He didn't want to know, really. He didn't want to start thinking about it.

At one point a spray of sparks flew up in his face. He turned his head to discover a first-sized hole in the Humvee wall just a few inches from his head. He hadn't felt a thing. When an RPG hit one of the trucks ahead, men came running down the street looking for space on the Humvees as tracers flew. One, Specialist Erik James, a medic, approached Sizemore's open back hatch carrying a Kevlar blanket.

"You got room?" he asked. He looked dazed and scared.

Sizemore and Private Brian Conner moved over to make a space for him.

"Just get in here and keep that blanket over your head and you'll be all right," said Sizemore. He figured it was always a good idea to have a medic close by. James felt Sizemore had just saved his life.

Specialist Steve Anderson was in a Humvee near Sizemore's in the column. He was in the back on the driver's side with his eyes pressed right to the night-vision viewfinder on his SAW. Whenever the column stopped, which was often, everyone was expected to pile out and pull security. The first time they stopped Anderson hesitated. He didn't want to stick his leg out of the car. He had just started skydiving lessons at home before this development, and now, suddenly, he felt immobilized by the particular fear of being shot in the legs—he'd received a minor injury to his legs on an earlier mission. Back home he had just made his first freefall jump. It had been such a thrill. What if he got his foot shot off and could never jump again? Anderson reluctantly forced himself out on the street.

At one stop he and Sizemore stood for a long time, it seemed like hours, watching the windows of a thee-story building for some sign of a shooter. They had been there for a time when Anderson noticed a dent and scrape on the roof of the Humvee right next to them. A round had ricocheted off it.

"Did you notice that before?" he asked Sizemore.

Sizemore hadn't. It hadn't been there when they got out either. Which meant a bullet had passed between them, missing them both by inches, without their even knowing it.

That was the way Anderson felt most of the time. Totally in the dark. He saw tracers and there were times the gunfire was so loud the night seemed ready to split at the seams, but he could never seem to tell where it was coming from, or find anyone to shoot. Sizemore, on the other hand, was going through ammunition as fast as he could load his weapon. Anderson was in awe of his friend's confidence and selflessness, and felt both inspired and diminished by it.

Sizemore unloaded what must have been a full drum of ammo at the front of a building about fifty feet away. When he was done, Anderson could see rounds glowing and smoldering from the ground where he had been shooting, which meant he must have hit something. When rounds hit the ground or street or a building, they deflected off in other directions. But when they hit flesh, they would glow for a few moments.

"Didn't you see them?" Sizemore asked Anderson. "There was a bunch of them there, shooting at us."

Anderson hadn't noticed. He felt completely out of his element. Minutes later he noticed another dent and scrape on the top of the Humvee, right alongside the first one. He hoped his buddy had silenced the gun that put it there.

At one stop on a wide street, when Anderson and the men in his Humvee were positioned near a two-story building, a Malaysian APC pulled up about twenty feet behind them and its machine gunner opened fire. He was shooting at the roof of the building alongside Anderson. The rounds traced red lines through the darkness, so Anderson could follow their trajectory, and they were all bouncing off the building next to him. The wall was made of irregular stone. Any one of those rounds could easily come this way. There was nothing he could do but watch. One of the rounds hit the building and then traced a wicked arc across the street like a curveball.

Private Ed Kallman was somewhere else along the giant convoy, driving again, equally amazed by the light show. Kallman's left arm and shoulder were massively bruised from the unexploded RPG that had hit the door of his Humvee the previous afternoon and knocked him cold. He felt fine, excited again, and reasonably safe in such a massive force. There would be long periods of relative quiet, then suddenly the night would explode with light and noise. One or two shots from the dark houses or alleys on both sides of the street would trigger a violent explosion of return fire from the column. Up and down the line tracers splashed out from the long line, literally thousands of rounds in seconds, just hosing down whole blocks of homes. His NODs framed the scene in a circle and offered little depth perception. It also gave off heat just a half inch from his face that after a while started to bother his eyes. Then he would take a break and just look straight down or off to the side.

They eventually stopped and waited in the same spot for several hours. Kallman was asked to pull his Humvee back down the road, about a half block, which he did, and no sooner had he moved than an RPG exploded on what looked like the spot he had just left. He and others in his vehicle laughed. An explosion on the wall above sent a shower of debris down on them. No one was hurt. Kallman moved the Humvee forward a few feet just to make sure it wasn't stuck.

Through the remainder of the night he just listened to the radio, trying to make sense out of the constant chatter, trying to figure out what was going on.

Ahead of them in the long column, Sergeant Jeff Struecker was shocked by all the shooting. He had heard a sergeant major from the 10th Mountain Division telling his men before they left, "This is for real. You shoot at anything," and clearly these guys had taken him seriously.

Struecker had warned his own gunner to pick targets carefully. "When you shoot that fifty cal, that round goes on forever," the sergeant explained. It was clear the rest of the convoy was not taking such precautions. They were throwing lead all over that part of Mogadishu.

Half of the rescue convoy had steered south to Durant's crash site, but had gotten stalled on the outskirts of the ghettolike village of rag and tin huts where *Super Six Four* had gone down. In darkness, the unmapped maze of footpaths leading into the village looked potentially deadly—it was like probing directly into the heart of the hornets' nest. Sergeant John "Mace" Macejunas, the fearless blond Delta operator, on his third trip out into the city, slipped off a Humvee and personally led a small force on foot, wearing NODs and feeling his way into the village toward the wrecked helicopter, where hours before Mace's buddies Randy Shughart and Gary Gordon had made their last stand.

Around the wreckage they found pools and trails of blood, torn bits of clothing, and many spent bullet shells, but no weapons and no sign of their buddies Shughart and Gordon, nor of Durant and three other crew members. The soldiers searched the huts around the crash site, demanding information about the downed Americans through a translator, but no one offered any. Risking drawing fire, they bellowed into the night the names of all six of the missing men: "Michael Durant!" "Ray Frank!" "Bill Cleveland!" "Tommie Fields!" "Randy Shughart!" "Gary Gordon!" There was only silence.

Macejunas then supervised the setting of thermite grenades on the helicopter. They stayed until *Super Six Four* was a ball of white flame, and then returned to the convoy.

Meyerowich's northern half of the convoy had been delayed by a big roadblock on Hawlwadig Road up near the Olympic Hotel, which the Malaysian drivers refused to roll through. In the past, such roadblocks had been heavily mined.

Meyerowich pleaded with the liaison officer. "Tell them small arms fire is ineffective against them!" he said.

Once or twice he got out of his Humvee and walked up to the lead PAC and shouted, waving his arms, urging the vehicle forward. But the condor drivers refused to proceed. So the convoy was stalled while solders climbed off the vehicles and dismantled the roadblock by hand.

Meyerowich and the D-boys decided not to wait for the roadblock situation to be sorted out. They ran up and down the line of vehicles banging on the doors, shouting for all the men to pile out of the vehicles. They knew they were only blocks from the pinned-down force.

"Get out! Get out! Get out! Americans, get out!"

One of those who emerged warily was Specialist Phil Lepre. Earlier in the ride out, when the shooting got heavy and rounds were pinging off the sides of the APC, Lepre had removed a snapshot of his baby daughter he carried in his helmet and kissed it good-bye. "Babe," he said, "I hope you have a wonderful life." He stepped out now into the Mogadishu night, ran to a wall with two other soldiers, and pointed his M-16 down an alley. When his eyes adjusted to the darkness he saw a group of Somalis a few blocks down, edging their own toward him.

"I've got Somalians coming down this way!" he said.

One of the D-boys told him to shoot, so Lepre fired down toward the crowd. First he shot over their heads, but when they didn't disperse he fired straight into them. He saw several fall. The others dragged them off the alley.

Out in the intersection, soldiers were pulling apart the barricade by hand under heavy fire. Lepre moved once or twice up the road with the rest of the men. They were spread out now on both sides of an alley a few blocks ahead of the APCs. They would move, stop, and wait, then move again, like parts of a human accordion slinking its way east. At one of the places where they stopped they began taking heavy fire from a nearby building. Men moved to take better cover and find an improved vantage to return fire.

"Hey, take my position," he called back to twenty-three-year-old rifleman private James Martin.

Martin hustled up and crouched behind the wall. Lepre had moved only two steps to his right when Martin was hit in the head by a round that sent him sprawling backward. Lepre saw a small hole in his forehead.

Lepre's voice joined others shouting, "Medic! We need a medic up here!"

A medic swooped over the downed man and began loosening his clothes to help prevent shock. He worked on Martin a few minutes, then turned to Lepre and the others and said, "He's dead."

The medic and another soldier tried to drag Martin's body to cover but were scattered by more gunfire. One of them ran back and braved the gunfire, firing his weapon with one hand and dragging Martin to cover with the other. When he got close, others ran out to help, pulling the body into the alley.

Lepre was behind cover just a few feet away, gazing at Martin's body. He felt terrible. He had asked the private to take his position, and then the man had been shot dead. All the dragging had pulled Martin's pants down to his knees. Few of the boys wore underwear in the tropical heat. Lepre couldn't bear seeing Martin sprawled there like that, half naked. So despite the gunfire, he stepped out into the alley and tried to pull up the dead soldier's pants, to give the man some dignity. Two bullets struck the pavement near where he stooped, and Lepre scrambled reluctantly back to cover.

"Sorry, man," he said.

The command bird continued to coax the force linkup at the first crash site.

—*They are leading the mounted troops by dismounted troops. The dismounted troops and the mounted troops are holding south of the Olympic Hotel. . . .*

Then, talking to the convoy, as they approached the left turn:

—*Thirty meters south of the friendlies. They are one minor block to the north of you right now. If your lead APC continued moving he can make the next left and go one block, over.*

Steele heard the vehicles making the turn. Out the door his men saw the dim outline of soldiers. Steele and his men called out, "Ranger! Ranger!"

"Tenth Mountain Division," came the response.

—*Roger, we've got a linkup with the Kilo and Juliet element, over.*

Steele stuck his head out the door.

"This is Captain Steele. I'm the Ranger commander."

"Roger, sir, we're from the 10th Mountain Division," a soldier answered.

"Where's your commander?" Steele asked.

It took hours to pry Elvis out of the wreck. It was ugly work. The rescue column had brought along a quickie saw to cut the chopper's metal frame away from his body, but the cockpit was lined with a layer of Kevlar that just ate up the saw blade. Next they tried to pull the Black Hawk apart, attaching chains to the front and back ends of it. A few of the Rangers, watching this from a distance, thought the C-boys were using the vehicles to tear the pilot's body out of the wreckage. Some turned away in disgust.

The dead were placed on top of the APCs, and the wounded were loaded inside them. Goodale hobbled painfully out to the one that had stopped before their courtyard, and was helped through the doors. He rolled to his side.

"We need you to sit," he was told.

"Look, I got shot in the ass. It hurts to sit."

"Then lean on something."

At Miller's courtyard they carried Carlos Rodriguez out first in his inflated rubber pants. Then they moved the other wounded. Stebbins was feeling pretty good. Out the window he could see 10th Mountain Division guys lounging up and down the street, a lot of them. He protested when they came back for him with a stretcher.

"I'm okay," he told them. "I can stand on one leg. Just help me over to the vehicle. I've still got my weapon."

He hopped on his good foot and was helped up into the armored car.

Wilkinson climbed into the back of the same vehicle. They all expected to be moving shortly, but instead they sat. The closed steel container was like a sauna and it reeked of sweat and urine and blood. What a nightmare this mission had become. Every time they thought it was over, that they'd made it, something worse happened. The injured in the vehicles couldn't see what was going on outside, and they didn't understand the delay. They'd all figured the convoy would arrive and they'd scoot home. It was only a five-minute drive to the airport. It was now after three o'clock in the morning. The sun would be coming back up soon. Bullets occasionally pinged off the walls. What would happen if an RPG hit them?

There was a brief mutiny under way in Goodale's Condor.

"Shouldn't we be moving?" Goodale asked.

"Yeah, I would think so," said one of the other men crammed in with him.

Goodale was closest to the front, so he leaned up to the Malay driver.

"Hey, man, let's go," he said.

"No. No," the driver protested. "We stay."

"God damnit, we're not staying! Let's get the fuck out of here!"

"No, No. We stay."

"No, you don't understand this. We're getting shot at. We're gonna get fucked up in this thing!"

The commanders were also growing impatient.

—*Scotty* [Miller], *give me an update please*, asked Lieutenant Colonel Harrell.

Other than brief stops back at the base to refuel, Harrell and air commander Tom Matthews were up over the city in their C2 Black Hawk throughout the night.

Miller responded:

—*Roger. They're trying to pull it apart. So far no luck.*

—*Roger. You've only got about an hour's worth of darkness left.*

There were more than three hundred Americans now in and around these two blocks of Mogadishu, the vanguard of a convoy that stretched a half mile back toward National Street, which created a sense of security among the recently arrived 10th Mountain troops that was not shread by the Rangers or the D-boys who had been fighting all night. The weary assault force watched with amazement as the regular army guys leaned against walls and lit cigarettes and chatted out on the same street where they had just experienced blizzards of enemy fire. To Howe, the Delta team leader who had been so disappointed by the Rangers, these men seemed completely out of place. The wait for them to extract Elvis's body was beginning to worry everybody.

When an explosion rocked Stebbins's APC, men shouted with anger inside. "Get us the fuck out of here!" one screamed. Rodriguez was moaning. Stebbins and Heard were taking turns holding up the machine gunner's IV bag. They were wedged into the small space like pieces of a puzzle. Soon after the explosion the carrier's big metal door swung open and a soldier from the 10th who had been hit in the elbow was lifted in on a litter. He screamed with pain as he hit the floor.

"I can't believe it!" he shouted.

The Malaysian driver kept turning back, trying to keep things calm. "Any minute now, hospital," he would say.

After patching up the new arrival, Wilkinson sat back against the inner wall and saw through a peephole that darkness had begun to drain from the eastern sky. The volume of fire was starting to pick up. There were more pings off the side of the carrier.

The wounded who had been so eager to board the big armored vehicles now prayed to get off. They felt like targets in a turkey shoot. Goodale had only a small peephole to see outside. It was so warm he began to feel woozy. He removed his helmet and loosened his body armor, but it didn't help much. They all sat in the small dark space just staring silently at each other, waiting.

"You know what we should do," suggested one of the wounded D-boys. "We should kind of crack one of these doors a little bit so that when the RPG comes in here, we'll all have someplace to explode out of."

About an hour before sunrise, there was an update from the C2 bird to the JOC:

—*They are essentially pulling the aircraft instrument panel apart around the body. Still do not have any idea when they will be done.*

—*Okay, are they going to be able to get the body out of there?* Garrison demanded. *I need an honest, no shit, for-real assessment from the platoon leader or the senior man present. Over.*

Miller answered:

—*Roger. Understand we are looking at twenty more minutes before we can get the body out.*

Garrison said:

—*Roger. I know they are doing the best they can. We will stay the course until they are finished. Over.*

As the sky to the east brightened, Sergeant Yurek was startled by the carnage back in the room where they had spent the night. Sunlight illuminated the pools and smears of blood everywhere. As he poked his head out the court-yard door he could see Somali bodies scattered up and down the road in the distance. One of the bodies, a young Somali man, appeared to have been run over several times by one of the vehicles being used to pull apart the helicopter. Yurek was especially saddened to see, at a corner of Marehan Road, the carcass of the donkey he had watched miraculously crossing the street back and forth through all the gunfire the day before. It was still hooked to its cart.

Howe noticed among the bodies stacked on top of the APCs the soles of two small assault boots. There was only one guy in the unit with boots that small. It had to be Earl Fillmore.

Everybody knew the respite here was about to end. Daylight would bring Sammy back outdoors. Captain Steele stood outside the courtyard door checking his watch compulsively. He must have looked at it hundreds of times. He couldn't believe they weren't moving yet. The horizon was starting to get pink. Placing three hundred men at jeopardy in order to retrieve the body of one man was a noble gesture, but hardly a sensible one. Finally, at sunup, the grim work was done.

—*Adam Six four.* [Garrison], *this is Romeo Six Four* [Harrell]. *They are starting to move at this time, over . . . Placing the charges and getting ready to move.*

Then came the next shock for the Rangers and D-boys who had been fighting now for fourteen hours. There wasn't enough room on the vehicles for them. After the 10th Mountain Division soldiers reboarded, the anxious Malaysian drivers just took off, leaving the rest of the force behind. They were going to have to run right back out through the same streets they'd fought through on their way in.

It was 5:45 A.M., Monday, October 4. The sun was now over the rooftops.

So they ran. The original idea was for them to run with the vehicles in order to have some cover, but the Malay drivers had sped out.

Still hauling the radio on his back, Steele ran alongside Perino. Eight Rangers were strung out behind them. Behind them were the rest of Delta Force, the CSAR team, everybody. It happened so fast, men at the far end of the lines were surprised when they made the right turn at the top of the hill to find that the others had moved out already.

Yurek ran with Jamie Smith's gear. Nobody had wanted to touch it. It was like acknowledging that he was gone. The whole force ran the same route the main force had used coming in, stopping at each intersection to spray covering fire as they one by one sprinted across. As soon as they began moving the shooting resumed, almost as bad as it had been the afternoon before. The Rangers shot at every window and door, and down every cross street. Steele felt like his legs were lead weights and that he was moving at a fraction of his normal speed, yet he was running as fast as he could.

When they got up to their original blocking position there was withering fire across the wide intersection before the Olympic Hotel. Sergeant Randy Ramaglia saw the rounds hitting the sides of the armored vehicles blocks ahead. *We're going to run through that?* It was the same shit as yesterday. He had made it up to the intersection when he felt a sharp blow to his shoulder, like someone had hit him with a sledgehammer. It didn't knock him down. He just froze. It took a few seconds for him to regain his sense. At first he thought something had fallen on him. He looked up.

"Sergeant, you've been shot!" shouted Specialist Collett, who had been running beside him.

Ramaglia turned to him. Collett's eyes were wide.

"I know it," he said.

He took several deep breaths and tried to move his arm. He could move it. He felt no pain.

The round had hit Ramaglia's left back, taking out a golf-ball sized scoop of it. The round had then skimmed off his shoulder blade and nicked Collett's sleeve, tearing off the American flag he had stitched there.

"Are you okay?" a Delta medic shouted at him from across the street.

"Yeah," said Ramaglia, and he started running again. He was furious. The whole scene seemed surreal to him. He couldn't believe some pissant fucking Sammy had shot him, Sergeant Randal J. Ramaglia of the U.S. Army Rangers. He was going to get out of that city alive or take half of it with him. He shot at anyone or anything he saw. He was running, bleeding, swearing, and shooting. Windows, doorways, alleyways . . . especially people. They were all going down. It was a free-for-all now. All semblance of an ordered retreat was gone. Everybody was just scrambling.

Sergeant Nelson, still stone deaf, ran alongside Private Neathery, who had been shot in the right arm the afternoon before. Nelson had his M-60 and carried Neathery's M-16 slung across his back. They ran as hard as they could and Nelson shot at everything he saw. He had never felt so frightened, not even at the height of things the previous day. He and Neathery were toward the rear and were terrified that in this wild footrace they would be left behind or picked off. Neathery was having a hard time running, which slowed them down. When they caught up to a group providing covering fire at the wide intersection they were supposed to stop and take their turn, cover for that group to advance, but instead they just ran straight through.

Howe kicked in a door of a house on the street and the team piled in to reload and catch their breath. Captain Miller stepped in, breathing hard, and told them to keep moving. Howe went around the room double-checking everybody's status and ammo and then they pushed back out to the street. He was shooting his CAR-15 and his shotgun. Up ahead the APC gunners were shooting up everything.

Private Floyd ran with his torn pants flapping, all but naked from the waist down, feeling especially vulnerable and ridiculous. Alongside him, Doc Strous disappeared suddenly in a loud flash and explosion that knocked Floyd down. When he regained his senses and looked over for Strous, all he saw was a thinning ball of smoke. No Doc.

Sergeant Watson grabbed Floyd's shoulder. The private's helmet was cockeyed and his eyes felt that way.

"Where the hell is Strous?"

"He blew up, Sergeant."

"He blew up? What the hell do you mean he blew up?"

"He blew up."

Floyd pointed to where the medic had been running. Strous stepped from a tangle of weeds, brushing himself off, his helmet askew. He looked down at Floyd and just took off running. A round had hit a flashbang grenade on Strous's vest and exploded, knocking him off his feet and into the weeds. He was unhurt.

"Move out, Floyd," Watson screamed.

They all kept running, running and shooting through the brightening dawn, through the crackle of gunfire, the spray of loose mortar off a wall where a round hit, the sudden gust of hot wind from a blast that sometimes knocked them down and sucked the air out of their lungs, the sound of the helicopters rumbling overhead, and the crisp rasp of their guns like the tearing of heavy cloth. They ran through the oily smell of the city and of their own bodies, the taste of dust in their dry mouths, with the crisp brown bloodstains on their fatigues and the fresh memory of friends dead or unspeakably mangled, with the whole nightmare now grown unbearably long, with disbelief that the mighty and terrible army of the United States of America had plunged them into this mess and stranded them there and now left them to run through the same deadly gauntlet to get out. *How could this happen?*

Ramaglia ran on some desperate last reserve of adrenaline. He ran and shot and swore until he began to smell his own blood and feel dizzy. For the firs time he felt some stabs of pain. He kept running. As he approached the intersection of Hawlwadig Road and National Street, about five blocks south of the Olympic Hotel, he saw a tank and the line of APCs and Humvees and a mass of men in desert battle dress. He ran until he collapsed, with joy.

Part Five
Rescue Dogs

The Mercy Dogs

From *War Dogs: A History of Loyalty and Heroism*

BY MICHAEL G. LEMISH

It may seem oxymoronic, but sometimes the dogs of war are rescuers—ministering angels. Michael Lemish's *War Dogs* related the incredible story of World War I's "mercy" dogs, animals who traversed no-man's-land between the two great armies, searching for wounded men.

★ ★ ★ ★ ★

Astriking monument resides at the Hartsdale Canine Cemetery in Hartsdale, New York. It is simply dedicated to "The War Dog" for services rendered during "the World War, 1914–1918." The monument was erected in 1922 by contributions from dog lovers. Those who helped establish the memorial had no idea that this was not the "war to end all wars."

Cast in bronze, the German shepherd represented is more an animal of peace than an instrument of war. During World War I, Red Cross institutions of every country used many canines to aid and comfort the wounded men on the front lines. Although the Americans would not join the war until 1979, understanding the use of these dogs, and the others that provided a variety of services for the Europeans, is a key element and a useful comparison for future American endeavors. Dogs employed during the war provided three main services: ambulance assistance, messenger service, and sentry detail. Other dogs were recruited as ammunition and light-gun carriers and scouts, and Jack Russell terriers were enlisted to combat the hordes of rats that often infested the trenches.

The setting for World War I is unique, and it is difficult to comprehend the immense scale of destruction and human suffering endured by millions of people. Most of the time was spent in static positions, with little movement of the battle lines. Soldiers squatted down in trenches, each side facing the other, and furious battles raged to gain just a few scant yards of real estate. Between the combatants lay no-man's-land, and it was here, often under the cloak of darkness, that many dogs worked and achieved their great success.

The Red Cross dogs—or sanitary dogs (*Sanitätshunde*), as the Germans called them—provided wounded men with two essential services. These dogs sought out only wounded men and were trained to ignore the dead soldiers. Medical supplies and small canteens of water and spirits were typically attached across the dog's chest or in a saddlebag arrangement. The wounded man, if conscious, could then avail himself of the supplies at hand. All too often the men simply held on to the dog for a short time, a last moment of companionship before dying.

If the soldier could not move or was unconscious, the dog would then return, inform the handlers that a wounded person had been found, and lead rescuers to the location. These mercy dogs were taught not to bark under any circumstances for fear of attracting enemy fire. At the beginning of the war, the innate sense of retrieval bred into many dogs led to the way they were trained, meaning that the return of a cap or helmet indicated a wounded soldier. In one case a French Red Cross dog named Captain located thirty wounded men in a single day using this method.

If the dog was unable to find a helmet or cap, the animal would pull something from the body of the wounded soldier such as a bandage or a piece of clothing. He might even attempt to yank hair from the soldier's head if unable to find a cap or helmet. This problem increased in frequency until the handlers, the men who trained and worked the dogs, altered the method dogs used to announce the location of wounded men. The quest to retrieve needed to be subdued to a certain degree within the animals. Dog trainers accomplished this by changing their teaching techniques. Now upon their return, the dogs were taught to either lie down, if no wounded were found, or beckon the handler to return to the site.

The Germans, by comparison, devised a short leash called a *Brindel*, sometimes referred to as a *Brinsel*. Upon finding a wounded man, the dog would return with the leash in his mouth. Conversely, if the leash hung loose, no wounded or perhaps only the dead were to be found. It is reported that these dogs were also trained to distinguish the difference between friend and enemy, and disregard the latter. This is probably pure propaganda and more re-flective of the time than fact.

The mount of enemy activity in the immediate search area deter-mined whether the Red Cross dogs would be sent out during the day. Most often they worked at night, relying on their sense of smell, called their *olfactory ability*, rather than on sight to find the wounded soldiers. At this time people did not fully comprehend how dogs scented—only that they could. The scien-tific community did not have the capability to truly understand the olfactory ability of dogs or the extent to which this gift could be developed.

Slit trenches, barbed wire, and chemical bases were among the many obstacles faced by these dogs. Four-footed silhouettes searched no-man's-land quietly and efficiently in the dark for the wounded, with perhaps the flash of an artillery explosion illuminating the landscape. Every country had its own Red Cross organization, and dogs from opposing sides set incredible records. After a single battle, a French dog named Prusco located more than a hundred wounded men. The dog, wolflike in appearance and nearly all white, dragged unconscious and wounded soldiers into protective craters and trenches before alerting his masters. Several dispatches from different regiments mentioned the heroic efforts of Prusco. Hundreds of other canines performed similar services.

The French began using military dogs in 1906, but stopped abruptly in 1914, after the Battle of the Marne. This decision was made by Marshal Joseph Joffre, a lazy and bullheaded commander, and without logical reason. The battle swayed back and forth over a three-hundred-mile front in bloody confusion. Dogs were found to be ineffectual in such combat, probably influ-encing Joffre in his decision. Some rumors circulated that he just hated dogs. The battle, eventually won by the French, ensured only that the war could continue for a very long time. For the most part, the French maintained few military dogs for the next year, although there were some outstanding excep-tions. Coincidental with Joffre's removal, the army reactivated its dog program with vigor in 1915, calling it the Service des Chiens de Guerre. It continued to expand its scope of operations for the remainder of the war.

Many different breeds saw active duty during the war, depending on the job at hand. Bulldogs, retrievers, Airedale terriers, sheepdogs, and German shepherds were used in a variety of roles. Purebreds did not have any advantage over mixed breeds, and this is probably just as true today. The physical parame-ters preferred were dogs of medium build and grayish or black in color, with good eyesight and a keen sense of smell. Several periodicals of the time noted that if the dog did not display the proper "character" it did not see any wartime service. One passage in a 1918 issue of *Red Cross Magazine* stated that "the aristocrat with the shifty eye goes into the discard." This statement equates the characteristics of dogs with those of humans, and the practice occurs frequently throughout history to this very day. Scientists with a detached clinical viewpoint may argue that this has no basis in fact. But in World War I, as with all conflicts since then, the temperament and disposition of the dog usually came first, and if found physically acceptable, it continued to receive advanced training.

Hundreds of other dogs became useful in the transportation of wounded soldiers. Even though the war became increasingly mechanized, all combatants still relied upon animals in a variety of roles throughout the conflict. The ambulance dogs were larger breeds weighing more than eighty pounds; they pulled two-wheeled carriers especially designed for them. A single dog could pull one prone man or two soldiers in a sitting position. The dogs, often oblivious to the war that raged around them, transported the wounded from the front lines to aid stations located in the more secure rear areas. Once the wounded were removed, the dogs alone pulled the ambulance cart back to the battle lines to retrieve more wounded.

Draft dogs offered several advantages over horses—or even motorized ambulances. Horses presented a larger target and needed to be accompanied by a soldier, and they consumed a greater amount of food. Motorized ambulances were subject to mechanical failure, required gasoline that was scarce, and often cold not negotiate the rough roads cratered by artillery shells.

The mercy dogs of World War I have been immortalized in a painting that hangs in the Red Cross museum in Washington, D.C. The painting, by Boston artist Alexander Pope, depicts a Red Cross dog sprinting back to friendly lines with a helmet. In the background, creeping along with the draft of a light wind, is the nightmarish chemical gas.

Several thousand mercy dogs participated in World War I. Their accomplishments are often overlooked simply because of the immense scale of the conflict. Thousand of soldiers owe their lives to these devoted animals, yet the dogs could help only a small fraction of the casualties that numbered in the millions during the war, leaving their legacy as just a footnote to history. Trench warfare and stagnant front lines ended with World War I, and with it the necessity ever to employ Red Cross dogs again.

Except for the United States, every country embroiled in the war considered dogs a valuable commodity. When the United States entered the war, few American commanders grasped the advantages of developing the animals to their full potential and needed to borrow them from the French or British.

Although ambulance dogs saved countless lives, the messenger dog is also credited with indirectly saving thousand of lives. Much of World War I consisted of trench warfare and battle lines that remained fixed, often for long periods of time. Communication, most often by telephone or soldiers running with messages, remained a vital link to commanders in rear areas. When communications broke down, dogs helped to fill the gap by relaying messages.

In Belgium an entire battalion lost contact with its headquarters after the Germans cut the telephone lines. Yet their messenger dog was able to relay their position and their desperate need for reinforcements. In the midst of an artillery barrage, the dog escaped with a message to headquarters, and the fresh troops that responded kept the battalion from being wiped out. Some of the accomplishments recorded are truly marvels of not only a dog's skill at survival but also the canine's innate sense of completing a mission. An Irish terrier messenger dog named Paddy, although partially blinded by gas, completed a journey of nine miles with a dispatch. Days later, the dog recovered from the effects of the chemical and returned to active service.

Messenger dogs could carry dispatches four to five times faster than the average foot soldier and needed only a small metal canister attached to their collar that could carry several sheets of paper. Besides carrying messages, the same dogs often delivered messenger pigeons in a saddlebag arrangement designed just for them. Dogs also offered a lower profile than men, making them more difficult to locate and a challenge for the enemy to shoot at. In one battle near Verdun seventeen human couriers perished while attempting to deliver messages. A lone dog was able to complete seven message runs before succumbing to enemy fire. It at all possible, however, the enemy tried to capture the dogs rather than just kill them. Unlike their human counterparts, captured dogs were retrained and sent out into the field again—this time providing a service for the enemy in the conflict. Dogs were not considered traitorous, just pragmatic under the circumstances.

The French divided messenger dogs into two groups: *estafettes* and *liaison*. *Estafettes* carried messages or pigeons, completing one-way journeys to a predesignated point. More danger faced liaison dogs, trained to carry dispatches on round-trips, since their missions doubled their chances of being shot. Perhaps the most famous messenger dog of the war was a mixed breed named Satan, who is credited with saving what later became known as "The Lost Battalion." As the story goes, the French held a small village near Verdun but quickly became encircled by superior German forces. With their telephone lines cut and their messenger pigeons dead, no one knew of their plight. The

Germans understood the precarious position of the French soldiers and quickly moved field artillery pieces to a nearby hill. Artillery shells soon found their mark, and scores of soldiers lay dead.

Amid the turmoil and confusion, a strange apparition appeared from the smoke. It appeared alien because several soldiers recounted that it looked like a winged creature with an unusually large head. In reality it was the messenger dog Satan, with two pigeon carriers on his flanks flapping as he ran, and a bulbous gas mask covering his head. Satan approached in a zigzag pattern, as he had been trained to do to avoid enemy fire. When he was only several hundred yards from the French line, the Germans opened fire. Dozens of Germans began firing until a bullet finally found its mark. Satan fell, recovered, and continued at a slower zigzagging trot. A second bullet shattered his shoulder and the dog stumbled, now just a few scant yards from the French. Satan must have drawn again from the deep well of courage many dogs possess, and he stumbled onward to awaiting arms. He was greeted enthusiastically, and an army doctor tended to his wounds.

Satan had managed to deliver two carrier pigeons from the nearby French forces. The first pigeon flew skyward for only three hundred feet before enemy gunners shot it down. Only one more chance remained. A soldier released the second pigeon, carrying a small message of their predicament. Rifles cracked and the air filled with lead as the pigeon flew high above the soldiers and toward the French lines—only time would tell if the message got through.

Within the hour, long-range guns from the French began a barrage against German positions on the nearby hill. The explosives hit the enemy squarely, and allied forces were able to relieve the village during the same day. The Germans remained confused and regrouped, fearing a counteroffensive from the French. A key battle involving thousands of soldiers was ultimately decided by the determination of a single dog to complete his mission.

Two Missions, Two Results

From Ready to Serve, Ready to Save: Strategies of Real Life Search and Rescue Missions

BY SUSAN BULANDA

Ready to Serve, Ready to Save is a most unusual book: a collection of actual missions featuring rescue dogs from around the world, wherein their handlers tell of the difficulties and triumphs of the search in their own words. Following are two tales: of an avalanche victim sought and a 16-year-old girl saved.

★　　★　　★　　★　　★

Mission Type
This avalanche was one of many that occurred in the Colorado Rockies during the winter of 1991–1992.

The Victim
Takashi Fujii was an approximately 27-year-old male from Osaka, Japan. He was a high school ski coach and gymnastics instructor and was in excellent health. Fujii was also a technical executive with the Bolle sunglasses/goggles company, and a very strong skier. At the time of this incident, he was staying with friends in Dillon, Colorado. Fujii was an excellent, highly experienced skier. He had the normal gear for back-country skiing. His rescue beacon was rendered inoperable when it was ripped from his body. Fujii was not found during the beacon or the Recco search. During the hasty search, there is always a beacon search, a scuff search for clues on the surface, a coarse probing of the most likely points of deposition, and a dog search if a dog is available. He disappeared on March 29, 1992.

268

Any Other Special Information

We were given Fujii's sweatpants for a scent article, but we did not use them. Typically, avalanche dog handlers do not use scent articles. For one thing, scent articles are not normally available quickly enough for avalanche searching and time is always a crucial factor. Also, the avalanche dog is trained to alert only on the scent that is coming from underneath the snow and disregard scents on the surface.

Point Last Seen
Why did the incident take place?

At 1530 Sunday, March 29, Fujii was skiing an extremely rugged back-country area with a group of about ten snowcat skiers. Snowcat skiers are people who pay for a guide to take them up the mountain and ski down in the area that the guide directs them. They are transported up the mountain in a cab on the back of a snowcat, which usually hold about 10–12 people. Snowcats carry the skiers to the top of a steep chute and pick them up again at the bottom once they have skied. These are people who are bored with ski-area skiing and want an added challenge on ungroomed, steeper terrain. They ski terrain much the same as that skied by people who are doing helicopter skiing.

The snowcat and helicopter guide services are flourishing in Colorado because a certain element of the skiing public thrives on this form of "extreme skiing." Customers usually purchase a trip that either goes out for a day or half a day. All of the patrons are briefed on safe back-country skiing procedures since the areas they are skiing are not at populated skis areas. The terrain is usually steep, not compacted by skiers, and full of unmarked obstacles. The snowcat operators purchase permits that allow them to use the Forest Service land for such enterprises.

They had already been skiing the Montezuma area for about six hours. They were careful to make their turns one at a time, as instructed by their guide. This diminishes the odds that multiple skiers would get caught should a slide occur. Fujii did not follow the guide's instructions and skied beyond the "safe" zone. Safety is all relative in the back country. There are no guarantees. However, tour guides study the areas where they take guests. They know which areas are more prone to sliding depending on the time of the year, recent wind directions, recent snow depths, etc. When he triggered the slide, he was the only one caught. The other members of his skiing party watched as Fujii was carried through the debris and had a vague idea of his location at the time he disappeared in the snow out of sight.

Where did the incident take place?

The slide occurred in the Equity Chute, which is near Saints John, an old mining town southeast of Keystone and south of the town of Montezuma.

Terrain Features

The area we searched was all steep avalanche debris. In those places where the debris was deep, it was well consolidated. As we got closer to the flanks and the tail of the debris we post-holed, because of the effects the warm temperature had on the snow. In the early mornings in the spring, the snow is well consolidated because it is still frozen granular. However, as the day wears on, warm temperatures cause water to percolate through the snow pack, and the frozen granular become unconsolidated corn snow, like slush. Post-holing is when you walk through snow and it does not support your weight, and you end up sinking through up to your hips and waist. The travel was difficult on this search. The elevation was above 11,000'.

Weather

Spring days in the Colorado Rockies are warm and sunny, and this day was no exception. The winds were steady and light, 0–5 mph, which were ideal for an avalanche search. The wind direction was downslope Sunday night and upslope Monday morning. During this weekend, more than 100 avalanches were reported in Colorado, many triggered by skiers. About 26 inches of heavy, wet snow fell since Saturday—the day before the search—on top of older snow layers covered with an ice lens, creating dangerous avalanche conditions. The ice lens is created after a particularly warm day when the surface of the snow is saturated with water. Over night the lower temperatures cause the surface to freeze. The Colorado Avalanche Information Center had rated the hazard for the Montezuma area as high. On March 29 there was also a rockslide in Boulder Canyon indicating the high level of precipitation and runoff.

Special Dangers

The largest danger for the rescuers occurred Sunday night when we searched in an area that continued to have an avalanche hazard. With the approach of darkness, the danger increased. In the dark there is no way to find out whether a pillow of snow is being deposited in the starting zone of a slope over the search area. Also, the avalanche guard is ineffective because he has no way of telling if an avalanche is descending upon the searchers. The avalanche guard is a rescuer who stands in a strategic location from where he can see if there are any new avalanches that might descend upon the rescuers so that he can alert them to the danger. He is in a location where he will not be hit by the avalanche himself. Keep in mind, that it is rare that rescuers will go in if there is any remaining danger; however, you cannot always be 100% sure.

Search Personnel and Equipment
The only resource that I wished we'd had was the ability to cut through red tape Sunday afternoon to get the necessary explosives to mitigate the hazard. By not bombing the remaining hazard that was hanging over the areas we searched, we were in a great deal of danger ourselves. I doubt I would take the risk again if I were put in a similar situation. Putting the rescuers in danger doesn't make any sense.

The Summit County Rescue Group coordinated the mission, under the auspices of the sheriff's office. Alpine and Grand County SAR teams assisted along with ski patrollers from Arapahoe Basin, Keystone, and Copper Mountain. Approximately 40 rescuers were involved. We had five different search dog teams that worked Sunday night. The three teams from Copper Mountain were John Reller and "Skadee," Todd Goertzen and "Cache," and myself and "Hasty." The team from Keystone was Tom Resignolo and "Donner." And from Arapahoe Basin the team was Peter Heckman and "Alex." We were shuttled to the slide area via snowmobiles and snowcats.

Search Strategy
The size of the search is well defined for most avalanches. The victim's not going anywhere. Though we arrived at the site only an hour after the slide occurred, we had to wait until 1900 to enter the debris. The reason for the delay was that the mission coordinators were attempting to have control work performed. This could have been a fatal error. It had been 3.5 hours from the time of the incident before we began searching, and yet we still held out a glimmer of hope that he would be found alive.

Since there was still a possibility of hangfire a minimum number of searchers ventured out on the slide. An avalanche guard was stationed higher up the slide path to alert us if another slide were triggered. Rescuers included a few beacon searchers, coarse probers, all the dog units, and a navigator/prober for each. All five teams worked at the same time. As I worked, I received an alert from Hasty fairly close to where we entered the debris area. I had my navigator probe the area and he was not able to get a strike. A "strike" is that awful feeling that a prober experiences when he hits a buried body. (Note: The debris was 15–20 feet deep in places, this means that there were times when the 12–15 foot probe poles could not hit ground.) About an hour later, Skadee got a stronger, more specific alert in the same place. Unfortunately, again we got no strikes. By 2030, it was very dark, and the site commander called it a night.

Monday morning at 0700, the fireworks began. A helicopter transported snow safety technicians from Colorado Heli-Ski to reduce the remaining avalanche hazard by throwing hand charges from the helicopter. These are usually two-pound primers with an igniter fuse. The shot placements effectively started a slide that covered a large portion of the area we had been walking on the previous evening. This was extremely sobering for me. We had three search dogs Monday: Hasty, Donner, and Alex. We took a different strategy this time and decided to work each dog separately for 15 minutes. With the different wind directions (downslope Sunday night and upslope Monday morning) Hasty alerted about 40 feet above his and Skadee's alerts from the previous night. He also did an article alert where Fujii's ski pole was buried. An article alert is much more subtle—and in some ways, more incredible—than a live or dead body alert, since a metal ski pole buried under the snow gives off very little human scent. At 1030 the Site Commander sent a probe line directly through Hasty's and Skadee's alerts and got a strike exactly between the two. This was a perfect example of where wind changes worked in our favor. Fujii was buried under ten feet of snow, another factor that affected the distance of the alerts from the body. In most avalanches, the mostly likely places of body deposition are at the toe of the slide, below ledges (terrain variations), above trees and other obstacles, and on the outside of turns.

Suspension
It is difficult to say whether the mission should have been called off on the first night any sooner or later than it was. The consensus was that the possibility of a live recovery was worth the risk. However, the one constant in an avalanche rescue is that the safety of the rescuers should always be paramount (Dan Burnett).

Results of the Mission
Success. We found him, finally, on the second morning.

What Are Your Feelings About the Mission?
The mission was a tremendous success in interagency cooperation and coordination. The tragedy of a vibrant life lost and the use of resources in an avoidable accident are memories that many rescuers will carry for a long time (Dan Burnett).

Missing Hiker: Mountain Scent Specific
Julie L.S. Cotton and Dave Bigelow
Larimer County Search and Rescue
Mission Location: Rocky Mountain National Park
Mission Date: August 10 and 11, 1995

Mission Type
This search is a long search utilizing extensive resources of various types. It illustrates that while the dog team may not be directly responsible for finding the subject, it can contribute information that leads to finding the subject by other resources.

The Victim
The subject of this search was a 16-year-old female in good health. "Sara" was described as athletic, adventurous, active, and levelheaded. She was not considered a risk taker and had no history of drug or alcohol abuse. Sara had a positive attitude toward her first overnight solo hike. She had learned about the hike at summer camp and planned to do it on her own while vacationing with her parents in the Rocky Mountains.

Sara was from Tennessee. She had attended the summer programs at Cheley Camp near Estes Park, Colorado for several years. Sara had extensive experience hiking in the Colorado Rockies because the program, designed for children ages nine through seventeen, included hiking in and around Rocky Mountain National Park. A particular hike in Rocky Mountain National Park, "The Mummy Kill," had been mentioned at camp as one of the "cool" hikes to do. The Mummy Kill entails hiking to the top of six mountain peaks in the Mummy Range. The hike begins at Chapin Pass (11,140' elevation) and continues to Mount Chapin (12,454'). From there it goes to Mount Chiquita (13,069'), Ypsilon Mountain (13,414'), Fairchild Mountain (13,502'), Hagues Peak (13,560') and finishes at Mummy Mountain (13,425'). The hike extends about 14 miles and is mostly above the timberline. In addition, over half the hike is off-trail. It is a hike that can be completed in a very long day. Most people begin the hike in the middle of the night.

At the time of this incident in August 1995, Sara had just finished another summer program at Cheley Camp. After joining her parents, she mapped a route to attempt "The Mummy Kill" on her own. Sara was well prepared for her first overnight solo hike. She had with her a wool sweater, long-sleeved shirt, rain gear, and she was wearing leather hiking boots. She was carrying a day pack that was well-equipped. It included a compass, topographic map of the area, emergency blanket, wool hat, first-aid kit, whistle, matches, food, and water. Additionally, through her participation in the summer programs, Sara had learned what to do if she ever became lost.

Point Last Seen

Sara's parents dropped her off at the Chapin Pass trailhead at 0300 Wednesday, August 9, 1995. After ascending the six peaks, she was to complete the hike by descending the Lawn Lake trail to join her parents at their back-country campsite in the Roaring River drainage. Her parents expected her at the campsite around 1800 Wednesday evening, several hours before dark. When she was overdue, her parents hiked up the Lawn Lake trail expecting to meet her. Since it was possible the hike took longer than anticipated, Sara's parents waited, and slept, on the trail throughout Wednesday night. They hiked out to the Lawn Lake trail Thursday morning to report Sara missing.

The hike Sara set out to do was challenging but not impossible. From the beginning of the hike to the Lawn Lake trail, about a mile south of Mummy Mountain, the "trail" is above timberline across the tundra. The mountain slopes consist primarily of loose talus, which either shifts slightly or slides down the mountainside with each step. Where there is not loose talus, the rocks are large and passage requires jumping from one boulder to another. Good balance is required to stay upright and not twist an ankle. In some places fairly gentle slopes form the mountain ridges. In others, the steep slopes come together sharply forming a narrow blade of a ridge. There is no protection from foul weather, or the intense sun, while hiking the ridge line from mountaintop to mountaintop. For the portion of the hike between Mount Chapin and Ypsilon Mountain, a distance of approximately 3.5 miles, the closest protection is 2,000 feet below the ridge. This is where stubby and wind-twisted pine trees mix with the rock and tundra. Beyond the first three mountains, protection from the elements is scarce for another five miles until reaching the Lawn Lake trail. The ridge line between the final three mountains is rugged and does not allow for a fast descent if needed.

Wednesday afternoon, a particularly strong thunderstorm had passed through the Mummy Range area where Sara had been hiking. Aside from that strong storm, the weather before and during the search was fairly typical for midsummer. Thursday, the day was clear and temperatures were in the upper 70s—a hot day in the mountains. Thursday evening there was a light wind primarily out of the northwest, but down-slope winds predominated at nightfall. Near the Saddle, the proximity of the numerous mountain peaks created a whirlpool effect so that the wind swirled and switched directions continuously. Late Thursday night another storm system moved into the area. While it brought some precipitation, the storm consisted primarily of abundant thunder and lightning. With the incoming storm, the stable down-slope winds became shifting and unpredictable. Friday morning, the westerly winds were forty-plus miles per hour, which made it difficult to move across the boulder-strewn mountain slope without being blown off balance. The skies were overcast and the temperature was in the low 40s.

During her solo hike, Sara was exposed to several hazards typically associated with alpine mountaineering in Colorado. In the Colorado Rockies thunderstorms are nearly a daily occurrence; they form suddenly and lightning strikes without warning. It was possible that Sara was on an exposed ridge when the strong storm passed through the area Wednesday afternoon. Besides lightning, the storm would have created another safety hazard, rain-slicked rocks. Slick rocks are a hazard not only because safe footing becomes uncertain, but also because the rain loosens the rocks from their tenuous hold to the earth, sending them tumbling down the mountainside. The wind is a hazard because it can be so strong that it is difficult to remain upright. This was the case Friday morning when Sara was still missing. Although it was midsummer, there were still many dangerous snow fields on the steep mountain slopes that had to be avoided. Serious injury can occur if a person slips and falls several hundred feet down a snow field.

Besides weather and terrain, a serous danger in the mountains is altitude sickness. Although Sara had spent a couple of weeks near Estes Park, her hike was over 5,000 ft. higher in elevation than her camp was located. This made altitude sickness a good possibility. The symptoms include general malaise followed by nausea and a headache. As the sickness progresses, judgment is clouded and apathy and dizziness increase. In severe cases of altitude sickness, a person may develop a high-altitude pulmonary edema or cerebral edema. As a solo hiker Sara would be in additional danger since she had no one to assist her if she should succumb to altitude sickness. Moving to a lower elevation usually relieves the symptoms of altitude sickness. However, since a person may not recognize they are experiencing altitude sickness, they may continue to move to a higher altitude, which could worsen their condition.

Search Personnel and Equipment

Many different resources were requested for this search. Foot teams, airscenting, and trailing dog teams, and a helicopter was requested once Sara was reported missing.

A total of seventy-five people and five dogs were used in the search effort. Two foot teams made up of park rangers were fielded immediately early Thursday afternoon when Sara was reported missing. Two airscenting dog teams from Larimer County Search and Rescue and a helicopter was also utilized Thursday afternoon and evening. Friday, two additional airscenting dog teams and a trailing dog team were fielded along with six foot teams and one helicopter. There was the possibility that a television news helicopter would also be available.

Search Strategy

Overdue hikers and climbers are common due to inclement weather and underestimating the time to complete a hike. The report of a person who is overdue on the morning following a particularly long hike possesses no special urgency, especially if the hiker is as prepared as Sara was. However, since Sara had not returned by early afternoon Thursday, the situation was upgraded to urgent.

The search area was very large and remote, covering over 50 miles in rugged terrain. We used two initial foot teams along trails on two sides of the search area for containment. Other than that, there was no containment in effect in the remote northern section of the search area. Management at the check-in site at Corral Park, northwest of the primary search area, was notified about the missing subject in case Sara exited via the Mummy Pass trail.

The extended first operational period, from 1300 Thursday afternoon until 0600 Friday morning, was primarily a hasty search to get teams in along Sara's intended path of travel. Hopefully they would find clues to further direct the search effort. Segments and boundaries were determined for the second operational period, which began Friday morning at 0600 hours. The high priority segments were based on clues obtained by the hasty teams, the history of overdue hikers in the area, and hazards encountered along the route. The descent off Ypsilon Mountain to Fairchild Mountain was identified as a likely place where Sara could have lost the route, as it is a particularly tricky descent. It was the highest priority area for Friday.

The Cache la Poudre/Chapin Creek drainage formed the western boundary. The Fall River Road was the southern boundary. The Black Canyon trail formed the eastern boundary, and the northern boundary went up toward the Mummy Pass trail. Most of the exit routes off Ypsilon Mountain, Fairchild Mountain, and Hagues Peak put hikers and climbers in the Ypsilon Lake and Lawn Lake drainage—the segmentation was extensive in this area.

On Thursday, the two hasty foot teams were used for confinement, clue detection, and attraction. Rocky Mountain National Park authorities called for dog resources mid-afternoon due to the size of the search area. The dog teams, and a helicopter, were used for clue detection and attraction. Friday, foot teams were used to search segments thoroughly rather than move quickly as hasty teams. The dog teams were also used to thoroughly search segments Friday.

Assign Resources

One ranger patrol foot team was assigned to follow Sara's intended path and check the register atop each summit to see if Sara had signed in. Another ranger patrol foot team was flown into the Lawn Lake ranger station to do attraction and man the station throughout Thursday evening in case Sara showed up.

The first airscenting dog team to arrive, Dog Team One, consisted of a handler and two rangers. They were flown to the Saddle to try to narrow the search area into one of four quadrants: two quadrants to the west of the saddle, one quadrant below Fairchild Mountain, and one quadrant below Mummy Mountain. The direction of the search effort would be determined by the information that Dog Team One obtained. The trailing dog was unavailable, so the second airscenting dog team, Dog Team Two, was assigned to follow Sara's intended route using any up-slope winds to cover a wide area. Dog Team Two consisted of a handler, two additional Larimer County Search and Rescue Team members, and a ranger.

The last resource available for the search Thursday afternoon was a private helicopter contracted by the National Park Service. The helicopter flew the intended route and searched around the mountain peaks. After these resources were fielded, management began planning for Friday. Resources requested for the next operational period were one trailing and two airscenting dog teams, foot team resources from Larimer County Search and Rescue, and additional helicopter time.

Information Obtained from Resources

Dog Team One was flown from mission base to the Saddle around 1700 Thursday. The airscenting dog teams in Larimer County are trained to scent discriminate and the dog, a black Labrador Retriever with two years of mission experience, was given Sara's scent. Immediately the dog indicated that there was a large mount of Sara's scent near the Saddle. The dog began to run back and forth with her head in the air, however, the switching winds made it difficult to determine from which direction the scent was originally. The dog team made grids across the Saddle, around the base of Hagues Peak, and circled Mummy

Mountain. Based on the dog's behavior, the handler and search management thought that it could be possible Sara's scent was coming up out of the Hague Creek drainage; however, the handler thought it might also have just seemed that way because of the swirling winds. It also seemed unlikely to management that Sara was in that drainage since it meant that the dog had an alert from what was thought to be too far way. Additionally, since there was no response to attraction efforts made by Dog Team One, it was decided that, if responsive, Sara was not likely to be close below the Saddle on the north side. As a result, the Hague Creek drainage was considered only a slight possibility for Sara's location. However, the alert distance and the unsuccessful attraction methods combined with strong interest toward Mummy Mountain suggested that Sara was most likely in the Lawn Lake drainage. Dog Team One concluded its search for the evening around 2200 and stayed in the patrol cabin at Lawn Lake.

Dog Team Two started their search assignment at the Chapin Pass trail at 1900 Thursday evening. The dog, an Australian Cattle dog with five years of mission experience, was given Sara's scent and the team started up the trail. At the trail junction for Chapin Creek and Mount Chapin, the dog started on the trail toward the mountain. As the team moved along the barely visible trail, the dog acted as if she was trailing. The dog's behavior showed the team that Sara most likely had been through the area, although they were unable to obtain any definite signs. Because of communication problems resulting from the terrain and distance, this information could not be easily relayed to the mission base. As the dog team progressed toward Mount Chapin, the winds switched to blowing down slope after have been predominantly up slope. An incoming storm later in the evening created strong, unreliable winds accompanied by thunder and lightning. The dog team was forced to retreat from the ridge line around 2330 due to lightning. The team bivouacked that night on the scree slope and resumed searching early Friday morning.

Most of the teams were not in the actual search area until a few hours before dark Thursday. Therefore the only clues obtained by Thursday night were those from the dog teams. They were the alerts in the Saddle area from Dog One and the continuing progress of Dog Two along Sara's intended path. Using this information, the additional resources Friday were assigned as follows: One airscenting dog team was to be flown to the Saddle to see if they could confirm the alerts from Dog One. Another airscenting dog team hiked into the Fay Lakes/Ypsilon Lake area to rule out the possibility Sara had descended off the east side of Ypsilon Mountain. A trailing dog team worked on the intended route, a trail that was now over 48 hours old. Four foot teams had assignments as well. One foot team was sent to the Spectacle Lakes area to scan the slopes under Ypsilon Mountain in case Sara had fallen or attempted a descent. Two foot teams were sent to look on the Lawn Lake side of Fairchild Mountain in the Crystal Lake drainage. Another foot team was flown to the Saddle to further check the area around the Saddle and Mummy Mountain. They were sent there because Dog One had shown so much interest in that area. Unfortunately the teams to be flown in had to wait until midmorning when the raging winds had subsided and the helicopter could fly.

An airscenting dog team and a foot team were finally flown to the Saddle around 1000 Friday morning. The foot team worked its way around to the north-running ridge west of the Saddle. After about an hour, they heard three whistles in response to them blowing their whistle. The initial thought was "What kind of bird is that?" After a few cycles of this pattern they realized they were most likely in contact with Sara though they never could get voice contact with her. It sounded like she was directly below them at the bottom of the northern slope of the Saddle. They worked their way over truck-sized boulders as they descended. At times they had to remove their packs and pass them to another teammate to maneuver across the terrain. The helicopter flew over the area north of the Saddle while the foot team slowly worked their way toward Sara. The helicopter crew spotted Sara near a clearing in the Hague Creek drainage and could land and pick her up around 1200 hours. She was flown to mission base where she was reunited with her family.

Sara said she became disoriented after she was forced off the mountain ridge by the thunderstorm Wednesday afternoon. The storm passed through while she was preparing to cross the narrow ridge from Ypsilon Mountain to Fairchild Mountain. She opted to move westward around Desolation Peak rather than cross the narrow ridge between the other two peaks. The storm's intensity forced her to continue a descent off the mountain range, eventually leaving her in the Hague Creek drainage. She was unclear as to her location once the storm passed, so she decided to stay in one place Wednesday night. She figured out that she needed to move back to the south Thursday and tried to attract the attention of the helicopter crew Thursday afternoon to no avail. Friday morning she was able to get into a clearing and caught the attention of the helicopter crew after getting contact with the foot team via whistles.

The Searcher
Dog Handler Team

Who Are You?

I was one of the two initial dog handlers who responded to the search Thursday afternoon. Since my trailing dog was still in training, I responded with my experienced airscenting dog, Tassie, an Australian Cattle Dog.

The Callout

My pager started emitting a series of tones around 1400 Thursday afternoon while I was at work in a research laboratory at Colorado State University. Based on the tones, I knew that the information I was receiving on my pager was search-related and urgent. While my employer allowed me some flexibility, my mission response could not be at the expense of any ongoing experiments. I had just started an experimental protocol that would take about two hours to complete. Following completion of that stage of the experiment, I had to start an overnight procedure. After that, I would not need to do anything further until the next morning, so I determined that I could respond to the mission later. I arranged with my coworkers to place my experiments in cold storage Friday morning after the overnight protocol was completed. I left my workplace around 1630.

I had to load my gear and dog into the car and then drive up the Big Thompson Canyon to Rocky Mountain National Park during high tourist season. I didn't arrive at the incident command post for briefing until 1800. Fortunately, for this mission, I did not need to take extra time making arrangements to have my younger dog cared for, since I was the only one in the household responding to this mission. My team and I did not reach the actual search site until 1900.

The Search Sector
Who decided your sector?

When I arrived at the incident command post, search management had two primary search objectives. The first was to get a dog team to the middle of Sara's proposed route, and the other was to have a dog team follow along her intended path of travel. The first dog and handler, who were available immediately when the pager toned, had been flown in by helicopter to the Saddle. They had been searching for a few hours before I arrived. I was briefed about the circumstances surrounding the search and given the objectives for my search area. While following Sara's planned route, I was to use the wind to see if the dog would show that Sara might be on the west or east side of the mountain range. Management hoped that I could use up-slope winds to determine if Sara had fallen down or descended the treacherous east face of her intended route.

Before I could leave the incident command post, I needed to obtain a scent article so my dog knew to search exclusively for Sara. I was given Sara's suitcase to select something suitable for my needs. The contents had not been touched by anyone else. Because the clothes had not been worn during Sara's vacation, my best scent article was one of her clog shoes. I had no desire to carry something that heavy and large with me while searching. Therefore I placed a sterile gauze pad inside a shoe to absorb Sara's scent while I briefed my team members about our assignment. Afterward, I collected and stored the gauze pad in a plastic bag to use as the scent article.

Two Larimer County Search and Rescue Team members and a park ranger, none of whom had worked extensively with a dog team before, accompanied me on the search assignment. One of them was tasked with keeping track of our route on the map. One of the team members had to mark the locations and directions of any alerts or interest from the dog and write down the time we were at different landmarks. The rest of the team did attraction and looked for any visual clues. One team member monitored the radio traffic and communicated with the incident command post when needed. It was beneficial having the park ranger with us since he was familiar with the area.

How large was your sector? How long did it take to complete?

Because of the nature of my search assignment, the size of my search sector was vague. I was to follow Sara's planned route and use the wind to the dog's best advantage to cover the mountain slopes. The primary objective of search management was to try to cover the east face of the mountain ridge. The distance between the trailhead and Ypsilon Mountain entailed a hike of more than 3.5 miles across some tough terrain. This was only the first part of our assignment. We had three more mountain peaks to cover to follow the entire planned route. The wind pattern and terrain helped me to determine how much area the dog could actually cover. By the time we ascended to the ridge line, it became obvious that we would not cover any of the east face below the ridge line. The winds were down sloping rather than up sloping. I adjusted my search objective for Thursday evening and concentrated my efforts along the western slope of the ridge. The slope consisted of loose rocks that impeded our pace. It also got dark after 2100. We tried to work along the ridge line Thursday evening at an elevation of about 12,800', but a thunderstorm late Thursday night forced us to descend nearly 1,000 feet. We were between Mount Chiquita and Ypsilon Mountain. We had expended a lot of energy to reach the higher elevation, but the descent, at 2330, was necessary to lessen the possibility of being struck by lightning. Though we moved to a lower elevation, we were still on a very rocky slope that offered no real protection from the storm. We stopped for the night to get some rest. A few hours later, the rain stopped, the storm had passed.

Friday morning at 0600, after spending the night sleeping on rocks, we again ascended toward the ridge line. As we tried to move up and across the rocks, a 40+ mph westerly wind with strong gusts, hampered our movement. When we reached the ridge between Ypsilon and Fairchild Mountains at 0800 hours, we decided that the wind made it too dangerous to cross the ridge. I again adjusted my search sector. Though I could no longer cover Sara's intended route, I could search a sector from the ridge line down to the west toward Chapin Creek and work back to the Chapin Pass trailhead. We returned to the trailhead at 1300 Friday afternoon after having been in the field for 18 hours.

How did you decide where to start your sector?
Since our assignment was to follow Sara's intended route, we started our assignment at the Chapin Pass trailhead.

Problems Encountered
The problems that we encountered were expected due to the nature of searching in a mountainous and remote wilderness. The first problem became apparent almost immediately. I had a difficult time moving quickly along the trail. I had come from an elevation of 5,000' in Fort Collins and in less than three hours was as 12,000'. My body had a hard time adjusting to the fast altitude change. I was slow, sluggish, and had to make frequent rest stops. This was because I had not done much hiking at high altitudes that summer. My other team members were not having as hard a time as I was that night, so I set the slow pace. Typically I have problems with altitudes. However, the severity varies from incident to incident depending on the time of day and how much sleep and water I had before the mission.

Two additional problems our dog team encountered were weather-related and typical for the time of year and environment. The first problem happened late Thursday night when a thunderstorm moved overhead. All four of us were up on an exposed ridge and were the highest objects in the terrain. We were totally exposed to the lightning unless we descended below 2,000'. We opted to drop about 1,000 feet to reduce our exposure to lightning, yet maintain some of the elevation we had worked so hard to gain.

Friday morning we had to contend with the second weather-related problem, the wind. Maintaining our balance across the boulder fields with wind gusts was difficult. Because of the wind, we did not feel safe walking along the ridge line. Therefore, we could not get close enough to the ridge to see the east face of the mountaintops along our route. Further along the route, the wind prevented us from attempting to cross from Ypsilon Mountain to Fairchild Mountain. We were not surprised by the problems with the wind. I have participated in several missions in Rocky Mountain National Park where the winds were brutal above timberline. It can literally pound a person into the ground and force them to crawl across the terrain on hands and knees.

The last problem I experienced on this search assignment was rather unexpected. The problem was convincing my teammates to work to the dog's advantage. When the wind was up sloping, it made sense to my other team members to work along the ridge line, since that was presumably where Sara had walked. However, once the wind shifted to down slope, I could not convince them that we would cover more area with the dog by staying at a lower elevation. By doing so we could use the wind to cover the area above us. Not being familiar with working with a dog team, they felt their primary responsibility was to follow Sara's intended route, even if it hampered the dog's search efficiency. This mean that I did not search my area very effectively Thursday night.

Were you prepared for the conditions you encountered?
The Larimer County Search and Rescue Team is rarely requested to assist Rocky Mountain National Park on "easy" missions. Whenever I respond to Rocky Mountain National Park, I need to be well prepared for a search marathon, mentally, physically, and equipment-wise. This mission was no exception. I knew that since we did not start until 1900 Thursday and that we were doing a remote sector, I would be spending the night outdoors. I carried my bivy bag and a sleeping pad in case we took a break to sleep. Since it was summer, I did not carry a sleeping bag, but I did carry several layers of warm rain gear and some cold weather clothes in my pack, so I was prepared for the weather. I was prepared to minimize potential ankle injuries related to moving across the boulder and scree fields by wearing full leather boots. As far as preparations for my dog, Tassie could stay warm and dry during the storm since she was small enough to join me inside my bivy bag. Unfortunately, the rocks were abrasive on the pads of her feet. Her feet were tender when we completed the search. Booties, however, may have impaired the dexterity she needed to move from rock to rock.

The Dog
While Tassie is an airscenting dog, her initial six-month training entailed following the scent trail deposited on the ground during a person's passage through an area. Because of that training, she will indicate the presence of a scent trail under certain conditions. Shortly after the hiking trail begins at Fall River Road, it splits and continues either north along Chapin Creek or east toward Mount Chapin. At that junction, Tassie went east without hesitation. She did not appear to trail continuously, but she worked with her nose to the

ground along various segments of our route. We felt she was indicating the presence of Sara's scent and passage. We noted it on the map.

When the storm moved into our area, we were forced to descend for safety reasons. The slope consisted of loose scree—lots of shattered boulder pieces that gave poor footing and made an even poorer sleeping surface. Eventually we found one boulder large enough for me to curl up on. We found another boulder about 100 feet away that was large enough for the other three team members to sleep on. During the storm, I crawled down inside the bivy bag and brought Tassie in with me so she could also stay warm and dry. Being a small dog at forty pounds has its advantages! Since we could hear rocks crashing down the mountain slope as the rain loosened them, we wore our rescue helmets throughout the night, and I kept my search pack against my back.

After spending a restless night on the rocks, we began to regain the elevation we had lost the night before while between Mountain Chiquita and Ypsilon Mountain. But our movement was greatly hampered by the strong wind. With each step, my body would sway about until I had both feet firmly planted again. Slowly we moved toward the ridge. As we got closer, Tassie's behavior again appeared to indicate she was trailing. We continued north toward Ypsilon Mountain, being careful to stay off the ridge itself because the wind was so strong. Two of the team members hiked to the top of Ypsilon Mountain while another member and I and Tassie, stayed just below the peak. We wanted to reduce the team's exposure to the hazardous conditions. Because of the weather conditions Friday morning, we were all wearing winter-type clothing.

When we reached the ridge joining Ypsilon and Fairchild Mountains, we discussed possible routes across the ridge and potential hazards. As a team, we decided the risks were too great to cross over to Fairchild Mountain and that it would be best to redirect our search efforts. We no longer searched along the intended path of travel but chose to clear the sector between Chapin Creek and the ridge line, making up the route. As we moved west to the saddle between Ypsilon Mountain and Desolation Peaks, Tassie again began to act like she was trailing. I did not know what to make of it since, if it was Sara's trail, it was at least thirty-six hours old. I figured the wind had probably blown any residual scent from Sara's passage elsewhere so there should no longer be scent for Tassie to follow. Therefore, I did not feel it was possible she could be following Sara's trail.

As we moved westward off Ypsilon Mountain, we descended from 13,000' to about 11,600'. During the hike down the drainage, which was just northwest of Ypsilon Mountain, we had to cross running water from melting snow, little ponds that were formed from the running water, and wet moss. We then began to contour back to the south and toward Chapin Pass at 1030 hours. Rather than walking across rocks and boulders, we were now crossing the headwaters of numerous drainages. We walked through an open marsh and some willows. With the strong westerly wind that morning, I felt confident that our hasty search cleared from just below the peaks to possibly the 11,600-foot contour line. I came to this conclusion because Tassie only indicated she had scent along a trail and not in the air to the west. With our grid southward at 11,600', I hoped to cover the area down to the tree line, a distance about 400 feet below out intended contour/grid. When we were halfway back to Chapin Pass, around noon, we heard that Sara had been found and that she was in good condition. While proceeding to the trailhead just below Chapin Pass, I had one of my team members place Sara's scent article along the trail so Tassie could find it as she passed by. I did this for two reasons: first, it would reaffirm to me that Tassie was indeed still looking for, and aware of, Sara's scent. Secondly, after finding the article, she would get her reward, a Frisbee, for doing a job well done and working hard for over 18 hours. However, it did not work as planned. I had a support person place the article along the path. Just as we started to work Tassie, we noticed a bird swoop down and fly away with something in its feet. As we worked the path, we could not find the article. By the time we reached the support person, Tassie still had not given an alert. The support person took us back to the spot where he had placed the scent pad and then we realized that the bird had taken the gauze pad! To give Tassie a "find" we placed a scent article from one of the team members along the trail. I gave Tassie a new scent to find and she found the article and was happy. Normally I wouldn't switch scents on a dog like this, but under the circumstance's Tassie needed a find. Tassie can alert on an article that is 100 feet or so away. Under the right conditions we can alert on it even further.

Probability of Detection

The probability of detection was low for my assigned task. Both Thursday evening and Friday morning I had 0% coverage of the east faces of Mounts Chapin and Chiquita and Ypsilon Mountain. The wind was not conducive for coverage based on my location on the west side of the ridge. For the area between my grid Thursday evening along the 12,200–12,600 contour up toward the ridge, my probability of detection was around 20%, again because the wind was not reliable and constant. I felt the POD was not much better than 20% for the scree fields I covered Friday morning. I felt that way due to the size of some crevices she could have fallen into if she had been injured. However, the probability of detection was much higher for the sector between the 12,600-foot contour and tree line. Because the terrain was fairly open and even, and I felt the wind speed was high enough to cover much of the area, I assigned the probability of detection to be about 60%.

How Successful Were You?

Although we could not follow Sara's planned route beyond Ypsilon Mountain, we were successful in completing our search assignment. As we later learned, the dog correctly indicated that Sara had passed through the area. And although I did not believe Tassie could still be trailing Friday morning, she was also correct in indicating that Sara had changed her direction and had not crossed over to Fairchild Mountain. Sara confirmed this when she described how she became lost. Our probability of detection was low for the scree slope, but we did feel we had cleared the lower part of the mountain with the dog. As we walked back to the trail before Sara was located, the team discussed how we would summarize our coverage of the area. We concluded we could confirm Sara's passage, but that our area was not a high probability area for finding her. We completed our assignment to the best of our ability and adjusted our assignment as needed so that we could still give valuable information to the mission management despite the weather challenges we faced.

What Are Your Feelings About the Mission?

I felt good about this well-executed mission. In fact, this is one of my favorite missions because it so obviously demonstrates the overall team effort required to find the subject. I feel the team aspect is something that oftentimes gets overlooked because typically only one field team finds the subject. However, it takes the efforts from all of the other field teams to eliminate likely areas for the lost subject, or to provide clues that direct a team to the lost subject.

The team effort is clearly illustrated in this search. First, information from the first dog team and previous search experience in that area were required to keep resources concentrated in the upper region of the Lawn Lake drainage. While it was difficult to determine the correct side of the Saddle to search, it was deemed important to keep teams searching in that area because the dog had so much interest. Secondly, it was a foot team that established contact with Sara, but they were unable to actually get to her. She ended up being much further away from them than they had thought; however, they did determine she was down in the Hague Creek drainage, rather than in the Lawn Lake drainage. With this information, the helicopter crew expanded its flight path. It took the crew's efforts, and Sara's attempts to get their attention, to finally get a visual on her. And it was the helicopter crew that picked her up and returned her safely to her family.

Permissions Acknowledgments

Hamish MacInnes, excerpt from *High Drama: Mountain Rescue Stories from Four Continents*. Copyright © 1980 by Hamish MacInnes. Reprinted with the permission of Hodder Headline, plc.

Jack Melady, "The Crash at the Top of the World" and "All in a Day's Work" from *Heartbreak and Heroism, Canadian Search and Rescue Stories* (Toronto: Dundurn Press, 1997). Reprinted with the permission of the publishers.

Jim Nolan and Nicole Weisensee Egan, "Under the Rubble: Two Cops Learn About Life" from *The Philadelphia Daily News* (December 31, 2001). Reprinted with the permission of Tribune Media Services.

Jack Olsen, excerpt from *The Climb Up to Hell* (New York: St. Martin's Press, 1998). Copyright © 1962, 1990 by Jack Olsen. Reprinted with the permission of Barry N. Malzberg/Scott Meredith Literary Agency, LP.

Brendan Phibbs, excerpt from *Our War for the World: A Memoir of Life and Death on the Front Lines in WWII*. Copyright © 2002 by Brendan Phibbs. Reprinted with the permission of The Lyons Press, an imprint of The Globe Pequot Press.

Reporters, Writers, and Editors of *Der Spiegel* Magazine, excerpt from *Inside 9-11: What Really Happened*. Copyright © 2002. Reprinted with the permission of St. Martin's Press, LLC.

Dennis Smith, excerpt from *Report from Engine Co. 82*. Copyright © 1999 by Dennis Smith. Reprinted with the permission of Warner Books, Inc.

Steven Trent Smith, excerpt from *The Rescue: A True Story of Courage and Survival in World War II*. Copyright © 2001 by Steven Trent Smith. Reprinted with the permission of John Wiley & Sons, Inc.

Spike Walker, excerpt from *Coming Back Alive: The True Story of the Most Harrowing Search and Rescue Mission Ever Attempted on Alaska's High Seas*. Copyright © 2001 by Spike Walker. Reprinted with the permission of St. Martin's Press, LLC.

Jonathan Waterman, excerpt from *In the Shadow of Denali: Life and Death on Alaska's Mt. McKinley*. Copyright © 1994 by Jonathan Waterman. Reprinted with the permission of The Lyons Press, an imprint of The Globe Pequot Press.

Darrel D. Whitcomb, excerpt from *The Rescue of Bat 21*. Copyright © 1998 by Darrel D. Whitcomb. Reprinted with the permission of the Naval Institute Press.